Advice for New Faculty Members

Advice for New Faculty Members

Nihil Nimus

Robert Boice
Professor Emeritus
State University of New York at Stony Brook

Allyn and Bacon
Boston • London • Toronto • Sydney • Tokyo • Singapore

Executive editor: Stephen D. Dragin
Series editorial assistant: Barbara Strickland
Marketing manager: Stephen Smith
Manufacturing buyer: David Repetto

Library of Congress Cataloging-in-Publication Data

Boice, Robert.
  Advice for new faculty members : nihil nimus / Robert Boice.
      p. cm.
  Includes bibliographical references (p.) and index.
  ISBN 0-205-28159-1
    1. College teachers--United States. 2. College personnel management--United States. 3. Professional socialization--United States. I. Title.
  LB1778.2 .B63 1999
  378.1'2-dc21   99-051610

Printed in the United States of America

10   9   8   7   6   5   4   3   2   1   04   03   02   01   00

Dedicated to a researcher/writer
whose potentially useful efforts to improve human welfare
created more heat than light,
more political than practical interpretation:

Francis Bacon

Contents

SECTION II   *Write in Mindful Ways*   **103**

Preface

It has been a while since I wrote my first book of this sort, *The New Faculty Member* (1992). I intended that book for an audience of faculty development professionals—those odd individuals, like myself, who devote their careers to helping colleagues—and for campus administrators who plan, fund, and evaluate faculty development programs. In the early 1990s, studies of what new faculty experienced were relatively new, as were attempts to programmatically ease the socialization period of novice professors.

The success of my earlier book in that regard, I am told, was reasonable. But its popularity elsewhere, as a book of advice for new faculty, has far surpassed expectations, my own and the publisher's. Its continuing use as a guidebook worries me because that edition focuses on establishing needs for faculty development programs and then on setting up and assessing programs; it says far less about specific directives for novice professors than it could have. Moreover, my first book on new faculty development is now dated. It is time for a more practical and readable version and here, I, hope you'll find it.

In a way, I'm glad to have waited. Since 1990, I've learned much more about what helps new faculty survive and thrive—so have my colleagues in this area of research and practice, many of them newly involved since my first book. Together, we've collected a remarkable amount of useful information compared to a mere decade ago.

The recently deceased leader in this burgeoning field about new faculty members, Robert Menges, conducted impressively broad inquiries about the experiences and needs of new faculty. And he, with his unfailing humor and fine work, acted as organizer and mentor for the rest of us in this arena. It was he, predictably, who conspired with my publisher, Steve Dragin at Allyn and Bacon, to coax this guidebook from me. Other major contributors to the field have also taken a nurturing interest in my career and welfare, encouraging me to stay with my projects even as I took early retirement from academe to heal a jaw and back injury: Ann Austin, Jim Cooper, Ken Feldman, Donald Jarvis, Lisa Lenze, Ann Lucas, Bob Lucas, Raymond Perry, and Maryellen Weimer, among others.

My appreciation goes to the following reviewers for their helpful comments on the manuscript: Anne E. Austin, Michigan State University; Roger G. Baldwin, College of William and Mary; Joseph B. Berger, University of New Orleans; Margie Kitano, San Diego State University; and Robert J. Menges, Northwestern University. I also thank my copy editor, Lynda Griffiths, for her patience, tolerance, and clear-seeing. My editor, Steve Dragin, was saintly in his reassurances about the worth of this book, in his suggestions for improving its organization, and in his tolerance of the adjustments I made due to my injuries.

My current respite from academe, after 30 years as a professor of psychology and as director of two large faculty development programs, is proving timely. I needed a break from the political intrigues surrounding faculty development programs and from their sudden changes of climate as higher administrations came and went. Now I understand that I needed time alone, away from it all, to see more clearly the kind of manual of advice I've wanted this to be. Here, in the remote mountains of western North Carolina, I've had a pleasant time rethinking and redrafting this book from its predecessor.

Introduction

Why New Professors Need Timely Advice

If you're beginning (or even planning) a professorial career, I congratulate you. I can't imagine a lifestyle with more opportunities for satisfaction and growth.

Think of it: Professors work mainly at their own pace and on their own schedules; they generally do the things they like most, such as reading and thinking. They have many days off and long vacations, including entire summers, if they wish. Their involvement as teachers and as scholars provides a self-education that can surpass all expectations. Their interactions with students and colleagues can be stimulating and fun; indeed, the depth and worth of such friendships may be unmatched in other professions. And few professors, once settled in, would trade their careers for any other. Nor would I.

Even so, this idyllic career poses hazards; its attractiveness is matched only by its risks of failure—especially at the outset. Innocence of those perils is an invitation to disappointment and despair. Moreover, naivete about the socialization process of the professoriate is wasteful. One fact stands out in my 20 years of studying new faculty: Almost all the failures and miseries of these new hires owed to misunderstandings about effective ways of working and socializing. Never, in my close observations of over a thousand novice professors, did I see someone falter for reasons of inexpertise in his or her area of scholarship. Or from lack of desire. Instead, the most telling mistakes were easily correctable problems such as not understanding how to moderate student incivilities in classrooms, not knowing how to manage enough writing for publication in modest amounts of time, and not learning how to elicit effective collegial support. Something else marked the career beginnings of new hires who would struggle and suffer: The immoderation and excessiveness with which they worked—with far more misdirection, busyness, and disruptive distress than for their successful peers who simplified their work and their lives.

This book, *Advice for New Faculty Members,* never loses sight of the upside of professorial experience, but it remains firmly grounded in reality. Its admonitions are based on long and systematic observation of what distinguishes new faculty members who excel from those who struggle and disappoint, and on careful experiments about which habits and attitudes of exemplary newcomers are most readily mastered by struggling new faculty. *Advice for New Faculty Members* offers simple, practical information for making a good start in your own career—information that too often remains unwritten and untold. It reveals how academic culture customarily winnows its "successful" members from its "failures." And, more important, it focuses on how newcomers can thrive, basically by way of practicing constancy and moderation—what our predecessors in the professoriate, still conversant in Latin, would have termed *nihil nimus* (loosely translated, "everything in moderation"). The idea is anything but new:

> *The [person] who works so moderately as to be able to work constantly, not only preserves his [or her] health the longest, but in the course of the year, executes the greatest quantity of work.—ADAM SMITH,* Wealth of Nations, *1776*

But even if all this is true, why attend to it now, when you are busy with graduate work or enduring the overscheduled first few years of a novice professor? Why not wait until you are caught up and settled?

Why This Usually Tacit Advice for Survival/Success Needs Early, Explicit Communication

The first few years in the careers of professors, beginning at the time they interview for their initial positions in academe, are an enormously critical period. Then, applicants and new hires *most* need useful advice but are least likely to receive it. Then, lasting patterns of success or failure develop with astonishing rapidity. And then, oddly, initiates to professorial careers are *least* receptive to advice.

Too often, novices begin inquiries about survival strategies after their careers are unsalvageable. When that happens, thwarted novices give a uniform reason for not having consulted proven advice such as this earlier: *Busyness.* Only when it is too late do they admit that a few hours a week spent learning and practicing constancy and moderation would have been a wise investment.

You may already sense three other common reasons for resisting advice books (in addition to whatever aversion I've induced with the moralistic warnings previously mentioned):

1. The professoriate attracts self-starting, self-reliant individuals who place high value on solving problems on their own. To seek or accept help, to take direction that might encourage conformity or submission, could signal unsuitability or weakness.
2. The professoriate quietly subscribes to a kind of Social Darwinism that supposes those of us without the "right stuff" will weed ourselves out of the profession. Perhaps because we experienced and survived the same unspoken arrangement in graduate school, we accept its continuation into the professoriate.
3. Usual advice for new faculty is sporadic, anecdotal, and unproven—no matter how well intentioned. In the midst of often conflicting and confusing advice, you may be tempted to ignore all of it.

Harbingers of Change

But there are signs that academe is at last offering useful advice to its new hires; orientations, for example, grow increasingly common and substantial. Indeed, you can spot a traditional Social Darwinistic campus by its absence of orientation programs for new faculty, or in orientations that offer little more than a parade of administrators delivering forgettable depictions of who they are and what their offices do (old-timers call this exhibition a "dog-and-pony show"). You can just as easily tell if a campus has embraced recent research by exposing new faculty to at least some of these aids:

- Introductions to peers in their cohort of new hires, in part to provide possibilities of friendship in what can ordinarily be a socially isolating job
- Meetings with junior faculty who have been on campus from 1 to 10 years and who offer useful, optimistic advice about good beginnings and hidden agendas
- Interactions with selected senior faculty experienced at noticing which new faculty most easily and satisfactorily navigate the socialization ritual
- Introductions to just the few administrators who need to be known from the outset (e.g., one's chairperson and dean)
- Direct contacts with campus faculty developers who provide long-term coaching in domains such as teaching, scholarship/research, and collegiality (e.g., workshops on cooperative learning/teaching)
- Written advice about how to find one's way amongst bureaucrats and regulations, about the local community, about campus and classroom demographics and customs, and about the hurdles of reappointment

Given usual budget constraints at colleges and universities, this ideal set of circumstances may not happen to you. If it does not, you can arrange equivalent experiences on your own or with the help of a book like this one. (I suggest alternative books in the Appendix, supposing that by then you will already own mine.) *Advice for New Faculty* provides first-order solutions to predictable hurdles (e.g., finding time for *both* teaching and writing amidst a busy schedule); it also emphasizes general strategies of planning and working that prevent most problems (e.g., starting manuscripts early and working at them in brief, daily sessions, instead of procrastinating and then rushing them in great binges). If that sounds too annoying or time consuming, compared to usual starts in professorial careers, keep this in mind: These simple strategies help produce more and better work in less time and with less strain. They characterize new faculty who succeed with ease. And they help newcomers survive and thrive. It's a fact.

Said another way, these fundamentals help simplify academic work. Here are several examples:

- Clarifications of generally unspoken rules for novice professors and specifications of instances (e.g., expectations that a newcomer will demonstrate independence from graduate school collaborations)
- Dilineation of common career "fault lines" that novice teachers should avoid (e.g., student incivilities in response to a fast and uninvolving pace of teaching)
- Advice from controlled studies about optimal ways of writing with ease, productivity, and acceptance (e.g., writing in brief, daily sessions, even before feeling ready)
- Directives for amplifying the benefits of mentoring (e.g., the necessity of confidentiality in interactions with mentors)

You could look it up, as James Thurber and Casey Stengel used to say; the literature in disciplines such as psychology, sociology, higher education, communication, composition, and engineering now teems with writings on new faculty experiences.

What Makes This Guidebook Unique

The sort of research-based information I've just overviewed, some of it new to the field of faculty development, is the substance of what follows in *Advice for New Faculty*. Its directive format—first about teaching, then writing, and then socializing—represents decades of empirical study as well as careful revision in handouts I once used in workshops for new faculty (and even in manuals for participants in my research-based programs). In a way, I'm saying the same old things over again because they work; but to an extent, I've simplified the advice and exercises ahead. You could find much of the same information in my separate publications about teaching (Boice, 1996a), writing (Boice, 1994), and socialization (Boyle & Boice, 1998). This book, as you might hope, pulls those efforts together.

In an important way, the book does less than before. Where I once interlaced my materials with every relevant bit of advice and expertise I could find from other faculty developers, I now limit such mentions to those consistent with empirical data about new faculty experience. The result, according to new faculty who read and used earlier versions of this book, is less distracting, less tedious, and more useful. I now focus on things proven to matter to new faculty in terms of what to expect, what to try to change, and what to accept.

Each strategy for constancy and moderation in the chapters ahead has four foundations:

1. Each has been documented as consistently distinctive and desirable in the new faculty I call "quick starters"—those 3 to 5 percent of novices who perform in exemplary fashion during their first few years on campus, without apparent help. Briefly, I have identified 21 exemplars—defined in terms of independent ratings of student approval of teaching, scholarly productivity/ acceptance, and social approval from gatekeeping colleagues—among the 415 new, tenure-track faculty I gradually tracked through their first years on campus.

2. The exemplars' habits and attitudes became models for normal new faculty— once those strategies were selected in repeated field studies as most helpful to the whole diversity of new faculty. While nontraditional new faculty were underrepresented amongst exemplars as I defined them, they were, without exception, just as able to adopt and benefit from exemplary practices as were White males.

3. Each exemplary strategy has been demonstrated to help novice professors, even those who had been identified by campus administrators as "in trouble," through R/P/T (retention, promotion, tenure) decisions with consistent success.

4. Each tactic has proven economical and enjoyable in long-term use.

Moreover, the broad, practical directives that comprise *Advice for New Faculty* have been verified as helpful for diverse new faculty at a variety of campuses. I first derived its principles at research/doctoral universities and at comprehensive campuses. (Comprehensive universities usually have large enrollments, public funding, and few, if any, doctoral programs. Examples are the California State University system and Appalachian State University, near my retirement home.) More recently, I've observed and interviewed new faculty at liberal arts colleges, technical campuses, and community colleges. Newcomers to the latter two sites benefit just as much as do others from advice based on their own "quick starters."

I've arranged the three sections of this book of advice and information in the order new faculty have told me they want them to appear. Section I explains proven ways of easing the surprisingly hard work of teaching, even at the most elite research campuses with the smallest teaching loads. Its strategies for action over the long run provide novice teachers with comfort, competence, and acceptance in the classroom at a critical juncture—during the first semester or two, when they might otherwise be overwhelmed and demoralized by teaching demands, including disaffected undergraduates and too little time for class preparations.

Section II reflects the first section in its similar principles for writing productively and painlessly. As a rule, these broad habits of writing overlap with those of teaching, but these more productive ways of writing reinforce an often shaky sense of scholarly competence in the nick of time—especially for those of us suffering from postdissertation trauma (a high-priced psychotherapist, as I once was, might label it *PDT*). Finding time for writing amid the busyness common to most new faculty helps in the domain that may count most toward reappointment/tenure: Scholarly productivity.

Section III centers on socialization of novices to professorial careers and it advises new hires about necessaries such as finding direction, mentoring, and collaboration before windows of opportunity close. Although these guidelines for socialization come last in the "preferred" sequence, their messages may apply first in professorial careers. So it is that I encourage you to look ahead to Section III early, before you feel ready.

The underlying principle of this common theme—about working/interacting with constancy and moderation—can be appreciated in another way: The advice in Sections I through III is more about *processes* of working as a professor (e.g., doing the right things in a timely manner and solving the essential problems first) than about *products* (e.g., how to format manuscripts for submission to editors; what, specifically, to include in grant proposals; how to make sense of end-of-semester teaching evaluations). Still, Section III extends practices of constancy and moderation to the fundamentals of "nuts-and-bolts" advice (e.g., what effective mentors can do to help you past the three most dangerous pitfalls just after arrival—social isolation, overpreparation of teaching materials, and an impatient pace that blocks writing).

And while I generally stay on course, I pause occasionally to make an aside like this one: You might wonder why my book isn't centered on the more specific advice found in most written directives for new faculty (e.g., "Don't become buddies with students"; "Don't plagerize your manuscripts"). The reason owes to a realization I came to while studying exemplary new faculty: The most useful advice begins with general ways of *working* in the professoriate with constancy and moderation. After new faculty learn *how* to work, they more likely benefit from specific advice such as *what* to do in constructing a classroom test or writing a well-formatted grant proposal. Once new faculty learn to work with constancy and moderation, they feel less busy, less threatened, more inclined to try new specifics. And because they slow down to notice the effects of how they work, they grow more likely to see how specifics can be put into practice broadly. So it is that I save most, but not all, "technical" advice until Section III. First things first.

A quick glance at the section and chapter titles and their brief descriptions can help prepare you for what lies ahead, most of it about moderation/*nihil nimus:*

Section I: Moderate Work at Teaching

Chapter 1, Rule 1: *Wait* actively, instead of rushing into tasks like lecture preparation, by practicing patient ways of slowing to notice alternatives and simplifications in what you can say and do. What usually undermines timely waiting? That great enemy of new faculty: Impatience. The same problem about holding back also undermines the moderate pacing of teaching necessary for student involvement and comprehension.

Chapter 2, Rule 2: *Begin Before Feeling Ready.* Once you are waiting actively, patiently, reflectively, you will be primed to begin early on necessary tasks, such as class preparations, before the work actually feels like work, before the work is rushed by looming deadlines. Preteaching can be done largely in spare moments. It generates surprising succinctness and creativity, and it saves time, compared to traditional ways of preparing classes.

Chapter 3, Rule 3: *Prepare and Present in Brief, Regular Sessions* instead of binges. That is, work in a pattern that not only affords a sense of being caught up but also allows time each day for other important things such as exercising, socializing, and writing.

Chapter 4, Rule 4: *Stop,* in timely fashion, both at preparing and then at teaching in class, before diminishing returns set in.

Chapter 5, Rule 5: *Moderate Overattachment and Overreaction* by assuming a more playful and tentative stance, by learning to seek out and learn from criticism while reacting less emotionally to it.

Chapter 6, Rule 6: *Moderate Negative Thinking and Strong Emotions* by working with an inclination to notice, dispute, and supplant disruptive and demoralizing self-talk; by preparing and teaching amid mild emotions to help moderate rushing and superficiality while working.

Chapter 7, Rule 7: *Let Others Do Some of the Work* as collaborators, even as critics.

Chapter 8, Rule 8: *Moderate Classroom Incivilities.* Quick starters show how to moderate classroom incivilities—partly defined as students who arrive late, noisily, and persist in talking aloud when someone else has the floor—with simple strategies of openness, pacing, and patience. This exemplary move is important because classroom incivilities often start with teachers' own incivilities, however unconscious.

Section II: Mindful Ways of Writing—Same Old Rules, New Perspective

Chapter 9, Rule 1: *Wait, Mindfully* by pausing reflectively to begin work in the moment and to resist old habits of rushing impulsively into prose.

Chapter 10, Rule 2: *Begin Early (Before Feeling Ready)* by way of freewriting and conceptual outlining that soon become prose and complete manuscripts.

Chapter 11, Rule 3: *Work with Mindful Constancy and Moderation* in brief, daily sessions and, after each, with ongoing awareness of what you will write the next session.

Chapter 12, Rule 4: *Stop, in Timely Fashion,* before a product orientation and its rushing subverts your process mode of working.

Chapter 13, Rule 5: *Balance Preliminaries with Writing* by spending as much time and energy on prewriting as on prose.

Chapter 14, Rule 6: *Let Go of Negative Thinking,* by noticing disruptive, distracting thoughts while writing and moderating them until you can write directly from mental images, without much intermediate thinking.

Chapter 15, Rule 7: *Moderate Emotions,* particularly the strong euphoria of writing in binges (and the depression that follows it).

Chapter 16, Rule 8: *Moderate Attachments,* chiefly by way of seeking out and listening mindfully to criticism; secondarily by learning to work with a sense of humor and mindful distancing.

Chapter 17, Rule 9: *Let Others Do Some of the Work* by learning from their criticisms, by employing their suggestions for improvement, by collaborating with them.

Chapter 18, Rule 10: *Limit Wasted Effort* by noticing whether you are solving the right problems, by seeing the savings in terms of time and energy, and by arranging more "success experiences" and their resulting resilience.

Section III: Socialize with Compassion

Chapter 19, Rule 1: *Learn about Academic Culture Early and Patiently.* And so, arrange realistic expectations by understanding customs, eccentric faculty members, and usual faux pas of novices in academe. Extend that inquiry to brief interviews with experienced colleagues, at first as casual then as more formal advisors.

Chapter 20, Rule 2: *Let Others Do Some of Your Work.* Do more than connecting regularly; accept direct help, even mentoring, from colleagues. Extend this social stance to cooperative learning and classroom research approaches in your own teaching.

Chapter 21, Rule 3: *Extend Self-Service to Service for Others.* Exemplary new faculty say, "Not until you take adequate care of yourself should you begin to perform service on and off campus" and "When you do begin to serve others, start close to home, where you are most readily qualified, by collaborating with other new faculty who need constancy and moderation in work." This exemplar-based approach to service begins with reading, observing, and interacting to understand new faculty experience, in general, then the special challenges faced by nontraditional new hires. I've abstracted some crucial readings about that latter experience, and then a pioneering study on the special pitfalls for women and minorities to illustrate how extremes educate and sensitize us. That experience, if carried out in exemplary fashion, often extends to service as cooperative collaboration with other new faculty most in need of help.

Feeling overwhelmed at the prospect of covering all that? Then please notice what I've just implied in the preceding schematic: For one thing, all three sections revolve around simple, proven ways of working at professorial tasks; every way of working is about moderation, about saving you time while enhancing your performance, survival, and happiness. Second, I've prepared all this advice and information with general brevity and directness, always based on tests of what is most effective for new faculty over the long run. And third, this book is *not* designed to be read and put into practice in a single sitting. Or even a few. In advising you how to read and use it, I repeat the advice of one of the greatest teachers of efficient ways of working and playing:

Be quick, but don't hurry. —*JOHN WOODEN*

All you need do is suspend your impatience with a book that tries to teach patience and moderation— during what may be the most impatient and immoderate period of your life. It's not as difficult as it sounds.

Section I

Moderate Work
at Teaching

Rationale for a Nihil Nimus *(Moderate)* *Approach to Teaching*

The truth about how new faculty begin as teachers is easily observed but not generally known: A close look reveals that too many novices struggle with seeming demands for classroom preparations and that that too few experience ready acceptance and comprehension from students. More important, poor starts as teachers are difficult to undo; they predict career-long ambivalence and avoidance. Another thing usually goes unobserved:

A clue to good starts in the classroom may lie with the minority of new faculty who begin with ease and acceptance. I call them quick starters. In decades of observing hundreds of novice teachers at various campuses, I found that some 3 to 5 percent of them made such exemplary starts as teachers that, compared to other new faculty, they showed:

- The lowest levels of incivilities in their classes (e.g., rates at which students arrived late, noisily, and talked aloud during the lecture)
- The highest ratings of student involvement, based on external observations of students attending and taking useful notes, asking questions, and engaging in discussions
- The most observed instances of moderately paced lecturing that allowed students to take meaningful notes and to comprehend the main lecture points
- The most balance between time spent preparing for class (e.g., writing lecture notes) and in class; that is, quick starters were most likely to show moderation

in the activity that other new faculty tended to carry to debilitating extremes (e.g., exemplars displayed a ratio under 2:1, other newcomers showed a rate of 4:1)
- The briefest, most tentative lecture notes taken to class

Yet another thing distinguished quick starters: They worked most often without rushing and busyness; instead, they generally displayed mild happiness and moderate emotions. So it was, they liked to say, that work at teaching gladdened rather than fatigued them. They were able to enjoy teaching as a process of discovery, their own and their students', without obsessive concerns about covering all the material, or about being seen as unfailingly correct and bright by students.

In explaining the eight general rules about good starts at teaching in the eight chapters that follow, I expand on moderate *(nihil nimus)* ways of working. Each has proven effective for the diverse groups of new faculty who tested them. Almost without exception, participants agreed that this *nihil nimus* approach surpassed customary trial-and-error methods of learning to teach.

Why Is This First Section of the Book about Teaching?

In my 20 years of observations, far and away the most suffering for new faculty occurred in relation to classroom teaching. Nothing else, not even writing for publication or coming to campus with few social supports, consumed nearly so much time and well-being. No other demand so effectively supplanted social life and professional productivity. And nothing else was so likely to get novices thinking about abandoning academic careers.

Why Teaching, at Least in Its Beginnings, Is So Perilous

Tradition in academe holds, mistakenly, that if you know your material, you can teach it. Said formulaicly:

good content knowledge = good teaching

That belief is part of the reason why traditional graduate training programs deliberately do little more than train scholars and researchers. And even when graduate years include teaching experiences, they usually amount to grading papers, leading discussion sections, and occasional lectures. Once faced with their first real teaching "loads," most novices repeat the process they learned in presenting those few lectures and a handful of graduate seminars: Extensive, painstaking preparation with a focus on understanding and covering everything—especially on avoiding criticism about a lack of comprehensiveness. Not only is this approach—one I like to call the graduate seminar method of teaching—time consuming in preparation but it also usually includes too little concern about how audiences understand and learn. It generates too much material to cover in the time allotted, too fast a pace of presentation to permit audience participation, and, in the end, exhaustion (perhaps even a bored audience). Imagine extending this time-honored pattern of preparing and presenting to classes that meet repeatedly—3, 6, 9, 12, 15 hours a week for 30 or more weeks a year—and you begin to see possibilities for inefficiency at a world-class level.

If, say, you have a teaching load of six hours in your first semester (a lighter than average assignment among new faculty I studied), this is how your time will be spent if you follow the norms I've documented:

- 6 hr/wk in class plus some 20 min/day interacting with students before and/ or after each class meeting (total = at least 10 hr/wk)
- 18–30 hr/wk preparing lectures/classroom materials via reading, notetaking, writing, plus another 2 hr/wk, on average, grading tests and papers, etc. (total = at least 18 hr/wk, often as much as 40 hr/wk)
- 6 hr/wk for office hours (total = at least 6 hr/wk, and much more for faculty who do not keep office doors closed past official office hours)

Keep a few things in mind about this discomfiting estimate of 30+ hr/wk for teaching responsibilities: First, it is conservative for most new faculty, except for exemplars and their mimics. Second, where campuses demand loads of 9 to 12 hours, time spent at teaching usually equals 50–60 hr/wk during the first two years. Third, these averages afford *far* less time than anticipated for good starts at scholarly writing, for setting up labs and research and field programs, for preparing grant applications, for reading of professional literatures, for keeping in touch with colleagues at other campuses, and for socializing on the new campus. Fourth, the dearest costs of this heavy demand come in social/family life, exercising, health, and sleep.

In my tracking studies of newcomers, exemplars were least often ill. Peers who spent the most time at teaching preparation most often suffered from influenza, headaches, and dysphorias.

Add to all that, if you can stand it, a final surprise in this disheartening picture of novice teachers working at the college level: Although excessive investments in time/energy at careful preparations for classes represent true conscientiousness and hard work, the typical results are anything but commensurate: (1) an unengaged, ungrateful reception from undergraduate students; (2) classrooms dominated by student noise and other incivilities; (3) poor student comprehension of key concepts and essential facts and equally disappointing performance on papers and tests; (4) mediocre ratings from students, sometimes accompanied by insults;

and (5) personal distress over spending so much time on so unrewarding an activity—especially one that excludes effective work at things with more apparent likelihood of reward, like research and writing. Why do these things matter? Gatekeepers who decide about reappointment/tenure expect that teaching should not keep new hires from making rapid, substantial progress in domains such as publishing, grant procurement, and university service.

Almost All New Faculty Take Teaching Seriously

Why, given the disheartening facts I've just presented, don't most new faculty simply do the minimum as teachers? In part, they've told me, because virtually all of them were inspired to professorial careers by at least one good teacher they'd like to emulate. In part, also, because they suspect their new campuses, even of the research sort, may terminate them for obviously poor, uncaring performances in the classroom. (In fact, at the research and comprehensive campuses I studied, new faculty were more often terminated for blatantly unacceptable teaching than for failures to publish enough.) And, most new teachers take teaching seriously because they want to enjoy teaching. They *do* desire to teach what interests them and what seems to be important material. Despite initial disclaimers, they do want to be liked by students. I can't recall a single new hire who didn't work hard at and care about teaching—although the least successful often masked their disappointment with cynicism and complaints about students.

Why These Facts May Dismay and Then Please

Have I exaggerated the usual experience of a new faculty member here? Not hardly, as John Wayne liked to say. This disheartening information may astonish you because the facts about initial teaching experiences are only just coming to light (e.g., Bullough, Knowles, & Crow, 1991); previously, novice teachers had supposed their struggles idiosyncratic and everyone else's lessor. Why has useful information about commonly difficult starts been slow in appearing? To an extent, academe has accepted awkward starts at teaching as inevitable. More often, campuses ignore the performances of new faculty unless they cause a rash of student complaints; new teachers are left to sink or swim, presumably because they must learn on their own or because they cannot be taught to teach.

Still, there is good news in all this. The new faculty I call quick starters can model for us ways of making far less painful, more satisfying beginnings as teachers. Those fundamental principles can be easily managed by the rest of us—with less effort than by trial and error.

What is deceptive about these fundamentals of moderation is their simplicity; they are so basic that they are rarely taught or even mentioned to college teachers.

One veteran teacher condemned my approach by publicly announcing, "Why, any fool could learn these things!" I agreed and included myself as one of many such learners.

Why hasn't tradition taught teachers this tacit knowledge? The equation about good content equaling good teaching is at the heart of it. Whatever help tradition provides for college teachers is usually more about content than about ways of working (i.e., more about product than process). So, for example, workshops for new teachers often focus on planning course material and getting the plan into a syllabus. Something else can keep us from learning how to work effectively as teachers: Historically, professors have disliked labeling teaching as "work." Its usual pain and struggling—along with the common assumption that good teachers are born, not made—seem more consistent with an "art of teaching." In that view, good teaching cannot depend on rules of the sort presented here, although the alternatives, except for good luck and good genes, seem vague. Said another way, tradition leads us to suppose that excellence in teaching can only be learned through experience that lies beyond advice in books. Even some authors of books of advice on college teaching make this curious claim.

Fortunately, observations of quick starters—and of other new faculty practicing their distinctive strategies of moderation—suggest that an alternative approach works better than the sink-or-swim mentality of tradition. What exemplars do that distinguishes them from struggling teachers is largely a matter of simple skills, such as the pacing and patience that limit fatigue and enhance student involvement.

What Nihil Nimus *Means in Practices of Teaching*

The *nihil nimus* (i.e., nothing in excess) approach of this book is at first more about learning to work efficaciously than about content issues. It is, as you know, more about the *process* of teaching in ways that promote involvement and learning than about the *product* orientation of getting through all the planned material correctly, brilliantly. After all, content tends to be more specific to disciplines and types of courses, even to the individual styles of teachers.

Once teachers learn to work with moderation and a process orientation, content matters take care of themselves. Why? Because, almost without exception, novice professors already know (or are learning) their subject areas. Where they struggle, as a rule, is in finding effective ways of communicating that massive knowledge economically and effectively to undergraduates who know (and care) far less about it.

The *nihil nimus* approach means looking for simple, effective strategies that allow new faculty to work efficiently amid a seeming overload of demands for their time and energy. A catch in depicting the simplicity of this usually tacit knowledge is the redundancy it requires. Principles of the *nihil nimus* sort are so uncomplicated and useful that they reward brief repetition in each new context. In the chapters ahead, I apply the same general principle—moderation in working— over and over, albeit in slightly different ways. Why is this problematic? In earlier versions of this book, I found this redundancy tries the patience of already impatient readers. "It is," said one of them angrily, "a book about patience that makes me even more impatient." Readers who benefited most practiced these repetitive methods with the clearest displays of tolerance and trust: Tolerance to rehear and reconsider principles that initially sound too counterintuitive or self-evident for careful listening, and trust to take the plunge and try some ideas and strategies that seem too foreign or time consuming. While you may profit in beginning with a brisk perusal of the pages ahead, real benefit awaits more patient and tolerant immersion—at least that is what the great majority of my program 'graduates' have told me in earnest.

Why Moderated Ways of Work Prove Tolerable

Let me recount or anticipate the ways:

- These *nihil nimus* principles nurture fast and easy success at classroom teaching.
- These same basic ways of working generalize, almost effortlessly, to other priority tasks, including writing for publication/funding (more about this in Section II).
- The tolerance and experimentation they teach helps novices make better use of traditional advice about teaching.
- These simplicities take less time and energy than expected and they soon save more of both than they cost; they may even reward novices who want only a brief look.

Why This Approach Elicits Initial Objections

Folklore holds that efficiencies interfere with creative acts, including teaching. Traditionalists often assume that teaching, done well, must be spontaneous and completely unique to each individual, without rules or constraints, without concern for economies of working. And, as we have seen, these conservatives implicitly believe its true mastery can be managed only by those of us born to teach. Empirically based arenas of academic work, such as physics, suggest a reason why we need to rethink those customary notions:

Physics is experience, arranged in economical order.—ERNST MACH

So is teaching.

The Plan for Section I

I've arranged this initial collection of chapters in an order that begins with the simplest strategies for preparing teaching materials and moves to a more complex demonstration of how *nihil nimus* principles apply to real-life problems with students.

I first address the related problems of busyness and overpreparation. New teachers often want to know how to find enough time to prepare classes that will include essential and stimulating information. So it is that Chapters 1 through 3 teach ways of preparing in brief, regular sessions of work that begin with patient noticing and noting of what you might teach, and then move you to initiate informal preparations long before you feel ready. Where do moderation and its constancy come into play? First, these early chapters explain exemplary ways of practicing patience and calm pacing—and other things that help teachers feel comfortable and in control long before they go to class. Second, the initial chapters center on beginning work early, before you feel fully ready or inspired (cf. the immoderation of working at the last minute, under deadlines). The most effective, reliable inspiration and motivation come in the *wake* of working, not in advance of it. And third, we begin with ways of segmenting work into brief sessions in order to better clarify and simplify the work.

Chapters 4 through 7 focus on slightly more demanding forms of moderation. Chapter 4 shows why stopping when enough has been done for the moment is an essential step in learning the control that undergirds moderation. Stopping is just as important a skill as starting. Chapters 5 and 6 teach ways of reining in negative thinking and letting go of excessive needs for control/attachment, even allowing other people do some of the work of teaching (Chapter 7).

Finally, Chapter 8 deals with tough but manageable issues of *classroom comfort* and *control*. It uses *nihil nimus* principles to moderate classroom incivilities. This step may be most fundamental in learning to work at teaching with ease and discovery, with optimal student acceptance and comprehension, with career-long commitment to teaching excellence. Chapter 8, which the brave among you might want to peruse first, includes a brief overview, one of the first of its kind, of how classroom incivilities derail or at least demoralize teaching careers. It then demonstrates how distinctive actions of quick starters, such as "positive motivators" and "social immediacies," help reduce those distractions. Why might you want to begin at the end of this section on teaching? Because initial classes can easily get off to poor starts within the first week or two of class meetings. Why do I put this information last? Because the unpleasant nature of classroom incivilities has discouraged some early readers from persisting in the *nihil nimus* approach; more so because the chapters that precede it gradually build the skills needed to deal with classroom incivilities; and most so because it fits nicely at the end of our journey through the fundamentals of working at teaching, as a practical example of how moderation helps novice teachers manage so difficult and pervasive a problem in real-life situations.

I've already hinted at some of the research-based outcomes for novices (and even for veteran teachers) that underlie all eight of these chapters: Moderated time spent preparing for class, more comfort and acceptance in class, fewer incivilities and more student attentiveness, more student comprehension, and significantly higher student ratings at semesters' ends. Notable among these benefits are stronger self-ratings of commitment to teaching excellence and to efficiencies in achieving it.

This is the plan:

Eight Rules for Working at Teaching with Moderation

There are more, but these eight have proven most effective and timely for new faculty.

1. Wait, patiently and actively
2. Begin early, before feeling ready
3. Prepare and teach in brief, regular bouts
4. Stop, before diminishing returns set in
5. Moderate negative thinking and strong emotions
6. Moderate overattachment to content
7. Let others do some of the work
8. Moderate classroom incivilities

I hope, much like a teacher starting a class with some intriguing propositions, to have attracted enough curiosity to keep you involved.

1

Wait

Most of us already know how to wait before getting to work at teaching preparations—at least in the usual sense, passively but amid an unproductive and unpleasant mixture of impatience and apathy. Passive waiting wastes time and energy in at least five ways:

1. It puts off preparations until we have ideal conditions, including a big block of undisrupted time.
2. It spends our time in the meanwhile on less important, more immediately satisfying tasks such as writing memos and making phone calls.
3. It rushes work, once we get to it, until we have completed it all—preferably in one sitting.
4. Its all-or-none attitude about working dichotomizes teaching preparation from our daily experience, as something to be contemplated and done only at specific times when we do nothing else.
5. Its associated habit, of waiting and then rushing, brings hurried classes and "distanced" students.

Active Waiting

What makes *active waiting* different from the passive kind? It is patient and productive. And, it means getting ready without an all-or-none decision to rush into work and finish it now or else put it off. The hard part of active waiting is the patience required, first to wait and reflect and prepare ideas and other material for teaching without insistence that the task be finished in one sitting, second to suspend work on a class preparation in order to do more with it the next day, while imagining during the interim how it will engage students as active learners. Active waiting means holding back, tentatively and briefly, during times when you might have put off preparations because you could not have done them perfectly and completely—or else worked at them to excess in a heated binge.

Because active waiting usually stimulates brief and casual outputs, it can be managed in the interstices of doing other important things. How do I know that active waiting can work this way? Quick starters reliably model this pattern for the rest of us. And, better yet, other novice teachers acquire its basics with more ease and benefit than they had anticipated.

How, exactly, is this sort of moderation managed? Active waiting, because it promotes early and contemplative starts at preparing a class, builds the kind of reflectiveness basic to good decision making and economical presentation. It helps teachers relax and see what is most essential. And it brings dividends in the longer run.

Active Waiting Aims for Long-Term Rewards

Active waiting teaches us ways of putting up with short-term discomforts (such as temptations to do something else more immediately relieving in an open moment) in order to gain longer-term rewards (such as, more reflective and succinct classroom preparations). It requires subduing the part of yourself that wants to put off teaching preparations until you've completely caught up on other things. But for all that, active waiting saves time over the long run. One way it does that is by freeing you to do two or more things at once—for example, preparing for teaching during the little openings that occur during even busy days, yet making enough progress on other things that matter.

This sort of active waiting—where you begin to prepare or revise class materials in odd moments—usually requires suspension of disbelief to get it underway. It might sound too scattered, too untidy, compared to completing preparations in a single long sitting. It might sound too time consuming. Or it might seem like a rule that would work better for other people than for you ("I like to prepare things at the last minute, when I'm forced to, when the material will be fresh for class; I think it's quicker that way and besides, I couldn't work in bits and pieces"). But before you dismiss the notion of active waiting, take another look at how and why it works. And, too, remember that this simple strategy is characteristic of quick starters and central to the improvements of other novice teachers in my programs.

Specifics of Active Waiting

- Active waiting means holding back, reflectively, instead of rushing.
- It means starting to work on teaching well before usual, formal sessions of preparing or teaching.
- It can amount to little more than merely making notes of thoughts about upcoming classes during lulls in other activities, such as waiting for an appointment or for television commercials to end.

- Active waiting helps teachers find imagination and motivation earlier and more easily, through playful, unrushed organization of materials and plans.
- It often gets teachers preparing classroom materials before they realize they are working; active waiting is more enjoyable and economical than passive waiting.
- And, because this patient reflectivity helps simplify material—by way of repeated exposures, reexaminations, and reorderings during early preparations—it means that lectures are presented with fewer main points and with more explanations of each. That pattern, incidentally, enhances student notetaking and is characteristic of exemplary teachers, novice and veteran. When preparations are patient and simplified, so are the presentations. Teachers who learn to pause and notice related things during and between these brief preparations show similar patterns of timing and listening in class. They even listen, patiently, to themselves.

So the pace of work at preparing classes is less taxing for teachers who practice active waiting. Enjoyment and learning grow as fatigue is lessened by way of brief, scattered work sessions. And as active waiting elicits informal preparations and revisions before they seem like work, the whole effort is easier—in terms of total time spent preparing and of teachers' self-ratings of effort.

Active waiting also enlightens teachers. Its tentativeness and repeated reacquaintance with the materials in their formative stages help us see new connections. Its experimentalism shows us what kinds of moderation work best: (1) calming and slowing during preparations to consider links between points we're making; (2) pausing again in similar fashion once in class, with the same patience, even the same nonverbal cues of immediacy, such as calm smiling, until students help solve problems; and (3) remembering aloud, in class, how we worked to solve the problems during preparations. Good teachers reveal both process and product.

Because active waiting is almost always experimental and explorative, it helps us moderate the perfectionism of supposing that we should make no mistakes, that we must know everything, that we ought to be in constant control as teachers. It does this by showing us that early preparations, even when still diagrammatic and imperfect, often suffice to say the necessary in class. It teaches us that preparations can almost always be done and said differently. And that remaining imperfections will be a stimulus to pausing and reflecting, aloud, as part of a more spontaneous and involving presentation. In my studies of student notetaking, comprehension is best when teachers talk aloud the ways they solve problems of understanding things, especially if they rethink statements that now seem unclear or mistaken. This tendency to openly admit confusion and then resolve it is, incidentally, by far most common among exemplars—the same teachers rated as most knowledgeable, competent, and likeable by students.

While active waiting takes practice and patience, research demonstrates its worth. In fact, active waiting proves more economical and effective than traditional delayed, rushed, and prolonged preparations. The principle involved proves to be surprisingly simple and old:

Make haste slowly.—NICOLAS BOILEAU

There are still more benefits in active waiting, some of them unimaginable until experienced. It allows serenity and creativity in work because it is neither tense nor hurried. It generates a growing mindfulness of having done something important and worth saying before saying it. It tolerates a more casual but focused attitude toward preparing and presenting; teaching presentations that once had to be fully written out are more easily and enjoyably done from conceptual outlines and diagrams that often fill but a page per class meeting.

With active waiting, decisions about the *final* structure of the content are put off, actively and deliberately, sometimes until in class. Consequently, classes grow more spontaneous, more involving of students as active participants. And, once more, active waiting—because it spreads the task over time and circumstance—allows more opportunity for discovery in teaching. Discovery, in turn, generates enthusiasm and hooks people on teaching, even at campuses where teaching is not overtly encouraged or rewarded.

Why Is Active Waiting Unfamiliar?

Part of the reason may be obvious. We persist in passive waiting, unquestioningly, because it is how almost all of us learned to prepare seminar papers and the like. Moreover, usual educations do not encourage us to notice how passivity and impatience work quietly but in vicious circles. Their usual results are procrastination and stage fright (Boice, 1996b).

The impulsivity and power of passive waiting customarily go as unseen as its kin, procrastination. Meanwhile, accepted notions of passive waiting, including the mistaken belief that geniuses work best by awaiting maddening binges, can make us too busy or proud to follow rules about patience. Passive waiting is so strong and unquestioned a habit that I'll remind you about the benefits of replacing it with active waiting:

- Active waiting finds time for small, informal beginnings that cause little disruption in the daily scheme of things.
- It encourages playful and reflective approximations to what will be done during serious work sessions.
- It gets the real work of teaching underway without obvious or aversive effort.
- It avoids usual inefficiencies such as procrastinating by working, busily, on something unnecessary to survival in academe or well-being. Exemplary new faculty tend to work at and solve the right problems (e.g., finding ways to moderate preparation times for classes), whereas strugglers do not.

Traditional books of advice about teaching rarely say much about the importance of patience and active waiting. There, too, we may already know the reason why. Custom directs novices to attend to content (e.g., organizing lecture material, constructing internally reliable tests) and to style (e.g., how to dress, whether to insist that students call you "doctor"). Exemplary new faculty, in contrast, like to say that content-oriented matters are more easily and readily managed while already learning moderate ways of working.

Rule 1: Wait.

Exercises for Rule 1

The following exercises have proven the most practical in my research. I recommend that you try them in order but without expecting them to work perfectly, at least at first. In long-term practice, some teachers rework the scheme to suit themselves, often with success. After all, the point of this advice is to tempt you to learn patient, reflective practices as a teacher, not just my set of rules.

As you read these suggestions for exercises, imagine yourself seated and about to prepare material for a specific class.

Exercise 1. Pause Before Writing or Talking, to Reflect.

That is, WAIT! Actually pause for a moment, perhaps as long as two seconds. Be prepared to hold yourself back if you feel an urge to do something else more immediately comforting (e.g., "First I'll make that phone call, and then I'll settle down to this"). Then, use these brief pauses of slowing and calming to sketch ideas, diagrams—even to jot down a quote. As thoughts appear, even vaguely, talk them over with yourself. If you cannot think of anything, freewrite what you guess you might think, by writing whatever comes to mind and without stopping to correct or edit. Whatever else, write it down, at least in some kind of shorthand or diagram. And then imagine talking it aloud with your students and how they will react/interact. All this, believe it or not, can be done in a few minutes.

Now, as you begin to begin, hold back for yet another reminder of where this exercise will take you. It will take only a minute. Patience, patience, patience!

Even so simple an act of active waiting brings the following, reliable, changes in my own programs for once-struggling novice teachers:

- A growing reflectiveness, especially in terms of audience awareness, helps simplify teaching materials to their most memorable and connectable essentials. As teachers grow more calm and contemplative, they more often organize lectures and discussions into a few central points they hope to make for the day. They replace the additional points they were tempted to make with more examples and applications of the central points.

- A slower, more deliberate style of preparing and presenting leaves teaching materials less rigidly structured and more creative, exciting.
- A reduction in tension and fatigue is attributed by participants to working less hard, and to learning to anticipate student reactions.

What if you feel too impatient or unprepared to try these things? To get past your "blocking," even if you don't quite see it or believe in it, experiment with easy moves that ensure small successes. Again, start with pauses, maybe no more than a minute of reflection and noting before formally writing out classroom materials. And then practice a brief lapse at the outset of a class, perhaps for two to three seconds before lecturing (a near eternity until you are accustomed to it). Use that hesitation in class to calm yourself, to establish rapport with students by way of eye contact and smiling, and—horror of horrors for most academicians, including me—indulging in small talk. Use the pause to set a reasonable, unrushed pace for talking. In other words, *wait.*

Exercise 2. Use Pauses Playfully and Planfully.

Instead of trying to write or diagram final versions of classroom materials immediately, pause to make preliminary notes, doodles, and diagrams about what you *could* write and say. This bit of active waiting, done in moderation, requires only a few minutes. Its brief but playful stance in organizing your material often suggests new ways of seeing the message you'll want to impart.

Use this time and its preliminary thinking to begin to clarify your goals for class materials you will be preparing more formally later on. More specifically, reflect on what you want students to learn as you consider the content of a class. The earlier the planning and goal setting, the better.

Remind yourself that research distinguishes expert problem solvers as people who take time to pause and to consider alternatives, who make sure they are solving the right problem or answering the right question. They do this, incidentally, with especial benefit on time-limited tasks such as test taking, where other people tend to rush and act impulsively.

Exercise 3. Put Some of What You Think/Visualize into Writing.

One of the most productive ways to practice this combination of pausing and informal preparations is to put your first thoughts about a new or revised lecture into freely writing whatever comes to mind and without editing. If you feel stymied, begin with a bit of freetalking, or by talking aloud your ideas and plans to a friend before writing them down. These methods can help you improve as a self-listener who uncovers the deeper ideas that occur after the ones have passed that might have been acted on impulsively. If you don't listen to yourself, others won't either.

Notice how this kind of active pausing saves time. Once your ideas are written down and simplified, rewriting them into sufficient forms of class notes goes quickly and flexibly. Revision is almost always easier and better than original writing.

Exercise 4. Remind Yourself Why Active Waiting Is Economical.
One economy is about avoiding deadlines and their stresses. In my own programs, participants translated their prewritten and prediagrammed notes into class notes well before nonparticipants began preparing their classes of similar dates. Another economy is about succinctness. The notes/plans that participants took to class were more generally abbreviated and quickly apprehended in a glance than were those of nonparticipants. A third economy for participants is less total time spent getting ready for class, usually a savings of at least half the time spent preparing by matched nonparticipants.

Know, too, that these participants, apparently because they talked in class with only general points and directions in mind, spent less time looking at notes while making more obvious attempts to elicit the attention, comprehension, and involvement of students. They even tended to say things more directly, more simply, more memorably, probably because their notes were written in much the same way. And they brought more pauses to classes. After classes, it figures, program teachers reported less fatigue and more satisfaction.

If the advantages of active waiting sound too good to be true, I assure you they're not. Instead, they are simply uncommon and generally unknown, except among those odd individuals I've called quick starters—and in those brave souls who have emulated the working styles of exemplary novices.

Question: What Usually Keeps Teachers from Mastering These Practices?
One answer: The same thing that makes giving up impatience difficult—issues of control in the short versus long run. Impatience impels us to hurry to finish preparations at once because the rushing and its euphoria create illusions of control and brilliance; when we speed and finish quickly, we feel brilliant and we seem unstoppable. And, too, Western civilization teaches us that busyness displays are useful and impressive. Who looks more important than a professor rushing down a hallway, bent forward like a missile, facial expression defying any mortal to interrupt him or her?

Another answer draws on the power of custom:

All men command patience, although few be willing to practice it.
—THOMAS à KEMPIS

The alternative to impatience—active waiting—is easier, but only in the long run. In the short run, then, it helps to have a reminder at hand to pause, such as a bold note in your classroom materials that might say: "WAIT!" or to post the reasons why rushing undermines good teaching at your work site, even in the margins of your class notes:

- Rushing at teaching lowers student comprehension.
- It distances students and turns them into passive, often uncivil, class members.
- It narrows the focus and flexibility of the teacher.
- It fatigues.

Exercise 5. Pause **While** *Working.*

This major step resembles pausing and waiting before beginning but it is more trying. Once we are underway at preparing materials or presenting them, we grow more and more reluctant to pause. Part of the problem, of course, lies with impatience. You already know the scenario: The more we rush and binge, the stronger our impatience becomes. The harder we try to get everything done and said at once, the more we talk nonstop and discourage student questions. To see this, notice what happens as you attempt to do even more as classroom time expires: You exhaust yourself and throw yourself, almost like someone in a footrace, over the finish line; some of your students squirm uncomfortably and the others try to cue you about the time by closing notebooks or leaving as you speak. Then imagine how much of what you rushed to say was comprehended. My own examinations of what students noted and recalled after such classes confirm your worst suspicions.

A difficulty here is also about *letting go of control:* When we pause with a class looking at us, the act can make us self-conscious and insecure. When leaving pauses unfilled (e.g., without even an "uh-h-h" or "you know") is not a familiar act, we can easily suppose the class will instantly riot or at least conclude something is wrong. In fact, if you don't, they won't. While talking nonstop appears a good way to maintain control, it isn't in the long run. We will see more of the reason why in Chapter 8, on classroom incivilities: When students cannot keep up with our impatient pace, when they have no respites from listening and noting, when they conclude we do not care about their involvement or comprehension, they distance themselves from us.

Remember that good teaching is in some ways like good conversion; few of us like interactions where the other person talks without ceasing, without ever inquiring about us.

Excercise 6. Use Pauses to Relax and Contemplate *but* **Not** *to Worry.*

Once you make your practice of regular pauses easy with the aid of external cues, such as reminders within your class notes, work at using those interludes to calm and relax yourself by slowing your breathing for a moment and following its course in and out.

Try such a pause now.

Use pauses to take stock of where you are and where you will go next. This last act cues students to do the same, especially if you talk some of your reflection aloud. The simplest versions of this excercise are among the most effective:

- Attend to your breathing and, for the moment, consciously staying in the moment contentedly.
- Check and readjust your posture and facial expression for more comfortable, open, and optimistic versions.
- Stretch out to loosen up—for example, by shrugging and then letting your shoulders go as you exhale slowly; better yet, invite your students to join you in these respites.
- Notice where you build tension while preparing or presenting, such as your stomach, neck, jaw, foreheads and lower back; then use pauses to deliberately relax those places, perhaps by first tensing them even more and then relaxing them.

After keeping pauses brief, find ways to ease back into your work. Exemplars commonly spend the moment before returning by reflecting and asking, "What's next?" They look back on what they have just been doing, particularly on what worked best, while congratulating themselves on their successes. They consider whether any changes in plans are needed. And then, calmly and clearly, they rehearse the next few points and how they might be said. All this fits nicely into 5 or 10 seconds of reflection. Isn't it amazing that quick starters and their imitators have so much leisurely time while teaching?

There is even time for something else important in these pauses: noticing their benefits. Without active efforts at appreciating the benefits of things like relaxing a tense jaw or getting excited about what you will say next, active waiting may not persist long enough to become an automatic habit.

When do teachers find time for pauses that last even a minute or two? They find them right in the midst of class. They simply announce that they are taking a brief break to rest and reflect (and that students might want to do likewise, without leaving their physical places and mental sets). Despite the usual concerns of teachers facing this exercise, few of their students object or act out (as psychologists call it)—and those who do, impatiently, soon get used to pauses and tolerate them better. Surprisingly, these interludes do not interfere with presenting enough material. In fact, the same teachers who work with pauses in one class and then without them in other classes get more planned presentation done in the former situation. How can that be possible? Because the pauses help them economize, in part by seeing ways of saying things more simply, in part by doing some of the teaching while answering the student questions that become more likely during and after pauses.

This sort of active waiting also introduces teachers to an unexpected benefit: Because pauses punctuate the flow of the class, teachers begin to see that they can easily set up different rhythms. Sometimes they accelerate material to accent it; other times they slow for emphasis. By changing pace, teachers learn a way of holding the attention of classes.

As teachers find comfort with active waiting, they are already mastering the next rule, another one first modeled by quick starters.

2

Begin Before Feeling Ready

At first glance, this second rule (Begin Early) seems to contradict the first (Wait). Resolution lies in remembering that active waiting (Rule 1) is a matter of beginning early, with preliminaries that get the work underway before it feels like real work. In fact, Rule 1 presages and overlaps with Rule 2.

So, as we already know, early beginnings get us working on task before it seems we are really working. And they establish momentum where we might otherwise ambivalate and procrastinate. The more effective and healthy the teacher, in my experience, the stronger the inclination to begin early and informally. The idea is familiar, at least to writers.

> *Don't loaf and invite inspiration; light out after it with a club, and if you don't get it you will nonetheless get something that looks remarkably like it.—JACK LONDON*

How Difficult Is Beginning Early?

In a way, this kind of moderation isn't as easy as it sounds, at least until it becomes an ingrained habit. Beginning early requires the patience and tolerance for regular practice before it seems beneficial. It also demands a great leap of faith in the face of impatience and its cynicism about something that seems so counterintuitive.

Because disbelief is impatient, it exaggerates the tentativeness, imperfection, slow pace, and other risks of preliminary work. It insists we will waste time with acts of "preteaching" (i.e., early starts at teaching) but it offers no better solution in the long run.

A Familiar Way of Seeing Obstacles to Beginning Early

We already know these hindrances, more or less. Here, I state the obstacles somewhat differently, in terms of society's labels for its various forms:

- *Procrastinators:* "I'm very busy; I have too many things to do. I wait until deadlines are near before doing most things and then I have to do them all at once. With a schedule like mine, early beginnings and so forth are an unaffordable luxury."
- *Perfectionists:* "I either do something well or not at all. Once I decide to prepare my lecture notes, I do make a point of missing nothing of importance. Once I get to work, I can't rest until I've done things right."
- *Elitists:* "If you're really bright, you just do it all in one sitting. You wait for inspiration and you don't settle for average, mediocre products. I wouldn't want students to hear me if I'm not at my best."
- *Blockers:* "The idea of preliminaries wouldn't work for me. If I dwell on things too much beforehand, I get nervous and I can't do anything. I do better if I wait until I have to do it, and then I do it fast."
- *Oppositionals:* "Good teaching isn't based on rules like yours. I know that much. Creative acts are too individual, too spontaneous to be rule-bound. Good teaching comes from within, not from external rules."

Note the striking similarities among these resistances to beginning early. In all of them, teachers want teaching preparations to be quick, easy, and unconstrained (except, perhaps, by deadlines). In all of them, teachers hope that magic will provide the motivation, the imagination, perhaps even the structure. And, always, there is a closed-mindedness about alternatives and an apparent unawareness about the common outcomes of their own traditional beliefs: Teachers who most dislike active waiting end up as polar opposites of quick starters on dimensions such as teaching satisfaction, student approval, and student comprehension. Impatience is no aid to good teaching.

A related reason why struggling teachers show reluctance is a lack of trust and openness that keeps them from plunging into the uncertainty of *nihil nimus* methods. When novice teachers cannot trust early starts, before feeling fully ready, they commonly:

- Feel insecure about their abilities to summon ideas, imagination, and patience.
- Fix on a plan that resembles notes from a class they once took or the plan of a textbook, and they do it somewhat mechanically, unreflectively.
- Comfort themselves in supposing that getting their facts straight and all the important points covered is the most important thing.

- Write most things they want to say, some of them word for word, but fear they will lose their place in the notes.
- Hold their breath while writing notes hurriedly and tensely, and, later, present them in similarly breathless fashion.
- Fail to visualize how the material will come across to their students.

Early beginnings of the sort modeled by exemplary novices help moderate those inefficiencies, discomforts, and distancings. Their patience and clear-seeing foster the kinds of easygoing but meaningful reflections that underlie really good teaching.

I first observed these acts of clear understanding in the comments of senior exemplars at work preparing class materials, then in quick starters, at least by their third and fourth years on campus. For example, their pattern of using an awareness of audience reaction to plan what to say is so similar to what exemplary writers do that I've combined here the essential strategies of both outstanding teachers and writers in the following list. In the doing, I've borrowed liberally from a friend and pioneer in the study of exemplary writers, Donald Murray (1995). These are the deficits that master writers and teachers look to avoid:

- *No territory:* There is no world of ideas, events, and personalities that the teacher and students (or writer and readers) will want to explore together.
- *No surprise:* There is no surprise in what will be said.
- *No teacher:* There is no clear individuality or personal voice in what will be presented; students will get little sense of who the teacher is (students learn better from and give higher ratings to teachers who are moderately self-disclosure about how they live and work).
- *Too few:* There are too few specifics to help the student comprehend the generalities (in exemplary teaching, there are fewer generalities or main points and more examples of each).
- *Too many:* The teacher tries to say everything he or she knows instead of picking out and simplifying a few dominant themes.
- *Too private:* The content makes sense to the teacher but not to students because its context and meaning are either left unstated or else do not connect with student experience.

Not all this sophistication needs mastering immediately; *nihil nimus* principles work by way of small steps and repeated practice. For now, simply reflect on the preceding list and contemplate when you should get underway and how you will do it. The answer to the first is, of course, is NOW. The answer to the second was also hinted at in the previous chapter. Work at teaching preparations early, before you feel ready.

Rule 2: Begin Early, Before Feeling Ready.

Exercises for Rule 2

Here, too, I ask you to begin by reflecting on what *early starts* mean. They mean beginning before feeling motivated or ready. They mean getting underway with preparations without having quite figured what to say or do. They mean letting go of the short-term control of rushing or avoiding, by letting things, especially surprises and discoveries, happen more calmly and reflectively (see Rule 1). Paradoxically, early beginnings also mean a disciplined holding back (waiting) in ways that begin to generate motivation, inspiration, and connectedness now. All this becomes easier and clearer with patience and trust—and with the outline of essential tasks that follows.

Exercise 1. Use Pauses in Other Activities to
Think about Teaching Ideas.
This pausing works best when your notions of a new or revised lecture/discussion are still vague, before they seem to merit praise. Its tentativeness also helps fit the work into these small openings for thinking (waiting to see the chairperson) or large opportunities for musing (waiting to see the dean).

Find times for early, informal work by noticing when you assume you can only read a magazine or watch a TV commercial. Don't spend every spare moment at noting and noticing; be moderate.

Make good use of these pauses by *carrying notecards and jotting down ideas and diagrams*. These props remind you to see what you could say when teaching, sometimes by noticing things related to teaching topics during the day in, say, a newscast or in an event you witnessed firsthand. Those preliminary notes and diagrams, as you begin to mentally relate them to your class, suggest ways of presenting the larger point more clearly, perhaps even more succinctly.

For example, I once noticed my dog, Sam, displaying the near-mania that came, almost instantly, when I excited him with fast and happy talking. As I made a note of this on my ever-present notecards, I realized that the pattern he showed would be comical and illustrative in my class discussion of hypomania—a near-relative of mania in humans. Better yet, it helped me see a way of shortcutting my explanation of the mechanism underlying hypomania, due to be taught in about a week. On further reflection on how Sam behaved, I was reminded how quickly his hypomania, once the excitement waned, turnd to sadness and depression. No one, I believe, displays this better than a dog. Maybe you needed to be there to appreciate my example, but I think you get the point. The class did, so they told me, especially when I mimicked Sam's facial and other postural expressions during hypomania and its consequent sadness.

Why go to all the work of making occasional notes such as that one? First, because external memories, such as notetaking or other kinds of hard records, are less often lost and forgotten than internal memories. Second, because external memories lighten the load on overwrought minds. And third, because they stimulate related thinking (imagination).

Practice pauses for early work regularly. In my experience with teachers in *nihil nimus* programs, pauses for early planning and preliminary work become enjoyable almost immediately. Still, they required regular practice to become reliable, useful habits. One way to help set up such a habit is to make its practice easy and productive by way of freewriting whatever comes to mind, without listening to internal editors. As a rule, this means writing for a minute or two about ideas for a particular class meeting or series of topics. Freewriting is spontaneous and it generates momentum by helping you ignore those internal censors who demand fully formed, conventional ideas, even correct spelling. And freewriting, because it promotes surprise and discovery, makes you want to resume this moment or two of freewriting again and again. Therein lies the basis of a strong, efficient habit.

Exercise 2. Add Collecting and Connecting.

C. Wright Mills (1959), the pioneering sociologist, was one of the first in the professoriate to share the secrets of what he called *intellectual craftsmanship:* practical, simple ways of working with success. For example:

> *Whenever you feel strongly about events or ideas you must try not to let them pass from your mind, but instead to formulate them for your files and in so doing draw out their implications, show yourself either how foolish these feelings or ideas are, or how they might be articulated into productive shape.*

This means doing more than just making notes. It adds the practice of taking *interpretive* notes, by beginning to explain each entry in terms of something you are, or will be, working on (e.g., when I made my note about Sam the Springer Spaniel's ready hypomania, I quickly restated/rewrote it in terms of how I interpreted its relevance to my class, and to my ideas of hypomania being followed by dysphoria).

These are some of Mills's other specific practices:

- Putting notes into files and so beginning to see them in terms of categories, with related points
- Rearranging ideas and categories in files to look for new meanings and connections
- Maintaining an attitude of playfulness and so not supposing any of your entries need to be perfectly conceived or written
- Casting ideas into categories and types to help make sense of them
- Considering extremes or opposites of important ideas
- Cross-classifying ideas to find perspectives and incongruities
- Mindfully looking for comparable or illustrative cases
- Tentatively arranging the materials for classroom presentation, perhaps as a diagram or conceptual outline, to bring the reward of tentative closure

The Mills approach, like the other early beginnings we've been considering, not only promotes discovery; it also moderates a usual cause of struggling, procrastinating, and blocking at tasks like teaching preparations: The aversiveness of getting underway with work that will be evaluated in public. In early beginnings, as Mills liked to put it, you never really start a project; instead, you are already working on a variety of ideas, facts, and figures—almost any of which could develop into classroom material. "To live in such a world," Mills said, " is to know what is needed to expand, connect, or re-see what you are preparing or presenting."

Exercise 3. Learn to Tell When You Have Done Enough Preteaching.

We already know that these preliminaries, what I call *preteaching,* can grow imperceptibly into more formal acts of teaching in surprisingly little time. Because preteaching can become so enjoyable and unthreatening an act in its own right, it can take on a life of its own and of practice to excess. So I advocate the following cautionary steps to make sure you do not continue past the point of diminishing returns. My advice is, as usual, about working with moderation.

One way to avoid overdoing preliminaries is to work through sets of increasingly complete conceptual outlines. It's simple. Conceptual outlines are outgrowths of usual outlines that add freewritten comments to each point in the outline. These informal comments approximate what might be said more formally when the whole is rewritten into prose or said in class. For example, my initial conceptual outline (COL) of this chapter, beneath my first notation under the outline point "Sam's hypomania" was this:

My note regarding his ready excitement followed by sadness did what? It quickly grew into a realization of how to use it in class.

That first approximation was easy to say and easier to translate into a close approximation of the final prose version in the second COL:

I noted his hypomania on my cards and I realized that the pattern he showed would be comical in the class discussion of hypomania.

That entry in the second COL stimulated a first approximation of the sentence that would follow in formal prose:

It helped me see a way of shortcutting explanations of hypomania.

What matters in a conceptual outline is getting the message or image down in a form that you can later expand and clarify. Subsequent revisions add detail, depth, logical flow, and, almost always, brevity. As another example, this is how I started a COL way back when I was getting ready for the first versions of the *nihil nimus* approach, in the handouts I gave workshop participants:

A. What exemplary novices do that brings patient, enduring motivation to teaching:
   1. Preliminary exercises in collecting information about teaching topics from formal and informal sources (with an eye for ideas that will connect with student experience);
   2. filing and ordering and rearranging materials for classes to see simplicities and themes;
   3. imagining the fun of presenting novel, connecting ideas in class;
   4. [and so on . . .]

This one-page COL, took about 15 minutes, according to my marginal notes. I did it during a brief respite from collecting data in my field research. In that way, I helped make the COL a pleasant activity.

I revised part of the COL in the next day's brief session of early preparation, during a similar break from field research. It is reproduced here in whole— although the original, handwritten version is not so neat as this:

A. What exemplary novices do that brings force/motivation to their teaching:
   1. They report that a regular, casual habit of noticing and noting things that might relate to teaching enlivens their work days in general;
      —when, for example, they see [and note] connections to their teaching in what they read (in news accounts or in scholarly pieces) or what they do (writing or conversing), they find themselves remaining more alert, mindful, forward-looking, and optimistic about teaching;
      —then, so they say, they look forward to working out the ideas and to presenting them in class.
   2. As they file, reorder, and then put ideas into revised conceptual outlines, they see ways to simplify and connect ideas and themes. They report being surprised and delighted by things they hadn't expected;
      —and so they grow more and more confident and excited about presenting the material.
   3. And, increasingly, they find themselves imagining how students will react as they expand their outlines;
      —and, just as important, seeing places where they can interact, even do some of the work.
   4. But, exemplars like to note, this conceptual outlining does something else useful. As they rewrite and expand them, COLs grow obviously sufficient to lecture or discuss from;
      —i.e., the hardest work is done before it seems like work.

This bit of work took less than 10 minutes; I spent the rest of my break meditating.

Later that same day, feeling even more primed to work on this segment and into another brief pause of about 10 minutes, I clarified that COL with the help of some freewriting and rethinking into a more expanded, detailed version. I had, I decided then, moved the process close enough to what I would write in the handout, close enough to allow me to speak what I meant to say in the workshop. But that decision was not made rigidly. I had finished these notes well before the workshop and I knew I might return to them with a new idea—but that I did not otherwise need to do more than type the handout. Indeed, I didn't do much more to prepare; I simply presented the workshop from the handout with small revisions during the typing. According to formal feedback from colleagues in that hour-long discussion, it worked well in terms of generating interest, comprehension, and specific plans for action. No complaints, no fatigue.

I'm sometimes tempted to let listeners and readers suppose that I invented this simple but effective strategy. But that would be untrue. I purloined most of it from exemplary faculty, novices and veterans.

Participants in my programs, at this point, don't seem to care much about provenances or confessions. They want more specifics about how I, and other teachers, actually moved the material along through those preliminary steps. Here, as there, I've restated my steps to imaginarily involve you in how I set up the story line in my COL:

1. I made a preliminary list of how I thought I might organize the workshop topic. I got three main points down by doodling with them while I talked them aloud and clarified what I meant to say.
2. The next time, I started over with experimental revisions to see if alternative arrangements of my list would work better. To help myself decide, I envisioned which of the discussions and questions would involve listeners and lead them to discoveries of their own. And, as a further aid, I recalled written, anonymous, comments from faculty in my other workshops.
3. I used another brief session to coach myself to be patient about what I had conjured so far. Amid the calm and clear-seeing, I grew quietly elated about the plan I had at last made clear and seemingly sufficient. To direct that enthusiasm into calm, reflective work, I next made notes in the margins of my newest COL about possible metaphors and examples I could use to explain ideas once in the workshop. All the while, I never trusted my memory or wanted to work hard enough to memorize everything I would say.
4. When I typed the handout, I made sure to handwrite one crucial set of notes on my own copy: Reminders about where to encourage audience participation, even where to assess audience comprehension. That, too, because of my earlier, marginal notes about these reminders, was easy.

All these practices, according to exemplars and to other new faculty who replicated them, work as nicely and painlessly for preparing classroom materials as I experienced them. Still, you might wonder about the wisdom of attempting COL when you are already overworked and behind schedule.

A quick review of the benefits of conceptual outlines (COLs): The method is quick and easy; preliminary versions can be done in but a minute or two. COLs help make a habit of getting fresh ideas on paper or screen, before they are forgotten or diluted. COLs provide a quick way of controlling and understanding the material because they display the roots of its organization prominently. They simplify. They delay closure so long as ideas and sequences remain tentative; they encourage critiques while changes are still easy and economical. And, almost without requiring awareness, COLs ensure reexposures to the material in ways that make later classroom presentations easier and more spontaneous.

Related Exercises in Exercise 3.   You can also find early focus and confidence by talking aloud what you might say in class to real listeners. Hearing yourself talking the material helps you notice what is unclear, unconnected, unneeded (even more so on audiotape—I advise putting off videotaping until you are far more comfortable and self-assured). Listener/observer feedback from class adds still more perspective on things otherwise hard to see or hear at first.

What if listeners are not readily available? Talk your ideas/plans and hear yourself while imagining yourself in the audience. Tape excerpts of what you will say and notice how well you pace and pause for emphasis, how clearly your organization comes across. Ask yourself things such as: Are my transitions clearly marked and explained? Are my main points clearly and memorably presented?

Exercise 4. Set Early Deadlines for Completing Preparations.
Exemplars commonly report the following as essential in doing enough during conceptual outlines:

- Taking enough time to construct a sensible plan with sufficient supporting details and examples
- Revising and expanding the COL only until cues of readiness become noticeable, especially an eagerness and confidence to share what you know
- Rechecking, throughout your early work to make sure you are solving the right problem (cf. unnecessary asides and redirections)
- Adding more regular and brief sessions to daily schedules to do this early work in ways certain to keep them early
- Setting an early deadline for near-completion, one that will allow sufficient time for reflection and correction before presentation

Exemplars manage this last and most difficult moderation by setting clear, realistic goals for brief, daily sessions, including minimal amounts of output they hope to accomplish. This precommitment, while casual, helps keep deadlines less urgent than when everything must be completed on one particular date.

Exercise 5. Let Go and Take a Few Risks.

This last practice in Rule 2 (Begin Early) is surprisingly essential to keeping dead-lines: It requires a letting go of perfectionism while preparing and, in particular, it means a willingness to go to class feeling imperfectly prepared. Why is letting go important? When you've left some of the details unspecified or incomplete, you'll be better able to keep teaching preparation to a reasonable amount of time.

What, in the end, makes this risky move difficult? First, it *is* risky. Second, and more precisely, all of us have concerns about staying in control and seeming all-knowing to students. All of us, I suspect, fear that things left to spontaneity might lead to blocking and embarrassment. Third, we are not ordinarily trained to appreciate the reality in this situation—in fact, almost all students will *not* see your use of pauses to find examples, to clarify definitions, to restate points, even to ask for student help, as signs of teacher weakness. Instead, students will like the greater involvement of seeing and hearing how you solve problems, especially if you talk some of your search aloud and let students help (in moderation). Students enjoy opportunities to generate meaningful materials, once past the shock of being asked. And they appreciate the changes in pace if they facilitate involvement and understanding. So will you.

Why are exemplars initially best at this sort of risk taking? In my studies, exemplars were the best risk takers, even though at least as socially shy as other novice teachers. They helped themselves by being forgiving when they made mis-takes in a good cause. They anticipated the value of taking risks as teachers. And they more readily let themselves enjoy the excitement of having to figure some things out in class— but not all things. They more deliberately used discovery and its occasional ambiguity to keep themselves fresh and enthusiastic as teachers. And, again, they more readily appreciated the value of letting students do some of the work. As a result, exemplars worried far less about losing face with students. In fact, in my own surveys of student perceptions of class sessions just ended, exemplary teachers were far less likely to lose face or to embarrassment than were other novice teachers.

> *[S]he has not learned the lesson of life who does not everyday surmount a fear.—R. W. EMERSON*

> *He who feareth to suffer, suffereth already, because he feareth.*
> *—MICHEL DE MONTAIGNE*

3

Prepare and Present in Brief, Regular Sessions

This third rule emphasizes more than moderation; it focuses on the constancy that comes naturally with practice of moderation. Recall, if you can, the quote from Adam Smith in the Introduction to this book. His point is that only with the moderation of doing important work in brief bouts are we likely to persist at it with the a constancy that brings greater productivity, health, and happiness in the long run.

What keeps most of us from following this wise old rule? Society teaches us to work sporadically and, too often, in great binges and under looming deadlines. We generally work at teaching as we learned to work at term papers, seminar orations, and convention performances: We wait too long and then binge at the preparation, sometimes in great marathons. This way of working is not only inefficient and unhealthy; it is also self-perpetuating as well as self-defeating. Because binges, so long as they last, exclude other important tasks that need doing, those too must eventually be binged. And because binges need long periods of uninterrupted time—whole mornings, entire days, weekends, vacations, sabbaticals, retirements, perhaps even reincarnations—we suppose that shorter periods, such as the remainder of a morning set aside for teaching preparation but disrupted until 10:45, are unsuitable for creative work: Said one binger to me: "The whole morning is shot; I might as well get some errands done at least; I couldn't get any good class prep done now, in what little time remains."

What society doesn't do to resist Adam Smith's advice, human nature does. At the base of our reluctance to work in brief, regular sessions lies the problem of impulse control. It amounts to what I've been calling impatience and its immoderation. When we feel stressed, our inner nature tempts us to put off difficult tasks, such as teaching preparation, until conditions for work are ideal. Why? It prefers the ease and immediate relief of doing something else now, something less demanding and threatening than teaching preparations. It tells us, in effect, that the work will be much easier and better when we are not distracted, not disturbed for long periods of time. And, moreover, our innernature tells us that if we wait, passively, we will somehow find such openings along with a ready, inspired mood to work, ideally by way of a Muse. Once in that mindless cycle, we can hardly imagine ourselves accomplishing enough teaching preparation in brief sessions of work to attempt writing out ideas for teaching: "I'm in the mood," said one binge preparer to me, "to do what I want to, not something I have to." Said Woodie Allen in one of his infamous struggles with women: "The heart wants what it wants."

This, in contrast, is how exemplars deliberately combine constancy and moderation for optimal output and well-being:

- They do almost all their "survival work," such as teaching and writing, in brief, regular sessions (BRSs).
- They initiate early work in sessions so brief that they necessitate no major scheduling of days (i.e., they work at first on early teaching preparations during interstices of already busy schedules). Only later, when early preparations are habitual, are they more formally scheduled.
- They start and restart early, before feeling in the mood, while reminding themselves that once underway, they will feel better about working. One common way of instilling momentum is freewriting; another is rewriting the last part of notes or conceptual outlines produced in the prior session.
- BRSs, because they tend to be brief and unhurried, help exemplars prepare for teaching in ways that keep efforts unpressured, reflective, constant, and timely.
- BRSs keep teaching preparations limited to durations that do not interfere with other important activities during the rest of the day, such as exercising, social life, and scholarly writing.
- BRSs avoid the three main costs of delayed, long, and uninterrupted work sessions: (1) the scenario of working under pressure and excitement until hypomania and its sequelae of sadness and disinterest set in, (2) the inefficiencies of preparing materials beyond the point of diminishing returns, and (3) the inconstancy of working that bingers evidence.

How This Combination of Moderation and Constancy Applies in Real-Life Teaching

In the classroom, BRSs translate into making brief segments of separate topics and strategies, each with a separate identity, each clearly related to segments that precede and follow. BRSs mean setting up distinctive periods in class—say, one for small talk and previews, one each for coverage of three main points for the day. And BRSs entail the clear separation of each of these segments with distinctive themes, breaks (including, perhaps, a stretch), summaries, and previews. Odd as it might seem, all this constancy and moderation take no more time or energy than traditional ways of teaching in nonstop fashion.

Rule 3: Work in Brief, Regular Sessions.

Exercises for Rule 3

Relevant practices from the preceding two rules get only a brief listing here:

Exercise 1. Wait, Patiently.
Ready yourself to prepare teaching with patience and tolerance. Practice simple ways of holding back during ordinary events: Pause and delay for two seconds before getting up or reaching out to answer the phone. Delay for two seconds before beginning to answer the question you've just asked students. Wait even longer when looking for ideas (and then, if nothing appears, leave a blank space and come back to it later—this is a real test of patience).

Be playful and optimistic when you can't think of something immediately by giving yourself hints and guessing at the answer in writing. Freewrite or rewrite. Use breaks, reflections, and brief work sessions to keep yourself fresh and on track. Imagine the good, the fun, and the excitement that will come when you present what you are preparing. Smile, wryly, while assembling all that deathless wisdom. Imagine the delight you might experience in mimicking the hypomania of a Springer Spaniel in class . . . or how fortunate you will be not to.

Exercise 2. Begin Before Feeling Fully Ready.
Don't feel that you should have motivation and certainty at hand before getting underway; these two things appear, as I've already mentioned, more reliably and more usefully once you are already working. Redundantly resaid, the best motivation appears in the wake of, not ahead of, constant and moderate work.

Exercise 3. Practice Tolerance.
Be patient instead of quickly accepting usual beliefs that brief, regular sessions are inadequate to produce or cover enough material in your case, or that BRSs, because they reflect a rule, will stifle your creativity and brilliance. Instead, wait and give Rule 3 a fair chance by practicing only its bare essentials over a short period of time. You won't really know if BRSs can work until you're patient and trusting enough to experience them repeatedly. If your present style of working seems more rushed and stressful, less productive and satisfying than you would like, what have you to lose?

One means of judging the worth of brief, regular sessions is already familiar: Comparing new versus old times spent in classroom preparations. Another consists of testing how well your brief but telling class notes, borne of BRSs, fare by by putting them on the board or an overhead projector. That bold move, I've documented, gives students a better sense of where you're going, of what you think is important, and of being part of the enterprise with you. Conceptual outlines, made public, also help teachers keep to clearer, more incisive presentations and interactions. A caution: Show students how to expand on what you have written, with notes of their own—much as you elaborate beyond what you have written in your COL. Then model it occasionally by talking the elaborations aloud, as an easy way of reviewing and prompting good notetaking.

With the first three exercises at practicing BRSs now familiar, you might be prepared to begin serious practice of the fourth, by consistently relying on brief, regular sessions of work instead of long and episodic bouts, including binges. The following exercises, according to my own studies, best facilitate this foreign habit.

Exercise 4. Establish a Brief, Regular Time for Preparing Classroom Materials.

BRSs really do mean *regular but brief*. They really do need small starts. If you feel too busy, too skeptical to allot, say, a total of one hour each workday, begin with one or two daily sessions of only 5 to 10 minutes. In this way, even the busiest of new faculty make a start toward BRSs. Whatever else, establish a regular expectation of working at teaching preparation on a daily basis—regardless. The hardest part may be trusting the rule enough to get its practice underway. Nothing in the *nihil nimus* program, participants have told me, seems more counterintuitive than the idea of BRSs at the outset; yet, nothing seems more obviously true and useful once it becomes a habit.

Once you've set a schedule, make yourself sit down at the appointed time with your notes and files, even if you do not feel like working on your preparations. At worst, you will sit and stare blankly for those few minutes; at best, you will begin to freewrite, take notes, or find other ways to get going. What, incidentally, do you have at hand to supplement a blank mind? Your early work at preparing, including notecards, diagrams, and conceptual outlines.

Remember: For now, the goal is constancy in simply sitting down, as though to work, and doing *nothing* else for a few minutes—not even brief errands.

Arrange a regular site (or sites) for reading about and writing classroom materials, one with few distractions (e.g., newspapers that tempt their reading or phones that demand answering). Ideally, the work site will contain nothing but teaching-related stuff. And it should be comfortable, almost to the point of decadence. Exemplars, more often than other new faculty, work in easy chairs that provide leg, neck, back support, and comfort. Why don't they fall asleep? Because they are less busy and better rested than other new faculty, and because, they say, their BRSs are stimulating and renewing, not wearying or soporific.

What typically hinders and helps in these practices? First comes the difficulty of breaking or even bending old habits; most of us are not accustomed to working at teaching (or almost anything else) in small, regular bits. Second, the prospect of a marathon bout where everything is finished in one sitting may continue to appeal. To combat this temptation, practice noticing the outcomes of brief, regular sessions versus binges over the longer run. A curious fact about working in BRSs is that they almost always produce more measurable gains in teaching *and* in other essential work, such as scholarly writing, almost always in less time overall than do binges. (I say more about this generality in the conclusion of Section I.) And, if you can stand it, manage other aversive things (e.g., housework) in brief, daily sessions of 5 to 10 minutes.

Struggling novice teachers typically undermine BRSs by (1) imagining they don't have time for the briefest of sessions on some days, especially if feeling pressed to finish things overdue; (2) supposing their mood for the moment rules out even a brief session of work; and (3) doubting the effectiveness of BRSs.

All these pessimisms disappear with some constancy of practice, but how do you manage even that? Try a strategy you already know in other spheres, one where you get yourself to do other disagreeable things, like going to a job on time, until they become habitual.

Exercise 5. Force BRSs Until the Habit Takes Hold.

Uncomplicated prods work best: Alarm clocks that signal times to begin; materials already set out and ready to work with; posted notes about ideas that translate into conceptual outlines; prearranged calls from spouses and other friends to remind you it is time to get started; and so on. In my experience, these methods remain aversive only until the habit settles in; after that, they may need implementing on the occasions where you backslide. The more you use them, the less you need them.

Consider an even more powerful strategy. Make the price of avoiding your scheduled brief regular sessions too costly for most days. This means making something you would rather do (e.g., reading the morning newspaper) contingent on first completing your brief daily sessions of preparing teaching materials. How strong a contingency should you employ? A moderate sort. Experiment until you find one strong enough to ensure regular practice of BRSs (e.g., earning your morning shower by first doing your daily ration of teaching preparations). But don't employ contingencies that imperil your health (e.g., earning lunch for the day and, supposedly, benefitting yourself with weight loss if you fail to work) or social life (e.g., no calls or visits to friends for the day).

Keep this practice of contingency management somewhat flexible and moderate. Allow yourself occasional days off for sickness or for a change of pace, and always during true emergencies. But keep them as occasional as, say, an average of one miss per two weeks. And, finally, keep the use of contingencies (i.e., making the desired activity contingent on first doing the writing) as brief as necessary, only until the new habit is fairly reliable and automatic on its own—usually for about three to four months. Overuse of contingencies turns them into aversions that become associated with teaching; in my experience, teachers work with more ease and creativity in the long run by relying on internal controls. Contingencies can always be reinstated later, when the need arises, perhaps for a week or two.

Many teachers, including me, find a social contingency more tolerable. They do this, for example, by finding a colleague with whom to share brief daily sessions of working at teaching preparations, someone they meet on a regular schedule at a comfortable work site such as the special collections room of the library. These "social contracts" work, at least initially, by way of the guilt we would feel if we let the other person down by skipping a meeting. And they work because they arrange social supports of seeing someone manage the same task—more so when that other person shares discoveries of working efficiently or when he or she provides encouragements while we are stymied.

handwritten note: like we do w/com between classes

Exercise 6. Transfer BRSs to Classrooms.

This, too, is about moderation, about dividing class meetings into easier, more memorable segments. For example, you might construct an initial preview of the day's class limited to a presentation time of, say, three to four minutes as a stand-alone unit. You might even plan an ending to the preview that will compel interest in the next segment of the lecture, perhaps as a question (e.g., you might find yourself saying to your class, "So what, you might wonder, does this idea about crop fertilization have to do with UFOs and the messages left in the wheat fields of Kansas? Stay tuned for the next exciting section of class").

Follow the same scheme for each of the next segments, with endings that set up the next segment, with moments of holding back for reviewing and eliciting questions by way of genuine breaks in the action. Depending on your preferences and the nature of the class you are teaching, you might want to experiment with a pattern of distinctively separate coverage of segments such as these:

1. Small talk, such as recalling preselected, individual students' participation in the prior class and a preview of this day's class
2. A few main lecture sections within a class period, each with a memorable central point
3. Discussion periods, perhaps preceded by small group meetings where problems are solved or materials are capsulized for presentation to the class
4. One-minute papers or brief daily quizzes that check for student comprehension of essential points
5. Brief, brief reviews that leave time for questions and clarifications—and for timely ends to class meetings

handwritten note: I do a lot of this already

Here, as in BRSs for preparation, most teachers in my programs report a *strong* temptation to persist in segments beyond planned time limits. Without brevity, it could go without saying, brief sessions and segments cannot be brief.

How strong is this temptation? Several teachers noted that the urge to rush on, beyond the planned stopping point, was accompanied by striking physiological changes, such as the hair on the backs of their heads standing up.

Two things help deal with this usual impatience. One is keeping the contents of each segment realistically brief and logically complete during preparations; you may need some trial and error to determine these boundaries. The other is to prearrange cues to tell you when time limits approach, even salient reminders in your notes to check for time as you move through each of the parts of a segment. This helps ensure the pauses that students value. For example, in the first of the main lecture sections for the day, you might want to arrange cues that signal the half-way point and the two-minutes-to-go point. The typical limit of such a section among experienced, exemplary practitioners is about 8 to 12 minutes. Said one to me: "You really can explain most things in about 7 to 10 minutes if you keep it simple." There are exceptions, of course. One advantage of depicting segments in terms of minimal content is that you can cover any one section with more generosity as necessary. This kind of moderation allows you to take advantage of moments where you and your class have a special rapport or unexpected needs—without having to worry about falling hopelessly behind for the day.

Regular practices of brief sessions and segments often take two to four months to become habitual and comfortable. Only then do their benefits become clear for teachers in my programs:

- More sustained, imaginative involvement, first by way of their own immersion and then that of their students
- Better coverage of main concepts and in less time overall
- Less fatigue during and after class
- Better teacher and student comprehension

I want to keep a teaching journal

Exercise 7. Monitor Your Progress.
To optimize benefits of working in brief, regular sessions, one more practice is important. I urge you to monitor and record how well you meet your goals for BRSs and brief classroom segments. Graphs, charts, or journals provide feedback about how consistently you conform day to day. These hard-copy recordings work far better than relying on memories and impressions of progress. Sometimes these records indicate a need to readjust your preparations or pacing. And almost always, once they show some constancy, these records reinforce the new habit. There is surprising pleasure in watching evidence of progress, especially in the gradual accumulation of substantial output.

> *It wasn't until I kept graphs of my daily practices that I began to make real progress here. I needed to see that I wasn't being as diligent as I had imagined. . . . When my graphs finally went up [i.e., when the levels of output rose] and pretty much stayed up was when I began to feel good*

about my progress. And I imagined that I would hate the graphing!
—PARTICIPANT IN MY TEACHING PROGRAMS

Record keeping helps in another important way we touched on earlier. It fosters a readier sense of having enough time to prepare and teach the essentials because the total times spent preparing becomes surprisingly brief compared to initial efforts. This, in turn, brings a surer feeling of being able to control and finish the work without rushing or bingeing. A relaxed awareness of time helps new teachers, so they say, find new confidence. How? Because their unhurried pace enables them to become better noticers and listeners who can, on demand, change course while preparing or presenting with ease.

With all this managed, have we done enough? Yes, for the time being. But because these rules of moderation always involve preparations for related rules, you might notice that you have already begun to work on the next one.

4

Stop

By this, I mean *timely* stopping—when you've done enough for the moment, when it is time to move on to other things. It also means holding back from saying yes to a request that you know will take you away from your priorities as a new faculty member. These kinds of holding back are no easy matter; indeed, timely stopping is harder and more important than starting on time. Why? Because *timely* stopping requires even more effort than timely starting—especially once we have momentum, when we are too euphoric or fatigued to fight off the excited impulse to continue. Holding back is the essence of moderation; stopping is central to self-discipline (Baumeister & Scher, 1988).

You can tell if you have a problem of timely stopping by noticing if you end preparation sessions only when exhausted or if you halt classroom meetings only when students are leaving to rush to their next classes. And you can begin to move past this problem by seeing that when you do not halt the trance-like state that keeps you busy and overextended, you make the work superficial and aversive at the time and more difficult to resume the next time.

Consider a usual sequence of not stopping on time among new faculty struggling as teachers: They have trouble tearing themselves away from something they're doing before class—writing one more line in their class notes, extending a phone conversation to mention just one more thing. Then they race to class, bound onto the podium, and launch the lecture without any warm-up or small talk. Having hurried into starting, they continue to speed through the lecture and then run overtime. One likely result of not being able to stop in a timely fashion just before class will be the distancing between these novice teachers and their audiences that induces classroom incivilities. A second result will be tiring themselves and their students with the incessant rushing that eventually hinders stopping on time. A third will be a hurried and impulsive pace for the rest of the day.

What, Exactly, Makes Timely Stopping So Difficult?

"Habit," William James once wrote, "is the great flywheel of society." It brings an automaticity that, once established, usually goes unexamined and unchallenged. Once we have the habit of rushing and its powerful momentum, we are unaccustomed, even unwilling, to interrupt it until we are forced to.

Not only has traditional education failed to teach us how to stop in ways that encourage general moderation; it unwittingly encourages us to binge on term papers or large exams because almost all their preparations can be put off without apparent penalty. Instead of reinforcing efficient and healthy processes of working, such as early starts and brief, regular sessions (BRSs), it looks only to final products. Worse yet, its tacit values suggest that last-minute preparations such as "all-nighters" are more noble than hard, regular work—even if we end up with grades of "incomplete."

An even deeper problem comes from not learning to stop other and less essential activities beforehand, in favor of crucial work—at least not until deadlines loom and the work that counts must be rushed in exhausting binges. So it is that most faculty live with chronic busyness and its attendant stresses. And so it is that struggling new teachers suppose rushing past the point of easy stopping brings the excitement and euphoria necessary to good teaching. (Records of student ratings and comprehension, of teacher satisfaction and health, say otherwise.)

Impatience and Intolerance

These are the core deterrents to stopping in a timely fashion. Impatience and its impulsivity reinforce feelings that we are doing something too important to cease and that stopping now will cause us to lose concentration, control, self-worth, and brilliance. Impatience tells us that if we stop a current task before it is finished, we may never again have an opportunity to complete it so splendidly. Impatience also builds on intolerances (i.e., fears) about changing familiar habits of rushing and other impulsivities. In particular, it leads us to believe that stopping before feeling fully ready will be too painful, too awful, to tolerate. Its arguments are remarkably sophisticated; one especially verbal and struggling newcomer wrote this to me in a note: "Genius must be unfettered by rules, by artificial boundaries, by arbitrary times for stopping. Truly brilliant teachers rely on spontaneity that keeps them going until inspiration runs dry."

Intolerance also crops up as skepticism about the value of patience in a workplace where busyness seems tantamount to importance. It also crops up as doubt about the scientific methods that show the greater health and efficiency of timely stopping. If I seem to be warning you against the Devil herself, note that that my concern is really about the devilishly hard work we make for ourselves—and for others—when we resist timely stopping. Students kept overtime often suffer over arriving late for subsequent classes; teachers who follow us in the same classroom must begin late and in classrooms still overheated and unsettled.

Said another way, working too long is overinclusion, a failure of doing more than necessary. Among writers, for instance, the problem is more readily seen as a deficit of omission.

> *The art of omission is hardest of all to learn, and I am weak at it yet.*
> —*JACK LONDON*

It is no less a problem for teachers.

Unassertiveness

Amongst new faculty, at least, one of the hardest kinds of holding back from impulsiveness concerns assertiveness. It is the inability to say no to things that will unnecessarily overextend their schedule and energy. This unassertiveness owes in part, of course, to fears of not being liked by those who make requests of us. That's understandable. What is less forgivable, perhaps, is the reluctance to make decisions about what really needs doing during these crucial first years on campus. And, instead, letting things that exert the loudest or strongest pull take over.

Exemplars, it figures, actively hold back from unnecessary commitments and stick to what they call "solving the right problems." Struggling novices, in contrast, too often opt for the easy, for the immediately rewarding and relieving. Specifically, struggling new teachers tend to:

- Rush and binge to complete and update lectures.
- Leave for class at the last minute and still be distracted by the tasks or conversations they had to interrupt.
- Begin class a bit late and impatiently and then hurry through it with few pauses for reflection or student involvement.
- Try to impart the most information per minute toward the end of the class, usually with poor student comprehension.
- Demand student attention beyond the bell by stating especially critical things as the class is trying to leave.
- Pride themselves on keeping their office doors constantly open and becoming the close friend and confidant of many students. ("I'd hate to have students complain that I didn't have time for them . . . I wouldn't dream of closing my door to them"—this comment came from a novice whose lecturing style allowed little or no time for student participation in his classes.)
- Volunteer to serve on campuswide or community committees and doing substantial parts of the committee's work. ("They really need me, and I'm good

at making all these calls and putting all the survey results onto the net"—this from a new faculty member usually too busy to meet effectively with her teaching assistants in a large introductory class.)

- Help colleagues with computer or data-analysis problems. ("Well it's hard to say no to someone like him if he asks for my help. How else is he going to get his data analyzed? He doesn't know much about statistics.... You know, I don't think he'd endanger my tenure."—this from a novice who spent so much time as the "department trouble shooter" that he had too little time to participate in teaching workshops, despite poor student ratings, or to complete his own research analyses.)

What tempts all of us to do such things instead of what matters more? Unassertiveness is easier in the moment because it offers immediate relief and satisfaction. The assertiveness behind timely stopping and refusing requires waiting, patiently, for rewards in the longer run.

Consider one usual way in which this temptation, and its cost, commonly go unnoticed among novice teachers: Participants in my summer programs for struggling novices aimed to (1) prepare the next academic year's course notes in a general format and (2) rehearse those presentations in ways to increase audience and self-involvement. They were paid the equivalent of a summer teaching salary beforehand. Even so, over a third of them took on summer jobs such as child care, house painting, or other commitments with local theatre and political groups that prevented them from completing significant work at teaching. How did they justify "bending" their contracts with me? Most often by admitting that they wanted to do something more immediately satisfying and concrete than dealing with the pain and vagaries of teaching, and that they had been asked to take on the extra task in a way that was hard to refuse. Said one: "I needed a break from that; I knew I'd be back at it in a couple of months, all too soon. You have to realize how hard it would have been to refuse to help my friends." Said another: "I'll probably be the better for it, for doing something more spiritual. I'm assisting with a ministry outreach and the experience was too interesting, too challenging, to miss." And yet another: "Don't forget how difficult teaching is for me. Remember? I'm the one who went to her car in the parking lot and collapsed and stayed there, slumped helplessly over the steering wheel for an hour after classes. I just couldn't face it again, not right now. I just couldn't make myself do it."

When those "avoiders" participated more fully in one of the next two summers, virtually all came to a similar insight about what needed to happen before they would make significant improvements as teachers: They needed to stop saying yes to things that were, in fact, less important than mastering teaching—*now:* "I'll have more time for animal rescue later—for years and years of summers; I need to say NO more often in order to rescue myself—not all of the time but some of the time, so that I'm not there 30 to 40 hours a week; this may be the only chance I'll get to become a good teacher who will have an impact on students ... that, you know, could be where I'll do the most good."

Rule 4: Stop in Timely Fashion.

Exercises for Rule 5

Because timely stopping depends heavily on preplanning, on knowing where you are going, on deciding beforehand how much will be enough, and on setting things up so that you will stop yourself from rushing or from going overtime, I begin with a preview of what I ask you to do in the exercises here:

- To practice already familiar ways of holding back by waiting, patiently and actively, instead of rushing and running over (these will be extensions of the Wait Rule, Chapter 1).
- To try more difficult methods of holding back by starting early, by stopping whatever else you are doing early (an extension of the Begin Early Rule, Chapter 2).
- To confront your old, maladaptive tendencies to impulsivity. Here, the methods of quick starters are especially worth modeling.
- To practice ways of holding back and saying no when you want to say yes, but shouldn't.

I warned you that stopping is harder and more important than starting. But it is still not all that difficult, as the following tried and true steps show.

Exercise 1. Reconstitute Practices of Holding Back.
You already know some of the best methods; these need continuance here: (1) slowing your pace at preparing and presenting by way of brief, regular sessions that moderate tendencies toward the euphoric rushing of bingeing; (2) taking time, regardless of mood, for routine pauses, for reflection and calming, (3) calming to help keep yourself working mainly in the present moment and not in the future; (4) moderating your pace enough to let students comprehend and, similarly, slowing to notice their notetaking behaviors; and (5) holding yourself back constantly asking yourself if there is a need to rush.

Exercise 2. Begin to Prepare Early for Stopping,
Long Before Feeling the Need.
The easiest way to stop in timely fashion is to begin early, well before you might have imagined you would. So, for example, instead of leaping out of bed in the morning and resuming old patterns of mindless rushing, try taking a few moments to stretch and breathe meditatively by consciously following your breath in and out. In that way, you will begin your days less stressed. And you will have stopped and given yourself the opportunity to wait and reflect on what really needs doing for the day (sounds like Rule 1, doesn't it?). Use this moment of stopping and patient waiting to precommit to limits you need to set in order to have a comfortable and effective day.

Plan, for example, to hold back from rushing just before class by spending the last half-hour (OK, 10 minutes) relaxing and reflecting. Many of the most revered and effective teachers of all time, William James among them, used this period to walk outdoors while reflecting on what they could say in class. Plan to get to class 5 to 10 minutes early. Commit yourself to wait before lecturing, to hold back to establish comfort and approachability with students. To do all that, of course, requires that you stop whatever you are doing beforehand, early. And the thing before that. First things first.

Plan to apply the same simple principle of this *nihil nimus* (moderation) approach to preparation sessions. Help ensure enough work that day by arranging materials ahead of time, in an otherwise idle moment such as commercial breaks on TV. Better yet, commit yourself to do these brief preliminaries at the ends of preparation sessions because, with early stopping, time will be left over to reflect on what needs doing at the next session. Imagine yourself precommitting, assembling materials into conceptual outlines with just a *few* main points, thereby limiting how much you will try to include in a class. Then picture yourself reminding yourself, when in class, of the time before it runs short. All this imagining and planning, while sitting abed or elsewhere during the day that follows, takes only a few minutes, once you are in the habit.

Exercise 3. Practice Ways of Saying No, the Earlier the Better.

How do exemplars manage to hold back, to say no when they want to please the person making a request? Imperfectly—until they have practice anticipating and meeting the special demands given new faculty. They do it, they tell me, by following three basic steps, two of them anticipatory:

1. Anticipating, once or twice per day, the demands likely to be made on them (e.g., requests for committee work), and rehearsing the reasons why they should say no or else keep their roles minimal.
2. Planning—in moderation, just often enough for clarity—to pause and hold back before acting or talking, much as they already do at other times when tempted to be impulsive. A particularly good strategy is to say that you'd like a day to think the request over before responding—that allows time for reflection and objectivity, time to feel less compelled to say yes when you should say no.
3. Listening carefully to the demand, request, or impulse and then reflecting on at least some of the reasons why you might want to comply or hold back, especially in terms of short- and long-term consequences.

Exercise 4. Hold Back to "Preteach" and "Prewrite" Briefly, Planfully, Playfully.

Preteaching means preparing early, perhaps by way of conceptual outlines and mental rehearsals. It also means stopping early, before the pressure of deadlines approach or the preparations grow too large. In class, holding back to preteach might take the form of previewing what you plan to do in that session. It could give you and your students a broad picture of what lies ahead and a rationale for pursuing it. This holding back sets a precedent up for more brief previews during class when you're ready for transitions or of sudden changes of course. It also encourages quick asides about what else you might have covered instead of trying to talk about them at length. How, then, could students get that information? Perhaps in readings and small group discussions outside of class.

An essential and often overlooked purpose of preteaching is setting a *context* for your teaching before you get to class and then again as you preview it in class. Exemplars clarify contexts by stepping back and reminding themselves and their students where they have been and where they are going (e.g., "Do you see where this fits in to what we've already covered? It is part of _____ and it relates to _____ in this way . . .). Failures to put things in context often turn otherwise well-organized presentations into confusing experiences for students who do not see why the material is important or how it connects to what they already know. Neglect of context setting is a common source of poor student involvement, comprehension, and ratings. Yet, few correctives are easier or more important. Exemplary new faculty model two with especial utility: First, they state contextual matters explicitly, repeatedly (e.g., "This is why it is important"; "This is how it relates to what you already know") as they prepare and present. Second, they provide clear signposts about where they are (e.g., "This is point 3 of 5") and emphasize transitions to next topics (e.g., "Do you see where we are going next? To _____, because _____").

What does preteaching have to do with timely stopping? When you specify your plan of what lies ahead in terms of clear purposes and goals and when you update your progress/context to yourself and your public, you are more likely to stick to essentials. When you mention what you might have said, and why you are not covering it directly in class, you refrain from trying to do too much. And when you imagine and rehearse how the points will flow and what is essential, you will prepare and go to class with clearer, more succinct material in hand. You will even have a sense of how much time to spend on particular topics. Said another way, when you decide what really needs doing, when you simplify what you present, and when you plan a schedule of timing, stopping almost takes of itself.

Exercise 5. Pause Regularly during the Preparing and the Teaching.

Pausing en route facilitates timely stopping a very simple reason: pausing is itself a kind of stopping. It is generally easier than complete and final stopping and it helps slow the pace of working from the kind of rushed, impatient, pace that makes stopping most difficult.

Pauses are already familiar in this scheme of moderation but they deserve a few reminders about specific practice; the first symptom of backsliding in my own programs is the omission of pauses. Pauses become most dependable when sched-uled in class notes and mentally rehearsed beforehand. I, for example, signal a pause with an asterisk or a *P* in the margin of my notes.

A general habit of paying attention to pauses, it turns out, encourages unscheduled but useful pauses in response to telling cues in all kinds of work, including teaching preparations: Bodily tensions and discomforts such as eye strain, anxiousness, fatigue—most tellingly in mistypings and misstatements.

Exercise 6. Stop Most Sessions Early.

Planning to stop early works even better than planning to stop at the bell because it leaves time for emergencies. Its cushion of extra time encourages more patience for student questions and contacts, for resetting or reviewing context. And its early stopping pleases students who need not rush to the next activity, who can push to reflect on the class just finished.

The most effective device for stopping a bit early may be the most surprising: Precommitting to stop in the middle of something you'd rather finish—a sentence or, better yet, a whole paragraph or concept. That way, the unfinished thought remains fresh in mind until the next time. And by completing what was left uncompleted the next time, we make restarting far easier than beginning with an entirely new thought.

A sure way to confound timely stopping is to insist on finishing everything you've prepared by rushing at the last minute. You might better tell students where to find the information on their own and what you want them to look for.

Extra Step. Monitor Your Progress at Stopping Early.

Start small by trying to stop only a minute or so before time officially runs out and then enter the result on a chart in your office, or wherever you and others will see it regularly. This record will discourage delusions about how well you manage the act of stopping in timely fashion. The act of keeping the record, I've noticed, greatly increases the likelihood of timely stopping over the long run—a small investment for so large and important a result.

One more thing bears mentioning, just the sort of thing that should appear toward the end of this chapter—as I get ready to stop while feeling I could write much more on this topic: Stopping early allows time to judge your work to see if it meets your standards. Why is it best to put off judging until the end? Judging too soon and too harshly can prevent you from getting to the end.

Finish, then evaluate. Perfect is the enemy of good.
—DONALD MURRAY

5

Moderate Overattachment and Overreaction

Here again, exemplary novices, those new faculty who work with the most effectiveness and appreciation, model the *nihil nimus* approach—that is, nearly nothing in excess, almost everything in moderation. Their pattern may by now be growing familiar. Exemplars see teaching as important but not as *the* most consequential thing in their lives. They work at teaching regularly, playfully, seriously, but they spend only modest amounts of time preparing because they keep notes informal, simple, and more focused. They work less overall at teaching than do lower-rated, less satisfied peers. (Exemplars, as we know, try to make only a few main points in class and they convey them more patiently, with carefully chosen examples and discussions.) Just as important, they keep some emotional distance from their teaching and students. The principle involved is best known amongst writers:

The worse the writer, the greater the attachment to the writing.
—STEPHEN NORTH

That maxim refers to struggling writers who get too invested in their work to see alternatives or to listen to criticism, who refuse to revise or deviate from original plans, who communicate in insensitive ways. You can see how the same principle applies to teaching.

What Makes This Moderation of Attachment Difficult?

Part of the answer is perfectionism and its secret ingredients—impatience and intolerance. Perfectionism is about control; overidentification with our work is a means of feeling in control of it. The narrowness of perfectionism is a kind of intolerance that keeps us blind to what is going on around us; ironically, it keeps us all the more likely to err or miscommunicate.

Why do we get so attached to things we present for public scrutiny? We want them to be perfect and perfectly admired. And we don't want disapproval. Still, we know, more or less, the costs of trying too hard, of being too attached:

- Rushing and premature decisions
- Tension
- Fatigue
- Doubts about being perfect enough
- Blocking, even paralyzing anxiety
- Humorless inflexibility
- Bingeing, because the work seems too important to interrupt
- Grandiosity
- Difficulties stopping when diminishing returns set in
- Overreactions to criticism, even to indifference

What Counters the Immoderations Just Listed?

Balance is the key to moderating overattachment and its overreactiveness. We've already seen how balance economizes on time and fatigue, where, for instance, exemplary teachers spend little more time preparing for most classes than in them. This balance, again, helps teachers prepare only what needs saying, displaying, and discussing; remember that one sign of expertise at teaching is presenting fewer main points but more examples of each. And that balance encourages teachers to go to class without having everything perfectly prepared. Without overattachment to teaching content, a clear, manageable scheme with some things prepared in detail, some not, suffices. Balance, because it limits excesses of overpreparation and overattachment, is essential to something especially valuable to new faculty: Better results from less effort.

Why You Might Resist This Moderation

If you respond like many teachers in my program, you might fear that this letting go of ownership and perfectionism will cause you to lose face when you make mistakes. And you could argue that if you do overprepare lectures, you are only following old, respected customs: "I'd rather be accused of being overprepared than lazy," said one participant. Or more likely, you'll feel skeptical, unbelieving, about the balance rule. "Come on now," one new teacher remarked, "I can't believe that. No way can you be properly prepared for class with so little time to prepare. *I* know how much time it takes to prepare [this new faculty member spent over 30 hours a week preparing for two three-credit, undergraduate survey courses] and my courses would be even better if I had more."

Another way of appreciating the nature of this overattachment and why it perseveres comes from my studies of struggling new teachers. They, compared to other new faculty, most often resisted modest preparation times while continuing to prepare more than they could present within class times. Some of them explained their actions as ways of remaining in control of class—for example, by writing a lot on the board and keeping students busy. Others simply claimed that there was too much material to be covered in so little time and that they felt compelled to try "to get it all in."

What, on the other hand, helps teachers get past skepticism about replacing overattachment with balance? Experience, particularly of one kind, has proven especially useful in my research-based projects: Gradual approximations in practicing strategies. As a rule, it means relying more and more on brief notes for classes than on having everything detailed and written out. It means beginning by basing only one small part of a class on notes that demand some spontaneity and student interaction, then two small parts, and so on.

With that foundation laid, the following practices work nicely.

Rule 5: Moderate Overattachment to Content and Overreactions to Criticism.

Exercises for Rule 5

Expect these exercises to be initially difficult and counterintuitive for good reason. They are a lesson in modesty and humility—no easy matter for academics, including me. The assignment is particularly difficult for newcomers to the professoriate who suppose that they must, first and foremost, never lose face in front of students.

Why might modesty and good-natured humility be uncommon amongst novice college teachers? First, of course, because public presentations, such as teaching, make most of us tense, at least initially. Second, because too few of us have been taught to see the occasional humor in ourselves, in our pretensions, in our work. Instead, the most memorable events in our education, such as doctoral defenses, teach quite different things, notably seriousness, perfectionism, and overattachment. Third, few of us are likely to have seen constructive humility and humor modeled among our own professors. My most compelling, intimidating mentor, my postdoctoral supervisor, liked to get his students together for depictions of how important social imperturbability was as researchers and teachers; none of us, while in his presence, I think, saw the careers that lay ahead of us as anything less than grueling struggles where we had to maintain the highest standards; none of us dared to make mistakes in his presence. He helped set that mood, I later discovered, by thoroughly memorizing his more formal talks to us beforehand and then presenting them as if spontaneous. The fourth reason we are inclined to overattachment is that few of us were schooled in ways of agreeing with and learning from criticisms—or to see mistakes and objections as opportunities for learning. The exercises that follow attempt to counter those powerful early experiences.

Exercise 1. Monitor for Overattachment.

This is the most basic move and its practice seems deceptively simple. During pauses in and out of the classroom, watch for signs that you are not maintaining your distance from excessive egotism. These are some clues:

[handwritten margin note: I think the I have to opposite preview...]

- Reluctance to slow or stop because your preparation or teaching seem too brilliant to interrupt.
- Annoyance with disruptions, even with something as impersonal as the noise of a passing airplane.
- Early feelings that your work will be superior to that of most teachers and that it must therefore be perfect, impeccable, brilliant.
- Anticipation, with delight, that your presentation will be so deep and complex that only the brightest, most deserving students will appreciate it.
- Diminishing joyfulness and humor about your work (notice, for example, if you and your students are frowning tensely or distantly apathetic).
- An urgency to rush and finish all of the planned content (i.e., paying more attention to product than process).

These feelings are not always inappropriate. All of us may have moments where we are impressively perfect and cleverly insightful. Problems arise when perfectionism and isolation in working are so excessive that we become overattached to all our teaching, all the time. Solutions include the modesty of admitting that not every moment of our presentations needs to be so perfect that we wouldn't want to make changes in another go-around, and that we need not be captivating every minute. In my studies, students fare better as notetakers and as comprehenders with changes of pace—some calming, and some exciting, and some dull. To overcome overattachment, we need the tolerance to learn from our critics.

Step 2. Practice Early Evaluations.

This brave act, like those before it, depends on proactiveness, on actually encouraging meaningful student evaluations early. It is, sadly, a most unlikely act amongst struggling novices I have studied. Why? These new teachers display bla-

feedback page

tant passiveness and pessimism about student evaluations They wait for student critics to come to them after class, not realizing or caring that this method yields an unrepresentative sample of student opinion—too much of it from ingratiators or whiners. Although some struggling novices ask, rather unconvincingly, for complaints and suggestions during classes, usually as public comments, most undergraduates are too shy to say anything substantial under such conditions, especially without anonymity. Similarly, struggling novices rely most often on formal student evaluations—usually administered at semesters' ends and fed back months later—to learn what might need changing, far after the fact and without useful specifics about what to do differently.

Notice four kinds of inefficiencies in this passive waiting for formal evaluations:

1. Teachers who wait for end-of-semester feedback express the most impatience in the meanwhile because they see few signs of student approval and have little information about how to gain it ("Why aren't they more responsive? I really don't know").
2. At many campuses I've studied, formal teaching evaluations were likely to end up in departmental files, unseen by faculty who remained unaware they had to ask for them (even though those ratings were later used in tenure considerations by their departments).
3. Standardized student ratings often leave new faculty with the impression that scores reflect teacher popularity and leniency, perhaps because the feedback fails to specify what needs to be done differently or better (e.g., slowing the pace of lecturing).
4. By relying on formal evaluations as the sole indicator of how well they taught, struggling novices shortchange themselves of opportunities to provide more useful—and usually more complimentary—information to themselves and to their gatekeepers.

Exemplary novices, once again, help model useful alternatives. They administer their own evaluation devices at intervals during the course of a semester. These evaluation formats show progress and prowess in dimensions that exemplars themselves value (e.g., teaching critical thinking about setting up research problems—something unlikely to be reflected clearly on a formal evaluation). A particular advantage of such evaluations, if kept credible by having someone else administer and score them, without any opportunity to identify individual student commentators, is that only the later evaluations from a series given over a semester need be submitted, as a rule, as part of information considered by reappointment or tenure committees. Never, in my experience, does a committee of evaluators of new faculty expect great teaching out of the gate; instead, they look for evidence of systematic work at improvement and of reasonable acceptance from students. To get them beyond their traditional, unthinking, reliance on end-of-semester ratings, you may have to take the initiative in collecting more reliable and valid information. Gatekeepers almost always need educating.

In my own programs for new teachers, the following sort of useful evaluation proved most effective for purposes of suggesting what needed doing differently and better. It also proved effective at informing gatekeepers what novice faculty had done well that mattered:

Early, Informal Teaching Evaluation

Date _____

A. Please provide specific written information, based on your experience in class today, about . . .
   1. What could have been differently, better (please be specific):

   2. What was done well (please be specific):

B. Please rate (on a scale of 1–10, with 10 = maximal) your perceptions of how successful today's class was in terms of these dimensions:
   1. Clarity and understandability of materials presented by the teacher ____
   2. Usefulness of the materials presented by the teacher today ____
   3. Pacing of the material in terms of your being able to take good notes and ask questions ____
   4. Worth of preview and reviews of what happened in class ____
   5. Warmth and concern displayed by the teacher ____
   6. Patience and helpfulness displayed by the teacher in response to student questions ____
   7. Classroom climate today (e.g., student noisiness and distractions *not* a problem) ____
   8. How likely you would be to recommend this class to a close friend ____

That format is only a suggestion, one weighing heavily on issues that distinguish struggling new teachers from exemplars. Three of the items in Section B (1, 2, and 8) represent the kinds of questions proven generally useful in traditional, end-of-semester protocols. You might want to add items from your own campus's end-of-the-semester form. Whatever, keep the total to 10 ratings items or less. Notice which of them help you see what needs changing and how to change. If you're starting with strong apprehension, employ only the first two items in initial applications (perhaps with students responding on both sides of a 3" × 5" card).

You might eventually want items that reflect how well you got a particular point across. Better yet, ask for a brief recounting, in just a line or two, from students about what was just taught—and make students aware that their answers will not be graded. This, you might have noticed, is the format for the "one-minute paper" you saw in earlier chapters. Or include items that index your progress at something as specific as timely stopping, smiling, or eye contact. You even might ask students for specifics of how well prepared they were for class today. And, no, you don't need my permission to use, modify, print, distribute, or vilify my format.

How early and often should you administer such an evaluation? Begin within the first week and repeat about every three weeks. How can you manage the seemingly onerous task of scoring and summarizing these evaluations? Easily, by appointing small groups of students, preferably relative strangers, to work together, before the next class, to capsulize the most common, useful written comments and to provide mean scores (even standard deviations if your students are competent to calculate them) of your quantitative ratings. How do students almost always react to such a request? By feeling honored and by carrying out the assignment with care. How can you clarify what the students' comments and ratings really mean? By not only reporting the outcome of your most recent evaluation but asking class members to speculate, as though explaining why someone else would have made such a rating or comment, and by suggesting your own interpretations and watching student reactions. How can you find time for all this in occasional classes? Have your student groups write their analysis on the board before class and then discuss it for but a few minutes unless something too important to cut short comes up.

What if you worry, reasonably, that such a report would mean loss of face for you? First, realize that most of what turns out to be painful criticism will already be obvious to your class: Your overly fast pace, your off-putting shyness, your seeming resistance to questions. Second, know that there is almost always less criticism than teachers anticipate. Third, employ "Olympic scoring rules" that instruct your compilers to eliminate extreme written comments of all sorts, and, of course, the very highest and lowest rating scores. Fourth, anticipate that a public airing of how most students react will help temper your excessive critics, most of whom will be surprised that not everyone else shares their low opinion of you. Fifth, expect that the mere act of soliciting and sharing this feedback seems to win more student approval and involvement, in part because they'll see that you care about them and are working to improve. Sixth, tell yourself that although getting this feedback is painful in the short run, it is an especially good way to attain excellence and happiness as a teacher.

Exercise 3. Encourage Criticism.
Struggling new teachers, far more than peers who enjoy teaching, tend to prepare alone, without discussing their plans and ideas with colleagues or graduate stu-

dents. They rarely invite colleagues to visit their classes. It follows, then, that their students more commonly remain anonymous transients. Years later, these struggling teachers cannot tell you much about individual students; their students, in turn, recall only the barest notions of what the class was about ("All I can remember is that he was a sharp dresser"). Why? Teachers who remain passive about getting early feedback, such as specific criticism and praise, learn too little, too late, about how best to change their working styles.

Efficient, effective, exemplary strategies of learning how to teach are public and open. Exemplary novices, if you can stand my mentioning them once again, deliberately collect information about how well they are received and comprehended. More impressive is the fact that they respond patiently to criticism and even encourage it—so long as it is civil and constructive. As you might expect, this practice of tolerance and patience with critics can be almost unbearably painful in the short run. The following strategies can help you progress somewhat gradually through the most difficult parts:

- At first, ask critics who will sit in on your class, beforehand, to limit their comments to only a few things that you yourself wonder about (e.g., "Did I pause and wait enough to encourage student questions/answers?"), inquiries where you know you will probably not be terribly hurt by the response. With practice, move to slightly riskier questions (e.g., "Could my reviews, during class, have been better?). Like any other kind of phobia, avoidance of criticism is best moderated by way of what psychologists call *exposure therapy* (e.g., getting used to going out on bridges by gradually walking farther and farther out as you grow more tolerant of the fear, more aware of how wasteful it is to fear that fear). If you or your critic worry about his or her sitting through a whole class, specify the 5- to 10-minute period you want judged.
- Ask critics to be specific in terms of what you might need to do to make your preparations and presentations better. This means not accepting vague criticisms (e.g., "It was great" or "Your presentation was confusing"). This means calmly asking for more specifics ("OK, please tell me what I should do to make it clearer"). And, as you muster more bravery, it means asking critics to begin with specific and positive comments about at least one thing you have done well (despite the proud tradition in academe of sticking solely to criticism). In actual practice, few critics refuse this request or even see it as an imposition; they may simply be unaccustomed to its practice.
- Remain relatively calm and nonreactive while hearing or reading your criticism. If you expect a strong self-response, get the criticism by way of an intermediary who edits and restates the critic's remarks or the written comments in gradual, tactful fashion. In that way, you will be better able to sort the useful message from what might have seemed intolerably personal and hurtful. In that way, you can expose yourself to criticism more slowly and more tolerably. Later, when you are ready to hear or read critics directly, maintain

your calm, open focus by taking careful notes on what might need doing differently. Stop your critic, calmly, for clarification if necessary. Doing this helps defuse what would otherwise be a tense situation.

- Practice ways of agreeing with criticism, at least some aspect of it. Begin by recognizing a basic truth about teaching efficiently: All critics, even the harshest or most ill informed, have something worthwhile to teach us. If the critic hasn't even listened carefully, find out what put him or her off from a closer and more patient look. If your critic has misunderstood your message, investigate to see where the confusion occurs. If your reader/listener is offended, inquire about the stimulus; it may be something minor that you hadn't noticed, such as too fast a pace; it may be something major, like a sexist style.

Find something in the criticism with which you can honestly agree (e.g., I can understand how some people might not find this interesting, but . . .). Thank your critic for her or his work; reviewers are rarely paid or properly appreciated. Then, request clarification of what needs doing differently or better. You will, at that point, be less tense and defensive, more inclined to appreciate the useful message.

Something else helps: Committing to keep at these practices until you reach the most difficult step:

- Enlist critics earlier and often—during preparations and in early lectures.

In the longer run, prepare yourself for the troubling kinds of critics—students who come to you in anger. Allowing the other person to vent and taking the risk that you will respond in kind is unhealthy and generally unproductive. Instead, learn to say, calmly, that you try never to answer criticisms or questions while you are (or might be) upset, that you would like to meet again at least a day later, when both of you are calmer. If your critic seems unlikely to calm down, insist that he or she submit the complaint/question in writing so that you can formulate a careful, thoughtful response. As a rule, critics put less venomous emotion into written versions of what they have to say; if not, you have the advantage of reading it without them present.

In the end, remember this: Even your acceptance of criticism is best done with moderation. Your responsibilities as a teacher do not include tolerating needless abuse. Indeed, in my observations, new faculty who tolerate excesses of student anger are most likely to opt for other, nonacademic careers. How did some new hires who began with that tendency change course? By practicing the strategies just listed.

Other ways of economizing your reactions to criticism appear in the next few rules/chapters. Because this point on our path together may be the most discouraging, I urge you to persist beyond this necessary focus on criticism. The way grows brighter as we continue.

Moderate Negative Thinking and Strong Emotions

What comes next when you're already moderating overattachments to your own teaching content and modulating overreactions to criticism from others (Chapter 5)? Managing the even tougher kinds of accusations—and of attachment to them—common in self-criticism. Excessive self-criticism wastes energy and demoralizes; it even paralyzes. When we beam our best doubts and self-rebukes on what we are doing, we not only dislike our work and ourselves but we also hesitate and block. Most bizarre, self-criticism grows to be so integral a part of us that we can be loathe to give it up.

Excessive self-criticism often leads to depression and pessimism, surprisingly common problems amongst new faculty. The immobility and indecisiveness of depression, in turn, usually necessitate another excess in order to get vital work done: The impulsivity of near-mania and of rushing under deadlines. The excessive emotions that come with bingeing start a viscous circle of depression and mania.

Nothing distinguishes struggling novices more dramatically than this pattern of passive sadness alternating with euphoric rushing. And yet, this problem in the new faculty experience is almost never mentioned or understood. Thriving new faculty suggest a solution; they, in contrast to new teachers caught up in busyness and disappointment, more often work with constancy and moderation, with generally mild happiness and consistent involvement in priority tasks. Adam Smith could have predicted that.

These are the related facts that need facing: First, cycles of depression/near-mania are common to most new faculty—probably more so than at any time prior in their lives. Second, while this cycling is not often so excessive as to require formal treatment, it definitely undermines optimism, productivity, sociability, and happiness. Said another way, it hinders progress toward excellence in teaching. Third, proven correctives for the negative thinking and impatience behind this pattern are simple to adopt.

Still, this is where participants in my programs often draw back in alarm. Here, it might seem, I'm the one being excessive. They hadn't, new faculty tell me, expected coaching about teaching to include something so personal ("I'm here about my teaching; if I need help with that [mania/near-depression], I'll ask my shrink"). They wonder if I'm being too "psychological" by adding concerns about mental health ("Until now, I felt comfortable with you but this makes me wary; I'm not sure I like psychology"). They sometimes assume that I'm mistakenly blaming *them* for their difficulties, not the real culprits, such as poor students and overdemanding administrators. But most of all, they wonder if I haven't simply gone beyond the proper boundaries of teaching improvement, off on a sidetrack like a teacher who has lost focus or is trying to do too much.

To counter those understandable doubts, I begin by reminding them, and you, of four related things. First, virtually everything about the *nihil nimus* approach of this book is unconventional because it attends to things usually ignored or suppressed. Second, it is unprecedented in assembling proofs of help for new faculty, and in attracting critics who dislike an entry ritual made egalitarian. Third, the *nihil nimus* approach emphasizes relief from depression/near-mania, and so runs afoul of romantic notions that brilliance and creativity need suffering and madness. Fourth, these problems of depression and mania are so readily dealt with that to ignore them would be wasteful.

To acquaint you with this uncommon perspective, I first overview ways in which excessive self-criticism affects teaching and then I move to general problems with sustained strong emotions.

Irrationally Negative Thinking

When we think too negatively, too self-critically, we make ourselves unnecessarily anxious. (Or, just as often, the anxiety comes first, perhaps as a result of feeling rushed and overwhelmed.) Anxiety not only induces a kind of intellectual stiffness and social distancing we know all too well but it also results in excessive caution and delay. It tempts us to put off preparations rather than face tasks that could discomfit or embarrass. And once in an anxious and self-critical mindset, we're likely to think of teaching as difficult and unrewarding—no wonder, given the discomforts our self-talk about teaching can create for us. Then, if we've let anxious self-talk put us off from work at teaching, we must eventually rush preparations and presentations, and thus set the stage for even more anxiety and its negative thinking. Each feeds the other.

Suppose, for instance, that you have a tendency to tell yourself that you are really a fraud under all those fine credentials, citations, and clothes. (If so, you're not the only one of us who feels that way, deep down.) When you struggle at teaching, that same inner voice, always the immoderate critic, may lead you to expect unforgivable mistakes and unforgiving students. That inner critic might even encourage you to take refuge in preparing factually correct, conceptually demanding lectures that cannot, whatever else, be faulted for unscholarliness.

Most predictably, negative thinking eventually exacts rushing and pain. If your inner critic tells you what a worthless and shameful person you are, you may try to work so fast that you leave its voice behind. If so, you will certainly find work tiring and inherently unsatisfying. Eventually, the pessimism of self-criticism brings a sense of helplessness that breeds still more depression and its inaction/indecision in work. And that passivity, immoderate in its avoidance of what needs doing now, induces related excesses, including anger that grows into irritability and overreaction to the slightest slight. In the meanwhile, the excessive self-focus that the inner critic produces in us (e.g., "I wonder if I'm blushing?"; "Can they see that my hands are actually shaking?") keeps us shy and isolated, apparently unapproachable and aloof, unable to find or accept social support or affection. The impulsivity of negative thinking, with its roots in impatience and anger, makes patience with ourselves and our students all the more difficult. The more impulsive we become, the more readily we opt for the quick, the easy, and the immediately relieving. In the midst of such negativity, we might even make an insulting reply that "one-ups" a seemingly impertinent student.

How Can You Tell When Your Thinking Is Getting in the Way of Your Teaching?

Begin by noticing when your thoughts drift to future or past events, to anxieties about what might happen and to regrets about what already has. You may discover that you spend much of your time trying to relive the past or control the future—without having appreciated how little consciousness you've had left for living and working in the present moment. When you do not live primarily in the present moment, you invite rumination, rushing, reproach.

Then look for instances when thinking outside the present moment discourages you and makes you want to do something other than work on teaching. Notice its tendency to painful negativity and its power of overreaction, including impatience, anger, pessimism, and helplessness. And then, as an unusual educational experience, try the strategies outlined below. After all, exemplars often extend their inclinations to experiment to themselves.

Rule 7 (Part 1): Moderate Negative Thinking.

Exercises for Rule 7, Part 1

Exercises for moderating negative thinking become easy with constant practice, even if you suppose yourself unqualified to practice psychology. Detailed strategies appear in a variety of best-selling books that help make self-therapists of readers (e.g., Seligman's *Learned Optimism;* Ellis and Knaus's *Overcoming Procrastination*). Strategies that work best in my programs for teachers are among the simplest of these.

Exercise 1. Habitually Monitor Your Thinking during Work.
This may be more difficult than it sounds, initially, because most of us are unaccustomed to listening, consciously and carefully, to the nearly constant self-talk that goes on in the backs of our minds. Even while much of that self-talk ordinarily goes unheard by the conscious self, it, more than anything else, undermines the *nihil nimus* ideal with its tendencies to impatience and impulsivity, to irritability and social distancing, to shyness and overreaction, and to all the other problems we've covered in the first five chapters about teaching. An idle, unattended mind tends to be a negative and counterproductive mind.

The keywords to becoming a useful observer of negative thinking are familiar—*patience* and *tolerance:* Patience to keep watching and listening, even when nothing seems to be there; tolerance to hear the amazingly negative, depressing, irrational things we often say to ourselves covertly.

Begin by noticing (and noting) your self-talk at just one critical time, the few minutes that precede the beginning of a brief daily session for preparing classroom materials or during your walk to class. Notice, for instance, do you find yourself worrying about needing to do something other than the task at hand (e.g., you need to mail a parking fine due at City Hall today), and then assuming, dejectedly, that you have too much to do? Or instead of thinking about your course—the task at hand—are you fretting about an injustice (e.g., in a faculty meeting just an hour ago, a colleague made a rude comment about a proposal you offered up to the group: "That doesn't seem well-thought out")? Or are you ruminating about the likelihood that the usual trouble-makers in your class will disdain even your best efforts ("Those guys in the back, with the thick necks and their hats on backwards," as one participant described them while talking aloud his thinking, as we walked to his class)? Or are you worrying about making your class preparations perfectly entertaining (e.g., "I should be much funnier, much more quick-witted, but I don't seem to be able to . . . I do, you know, want to be the most fascinating teacher they'll ever encounter")? If so, you're not using your time and mental energy economically or humanely. If so, you're engaging in too much negative or irrational thinking.

How many new faculty avoid negative thinking altogether? None from the hundreds that I've studied in this regard. What really matters is the degree to which they moderate it; exemplars and novices who model after them lessen negative thinking to levels that do not interfere significantly with ease and enjoyment in teaching. What these new faculty who work with moderation have in common is a habit of attending to their self-talk, especially its irrational aspects. Once negative self-talk comes under closer scrutiny, the next step comes almost spontaneously.

Exercise 2. Dispute Negative Thinking.

This second step also requires regular, moderate practice for optimal results. It means noticing and challenging the usual excesses of negative thinking by consciously listening to how rational the thought is as you repeat it and consider it slowly, calmly. If, for instance, you imagine that your teaching surely will be criticized, rejected, or unappreciated, consider this: Reflection will expose the irrationality of expecting that *all* your classroom comments will be disparaged or misunderstood. It also reminds you that expecting all your teaching to be adored and all your advice to be adopted is just as irrational. Awareness of irrational thoughts helps you avoid overreacting to them and helps you move beyond the usual pain and distraction they cause. The knack for noticing an inner critic or pessimist and then refuting it is not so difficult as you might suppose:

> *The main skill of optimistic thinking is disputing. This is a skill everyone has, but we normally use it only when others accuse us wrongly. . . . You can, with some discipline, learn to become a superb disputer of pessimistic thoughts. . . . Once you are good at doing it, it makes you feel better instantly.*—MARTIN SELIGMAN

Exercise 3. Replace Negativities with Constructive, Optimistic Thinking.

Once you have disputed and dismissed an irrational thought—or at least tempered its meanness and noisiness—turn your thinking to the present moment, to getting on with the priority task you had planned to do. This is the sort of self-instruction that exemplars report making: "Once I'm doing the teaching, I'll enjoy it. I might just as well go and do it and enjoy it; it only lasts 80 minutes." Sometimes the cue is more succinct ("Just do it").

Anticipate deeper changes. Teachers who practice these moderations not only discover the inefficiency of pessimism and the efficacy of optimism; they also learn to reinterpret things that happen in a more positive light. They, for example, more often report supposing that failures don't so much reflect inborn personal weakness or unfair working conditions as they do a correctable problem such as rushing.

Another general change is just as useful: When you find yourself and/or your class reacting negatively, you'll be more inclined to pause and notice the ongoing process—particularly the likely sources of that negativity. For instance, you might be presenting in ways that confuse and worry your students; if you see mostly worried faces, pause and ask students what they are thinking. Or you might notice, for example, that you are feeling angry toward a few restless students and allowing your negative thinking about them to affect your treatment of everyone. You might even see that your own negative thinking, quite unrelated to the class, has crept in and darkened your mood.

But that kind of emotional excess is only one side of the problem. The other, less well-known type is the high side of the emotional continuum.

Excessively High Emotions

Some reasons why we don't ordinarily resist high emotions in teaching are obvious. First, preparing or presenting with too little emotion leads to dull experience, weak motivation, and missed communication. Second, standard teaching evaluation devices often count enthusiasm as desirable, apparently implying that more is better. Third, there are times when bursts of high emotion regain the attention of students. And fourth, tradition favors anecdotes of teachers who always work with full intensity; the most impressive and misleading of these "ideals" are those teachers who never break from their stream of talking, those who continue nonstop while opening the door for latecomers ("What a show! He never misses a beat," said one admiring student about his manicky professor).

But in fact, too much emotion, even positive emotion, interferes with effective teaching and learning. Novices who try to emulate the fast-talking, entertaining style they suppose ideal tend to rush and distract their students from useful notetaking; they almost always leave class exhausted. New teachers who rely too much on enthusiasm to maintain student involvement risk becoming superficial entertainers whose students leave class, at best, still captivated but with few meaningful recollections about concepts and themes. Indeed, students in classes taught with high emotion report that they cannot keep up with so rushed a pace, that they need more pauses to reflect and ask questions, that they too leave class exhausted.

Practice at moderating emotion while teaching seems to work best when it starts during preteaching strategies that combine the excitement of discovery with patient reflection. Here, once again, we benefit in constant but moderate acts of pausing, slowing, and stopping—and in appreciating how high levels of positive emotion lead to teaching problems.

To Understand Problems of High Emotion, Look at Their Usual Basis

Hypomania is a near-state of mania and it is pathological (American Psychiatric Association, 1994). Hypomania typically originates in prolonged rushing and excitement. Its short-term benefits, including sustained attention and euphoria, are tempting and addictive but its long-term costs far outweigh them. True, rushing and bingeing at teaching bring a seeming creativity, euphoria, and charm. But the problem with hypomania goes beyond the superficial and disorganized writing/talking it often produces, even beyond the exhaustion that makes starting the work again, an hour or day later, difficult. Hypomania, because of its excessiveness, must eventually exhaust and disappoint us. It leads to fatigue and dysphoria, to sad inaction and negative self-talk—just as full-blown mania, among people who need professional help, begets dangerous depression and then more mania.

Consider why this cycle, even with the relative moderation indicated in the modifier *hypo,* actually keeps us working immoderately and inconstantly over the long haul. If our last bout of working was an exhausting binge, our mood may have been "down" since then. When we break out of our depressiveness and its negative thinking—because we must get to work—we tend to generate the emotional state that ensures the opposite experience of hypomania. Why? The passive and agitated waiting of depression, once deadlines approach, rely on bingeing and on its motivating euphoria to resume challenging work. Then, when we have once again exhausted ourselves with the impulsivity of a binge, we risk another bout of dysphoria. Why? Impulsive actions, especially binges, rarely feel good in the long run; their very excessiveness and superficiality, their attempts to do too much, too hurriedly, too indiscriminately, lead to disappointingly unreflective efforts. Worse yet, the eventual outcome of hypomania/bingeing, of doing things under pressure and deadlines, leads to a general style of working and socializing called busyness. The chronic feeling of being overwhelmed and overscheduled that comes with busyness encourages more depression . . . and so on.

Hypomania also ensures mood swings that interfere with everyday living. In fact, hypomania produces:

- A measurable wake of increasing depression (as indexed, for example, by self-report devices such as the Beck Depression Inventory; see Section II of this book for more detail)
- Observable reductions in the quality of teaching (as estimated by trained judges)
- Less comprehensibility to students (as indicated by examination of their classroom notes)
- More reported difficulty at timely pausing and stopping by teachers

Hypomania even seems to undermine the health and social relations of teachers; when we are either elated/grandiose or depressed/pessimistic, we stress and isolate ourselves. In my studies of new faculty, struggling novices not only exhibited the highest incidence of hypomania-depression cycles but they also reported the most bouts of influenza and distressing social interactions.

Still, Hypomania Has a Place in Efficient, Effective Teaching

Even moderation needs moderation. Teachers in my programs who prepared and presented with the highest levels of externally judged fluency and of self-reported happiness were most likely to report keeping their working emotions at midrange levels. Even so, they remained mindful of the value of changing their pace occasionally. Sometimes they used a burst of excitement to work past their internal censors or to convey the appropriate voice in their preparing or presenting. Other times they prepared dispassionately, just to get ideas out, knowing they could wait to find more imagination in revising them later. When doing what they and others judged as their best work, they displayed a rhythm based in mild happiness, one punctuated by occasional swings in mood. These exemplars and their followers liked to mention their specific goal for moderation: Not persisting in heightened emotions to a point that impeded returning to the base level of mild happiness. How did they learn to recognize such limits? Practice, practice, practice!

Rule 7 (Part 2): Moderate Emotions.

Exercises for Rule 7, Part 2

At this stage of my programs, teachers become close observers of their emotions in order to notice which impede or impel working. And here, teachers become patient experimenters who compare the effects of working under hypomania versus moderation. Said one, "Strange, isn't it, that I had so readily thought about experimenting with my approaches to research but not with my teaching?"

Exercise 1. Monitor and Record Emotional Levels and Types during Preparation Sessions.

Begin by rating your working emotions in a continuum with, say, high nervous tension at one end and calm confidence at the other. That emotional domain might be labeled *anxiety–relaxation*. Practice noticing affective states as simple as happiness while working (something most of us have not been trained to do); once you're doing that, more elusive emotions such as euphoria, anger, fear, or anxiousness become more readily apparent. Aim for gradual awareness of how all these emotions affect writing, speaking, interacting, and, of course, how they relate to your own self-talk. Is all this too much a demand for busy novice teachers trying to survive the toughest initiation rite of their lives? It isn't, according to program participants who found that tempering emotions makes the work of teaching simpler, less stressed.

It takes a few months of regular practice, in my experience, for teachers to become good observers of their working emotions. Meanwhile, though, the mere act of paying attention to emotional processes brings noticeable, redeeming results.

"am I happy?"

Exercise 2. Set Reasonable Goals for Emotional Management.

At the least, practice the calm pacing you already know about. Then add the emotion of mild happiness to it. Why? Both states, calm and mild happiness, optimize the kinds of problem solving essential to preparing and presenting. Both make teaching more enjoyable and rewarding.

How can you tell if you are calm and mildly happy? Stop and observe. Compare your feelings and expressions with occasions when you were undoubtedly calm and mildly happy (e.g., for me, a moment of listening to tree frogs and inhaling the damp evening air).

How can you induce these moderate states if they are not already there? Scan for and dispute negative thinking and supplant it with positive thoughts—better yet, with getting to work on a priority task without rushing. Plant a faint smile on your face (this, again, grows easier with practice), but not the fixed sort displayed in beauty contests or political arenas. Recall, for the moment, a pleasant experience, such as sitting near a waterfall with ferns fragrant in the sunlight. And, with practice, notice the components of pleasant emotions, such as joy:

> *Joy is sensed as pleasant, desirable, feeling . . . comfort and well-being and relaxation, even playfulness . . . movements seem easier, accomplished by strength and vigor and openness and receptivity and creativity.—CARROLL IZARD*

That well-being, with its calm and openness, makes the next steps easier. Now, I hope, you will be primed to notice anger or impatience growing excessive, even how similar they are. You will grow better able to rein yourself in, not only from the impulsiveness of impatience but also to stop yourself from persisting into more euphoria than is optimal for reflective, communicative work in the long run.

Expect to struggle, at least at first, in the absence of usual tension. You might suppose, mistakenly, that you are not working hard enough (or suffering enough). Exemplary teachers, in contrast, not only work with mild emotions but they also rely on changes of pace to keep them going.

What might, in the end, keep you from taking the leap into this unfamiliar state of moderation? Part of it might be that nagging feeling of not working hard and fast enough. And part could be the fear of losing touch with the euphoric hypomania that seems to bring out the genius in you. In fact, as we will see soon—in the chapters of advice in Section II about exemplary ways of writing—the best and most creative work experiences tend to occur amid constancy and moderation. It sounds dull and boring, but it isn't; boredom is rooted in impatience, not moderation.

You might first have to fully experience the benefits of constancy and moderation as a writer before you can as a teacher. Don't worry; we'll soon be immersed in the *nihil nimus* approach to scholarly writing; meanwhile, virtually everything you accomplish here as a teacher will help there.

For now, I encourage you to consider another rule/chapter about teaching drawn from quick starters and their followers, and then a final chapter on how these *nihil nimus* methods apply to the difficult problem of moderating classroom incivilities. Patience, patience, patience!

Let Others Do
Some of the Work

This may be the most counterintuitive of all the rules about letting go of control. Still, the fact is that the most efficient, effective teachers stand out for letting other people do some of their work. They, compared to most teachers, collaborate more by sharing the work of presenting in classes. And they encourage more observation and criticism of their work, even early in the planning and preparation process. When readers/listeners/learners mention overlooked sources and confusing transitions, they do some of our work for us. If these noteworthy acts, none of them difficult, save time and improve teaching, why aren't they more common?

Traditional Misbeliefs

Teachers often resist Rule 7 because they respect unproven traditions that grant special genius to artists, inventors, writers, and teachers who seem to work alone, without help. More specifically, we cherish myths about teachers who apparently produce finished, flawless work in a flash of brilliance, without any obvious preparation or notes.

On the other hand, we tend to believe that ideas and materials shared early, although still imperfect, will create irreversibly negative images in our readers and listeners. We suppose that asking for help with teaching is always an imposition. And, to complete the usual constellation of misbeliefs, we agree that brilliant teaching must be completely original, unique.

We are also likely to suppose that letting others do some of the work is tantamount to self-weakness or manipulation of others. Said one newcomer to me: "If it isn't all mine, all my own work, why bother?" Said another: "You have to understand that I value my autonomy above everything else. No way am I going to ask for help." And another: "I can't impose on busy, successful people" (even while admitting that she would welcome requests for feedback from other teachers).

Consider the counterarguments to these traditional claims and beliefs:

1. The most efficient and effective teachers delegate some of the responsibility, just as good managers do. They also cheerfully admit that most teaching is the borrowing and restating of old ideas. Indeed, quick starters actually enjoy sharing the credit for collaboration and assistance in their teaching. They also, as you may recall, get the highest student ratings and induce the highest student recall/understanding. Exemplary novices understand that appropriating other people's ideas but restating them and putting them into different contexts is not plagiarizing (particularly when mentioning sources). They know that soliciting early critiques and suggestions for change does not constitute shirking (even in academic settings where things like term papers and dissertations are traditionally not shown to anyone until seemingly finished and perfect). They particularly take advantage of other writers and teachers by studying their ways of working, such as modes of organization and emphasis, adapting what they like to their own work.

2. The best teachers I've studied sense the logical shortcoming in becoming a teacher who doesn't believe in learning from others. "If teaching includes sharing information and ways of making use of it," said one of them to me, "then why wouldn't learning to teach include those same things?"

Rule 8: Let Others Do Some of the Work.

Exercises for Rule 8

Involving others in the work requires letting go of some of the control and credit. Curiously, it also helps make teaching more public by letting others, even critics, see how you work and how you change. Most surprising, it makes teaching more publicly acceptable; as your well-intentioned motives grow more visible, more responsive to audience needs, so will your support. This act of accepting help is one of the most difficult of social skills for novice teachers; it is also one of the most commonly overlooked and underappreciated in advice for novice teachers. Once more, exemplary teachers suggest practical ways of acquiring these skills:

Exercise 1. Establish Social Contracts.
We first saw this practice as part of Rule 3, while setting contingencies to impel the habit of brief sessions of working at teaching. Here, in the seventh rule, it

broadens to finding a regular partner who will listen to parts of what you are writing and diagramming for a class—and you to his or hers. How does this help? The realization that you must talk aloud what you have prewritten to your partner brings more focus and clarity to your preparations for meetings. The act of actually hearing yourself, while noticing the reactions of your listener, suggests how students will respond and helps generate a mild excitement about shared ideas and discoveries even before class gets underway. With the aid of this early and ongoing feedback, teachers are more likely to make changes, according to my observations. And with repeated suggestions of where listeners will react badly, teachers report growing more habituated and objectively responsive to the criticisms and objections that lie, inevitably, ahead.

Exercise 2. Collaborate in Classroom Teaching, at Least Occasionally.

Yes, some coteachers disappoint because they don't communicate or cooperate well. But most can ease your load, add novelty over the long haul of a semester, and provide educational experiences that cannot be had elsewhere. How can you find good coteachers/guest speakers?

- Ask colleagues if you may sit in on a class of theirs to gain ideas for your own classes. If they refuse your entry, that tells you something worth knowing; if their class is tedious and their students riotous, that, too, might tell you to look elsewhere.
- Look for potential coteachers/guest speakers who will complement and instruct you.
- Don't limit possibilities for coteachers to colleagues on campus; bring in experts from your community (at first, at least, for brief stints).
- Don't leave the presentations of coteachers, even the most sophisticated, to chance; ask for a brief session in which both of you rehearse what you will do in class. This preteaching helps ensure some continuity between what you've been doing and what the other speaker will do. It also raises the likelihood you will participate along with your guest, at first as a running commentator, then in dialogue. After all, students and teachers report giving especial value to interactive coteaching.

There are still more advantages to this uncommon act of collaboration. Shared planning/presentation provides an opportunity to discover how other teachers think and work. Collaboration during classes (i.e., turn-taking at speaking) can bring a richness of combined styles and ideas that no one teacher could have conjured. Collaboration reduces the kinds of oversights and miscommunications that undermine public acceptance. And it can even produce a completed preparation and presentation in far less time than if done solo.

Exercise 3. Observe and (Compassionately) Critique Colleagues' Classes.

When you analyze the teaching of colleagues, you can learn a lot about becoming a better teacher in your own classes. You may see things to emulate as well as things to avoid. Almost always you will take the perspective of students around you. And, most useful, you will have practice at reflecting on teaching in ways that go beyond mere content—to processes such as nonverbal acts of teachers and students, even how classrooms themselves are experienced in domains such as lighting, acoustics, and ventilation.

How can you manage such visits without annoying or threatening your colleagues? First, of course, by asking for permission to sit in on a class of theirs. Second, by having them suggest a particular class or segment that they value. Third, by making clear your primary goal of seeing what they do well, what you might emulate. Fourth, by sticking to specific compliments, not general impressions (e.g., "I liked the way you paused for emphasis; that's something I need to work on").

Eventually, of course, you should ask for a reciprocal visit. This won't be so difficult as you might suppose, especially if you adopt the strategies we saw in an earlier chapter for tolerating and learning from criticism:

- Meet briefly (5 to 10 minutes), before your class, with your observer/critic and share your plan for the day with her or him (e.g., scan your notes and give your critic a copy).
- Ask your observer/critic, during that preliminary meeting, to rate you during class in specific fashion and to follow up with open-ended comments on what you did well and what you could have done better, perhaps with numerical ratings on dimensions such as pacing, pausing, eye contact, and reviewing.
- Unless you're stronger in the face of criticism than I am, have your observer leave those initial notes/ratings in your mailbox. Then, within a day, ask for clarification by phone or in person—while remembering to be brief and calm.
- Thank your colleague/critic/coach.

Exercise 4. Share Information about Yourself in Class.

Another act of sharing may surprise you because it seems quite different from the one with which we began this chapter: The best teachers I've observed let students know who they are, usually by way of occasional anecdotes that help make a point in the teaching (e.g., students especially like hearing accounts of how your research was done and what your interest was). This kind of openness, practiced in moderation, relates to the need for social immediacies, which we will see in the next chapter; so long as you remain mysterious to students, you will seem aloof.

This kind of sharing also helps make teaching easier for a couple of reasons. For one thing, an occasional anecdote provides a welcome change of pace. For another, sharing your own relevant experiences encourages students to do the same in return. In a sense, this mutual sharing is first a matter of accepting help from yourself, from that real person who exists beyond the classroom, and second another way of letting students do some of the work.

Exercise 5. Join an Even Broader Conversation.

All four of the exercises preceding this one let others do some of the work—and so move us away from the solitude, privacy, and autonomy that traditional teachers have claimed to prefer. That is, all of these practices amount to making work at teaching more sociable. The long-term result is more than just sharing and rehearsing as you prepare, and more than just coteaching, even more than stimulating/tolerating discussion by students. It also means socializing with other teachers working on courses like your own. It means recognizing that when you teach in an area, you become part of an ongoing conversation carried out by colleagues in other classrooms and on other campuses. If, as in any social conversation, you speak out in the group without listening to what others are saying, you will act naively. But if you listen to how others are posing problems, you can reshape your contribution while making sure you have something relatively new and interesting to add.

How could you manage such a conversation? Join Internet discussions about courses like yours and attend annual conferences for teachers of specific disciplines. The wealth of useful ideas in those forums is impressive. So is their social support.

To the extent that you learn from such conversations (e.g., how to state problems, how to present arguments effectively, how to stimulate discussions, how to keep up with the literature, how to formulate creative ideas, how to give effective tests), you let others do some of your work. To the extent you allow other teachers to help you, in and out of class, the more open and efficient you will become. Successful teaching isn't solely a matter of learning how to produce good classroom material. It is just as much a skill of accepting help from others, even competitors and critics. Indeed, one of the surprises in my studies of exemplars was the discovery that they regularly interact with more fans *and* critics than do normal teachers. Evidently, the boldness of exemplars means they encounter more praise and more criticism—the optimal way to get help and to learn, so far as they are concerned.

A Final Caution Near the End of These Rules about Teaching

If you're like the readers who responded to my early drafts of this book, you have reservations about the *nihil nimus* approach. Some of my early readers proceeded through these rules far more slowly and skeptically than others. Some were more timid or doubting about trying new strategies. But guess what distinguished early readers who got involved most readily and with the most documentable benefit? The same old duo: patience and tolerance.

Those readers who "let go" most readily (and who found the most productivity and acceptance as teachers) acted in these three distinctive ways:

1. They deliberately and repeatedly talked to themselves about how their generally traditional, self-reliant beginnings at teaching seemed less than satisfying or restful—that they would need to make deliberate changes if they were to benefit from alternatives. One of them put it this way: "Deep down, I know that I always have to talk myself into making changes that matter." Another added this point: "Where my pride is involved, and it was here, I need to be extremely specific and directive with myself and not rely on vague intentions."

2. They made an especial effort to practice the two things that I had repeatedly mentioned as most central: constancy and moderation (constancy in practicing exercises in regularly scheduled sessions; moderation in practicing them during brief sessions that stopped short of exhaustion or interference with other needful things).

3. They displayed a style of moderation that included a healthy and humorous distancing from my pronouncements. Some of the teachers who have displayed the greatest success with these rules liked to add this spontaneous comment:

The worse the participant, the greater the attachment to these rules.

In the end, these most readily involved novices admitted to having done something else crucial. They deliberately worked at letting me share what I have learned about good starts at teaching with them—despite my sometimes annoying or off-putting ways. The single-most distinctive thing about these early readers who benefited so quickly and thoroughly was not so much their own hard work as their willingness to let others, including me, work hard on their behalf. That, they noted, was among the hardest work they did.

8

Moderate Classroom Incivilities

This final chapter of Section I marks a shift in perspective. The first seven chapters concentrated on *nihil nimus processes,* such as brief, regular bouts of work somewhat independent of setting. This eighth chapter sets a real-life context where new faculty encounter real needs for *applications* of constancy and moderation.

No experience of new faculty as teachers, in my observations, is so dramatic and traumatizing as facing unruly, uninvolved students—especially in the large introductory courses traditionally assigned to newcomers. Nowhere else are they so unprepared and so uncoached about how to manage difficulty. Nothing else in new faculty experience takes so much time and energy. And at no other time do newcomers to the professoriate feel so disillusioned about their career choice. Put bluntly, initial classroom experiences too often make or break us as teachers.

We've already seen indications of what sets the stage for difficulties in first classes:

1. Newcomers to college classrooms prepare too much material and then present it at too fast a pace, at too difficult a level, for student involvement and comprehension. Amid that rushing, new teachers discourage questions or discussions.
2. Novice teachers don't set useful contexts to explain the rationale and relevance for what they present. Teaching presented in isolation from student experience risks student detachment.
3. Our graduate experiences rarely go beyond seminar presentations and occasional lectures to classes, roles in which we learn too little about the value of connecting with audiences.

4. Tradition implies that if we know a subject, we can teach it. Thus, we concentrate far more on product/content than on processes of working at teaching. And so we care more about teaching than learning.

Add to that list one other factor that I haven't yet mentioned:

5. Few of us enter teaching with a realistic picture of average students. During our school years, we generally excelled, not only on tests and papers but also as class members who paid attention, took notes, and even smiled and nodded at our instructors. Not until we stand in front of a class as its regular teacher do we begin to appreciate how more ordinary students behave. They don't always come to class and if they do, they may not pay attention. And they often covertly or overtly defy our attempts to elicit hard work or conceptual thinking. When we do not attend to that reality, we teach to ourselves and the few people in class like us. Old-timers call it "preaching to the converted."

But even when we know about these predispositions to experience trouble with students, we may not understand exactly what we will face. New faculty in first classes usually experience shock and disbelief at students' disinterest, distractions, and defiance. Adversarial relations with students, once underway, affect professorial experiences far beyond the classroom.

I hope you see, then, why I've chosen this aspect of new faculty experience to put the rules of constancy and moderation into real-life context. To emphasize the seriousness of classroom incivilities, I present my investigations and interventions in an academic format. It begins with an overview of the problem of classroom incivility (CI) and emphasizes research on what classroom incivility is, on why it matters, and how to moderate it with practices of constancy and moderation. Here, too, the *nihil nimus* principle is most fundamental.

An Introduction to Classroom Incivilities (CIs)

So vulgar a thing might seem remote to those of us in the ivory tower. Usually, we read about these misbehaviors in news accounts of violence directed at high school teachers. Yet in my own studies at college and university campuses, CIs dominated many classrooms, and its presence or absence in first classes proved a strong predictor of how teaching careers would proceed, even of how likely new faculty would thrive in the reappointment procedure. CI was the first and most telling sign of success or failure that I documented in initial experiences of new faculty. Indeed, CI turned out to be so crucial that I'll share a few impressions from its scattered and generally obscure literature, but not too much. (If you're a glutton for information, please see the original account of this study in Boice, 1996a.)

A Brief Overview of Traditional Literature Related to CI

In my own searches, I first wondered why CI is so generally overlooked at post-secondary levels. You may already know one reason: Only those transients in the university called students witness what happens in most of our classrooms; tradition discourages visits by colleagues, more so from experienced evaluators. Another factor in this silence owes to society's disapproval of noticing social failings, including those of our colleagues as teachers. Social psychologists explain why we do not persistently question people's foibles—or their excuses—and why we resist admitting to faux pas of our own, no matter how observable. Both are an embarrassment to ourselves and a social impropriety when mentioned to others.

CI Is More Publicized for Teachers with Less Status

We increasingly hear about primary and secondary schools with insolent, indifferent, even murderous students, and of programs for violence prevention. Students at those levels complain about mean-spirited, boring teachers, and so, they say, they react in kind. Their teachers, in turn, depict students as more and more likely to demand the good grades they need for college but without interest in working for them. This adversarial culture not only demoralizes and exhausts its teachers; it sends increasingly difficult students to college. From the news media, at least, you might think misbehaviors in college are generally limited to student alcoholism and rape or to faculty harassment of students.

CI as Higher Education Researchers Have Approached It

Experts on college teaching have resisted empirical evaluations of what affects success or failure among teachers in domains, including classroom incivility (Weimer & Lenze, 1991), perhaps because they do not want to embarrass some professors or because they suppose teachers are born, not made. When most authorities on college teaching address trouble in the classroom at all, they do so vaguely. They mention the breakdown of traditional student/faculty relationships but say little about its nature or how it demoralizes faculty. They blame democratic tendencies to admit underqualified students into college, but they overlook the immediate problems of ever more crowded classrooms. Most of all, they respect beliefs that professors' classrooms are inviolate, but they do so without apparent recognition of the resulting disservice to both new teachers and their students.

Amada (1992) was one of the first to document CIs as mental health problems; schizophrenia, manic-depression, and personality disorders are all on the rise at college campuses. Thus, he advocated treating CI in campus mental health centers or with legal actions. He, too, shuns interventions in professors' classrooms. By focusing on extremely disruptive or disturbed students, Amada neglected the more common kinds of CI that need to be dealt within and near the classroom by teachers themselves.

Much of the rest of the research on CI proves the obvious and is based on surveys. Students report that they more often cut classes they do not like. They indicate that not just absences but cheating, a form of CI, relate to disliking a class, particularly when they see classes as irrelevant to their careers. Both teachers and students report disliking people in the other role who come to class late. Students resent teachers who run overtime; teachers loathe class members who pack up early. And both complain about counterparts who cut or cancel classes.

The thing usually left unspecified in conventional accounts of CI is the teachers' own role in it. My own samplings of core courses at large, public universities suggest that one-third of the faculty treat students with unmistakable rudeness and condescension, over 85 percent with insufficient warmth and approachability to optimize student involvement and learning. In a few cases, they physically assault students who press them for answers or help (Boice, 1986, 1993b), perhaps about as often as students assault professors. In many more instances, professors take advantage of teaching situations to intimidate and compromise students.

Thorough studies of CI are recent and their breakthrough lies in showing that students and teachers are partners in generating it. For example, in a class of 30, 5 or 6 students resist doing what the teacher wants; one such student can ruin an entire class for everyone. According to these studies, student CI typically consists of missing classes, cheating, refusing to participate, coming unprepared, and distracting teachers and other students. Among the researchers who first made these facts known, Kearney and Plax (1992) found that some kinds of student (and teacher) resistance can be labeled constructive—as when substantive questions are pressed—even though most teachers reacted to any kinds of confrontations as problematic. Kearney and Plax also demonstrated that the ways in which teachers present themselves socially may be most telling in initiating CI. In laboratory simulations, at least, students decide to resist and misbehave depending on the directions that two teacher behaviors, in particular, take:

> In the first continuum, teachers tend to use prosocial motivators (such as "Do you understand?" and "You can do better!") or antisocial motivators, such as threats and guilt induction.

> In the second critical continuum, teachers are labeled as "immediate" (because of verbal and nonverbal signals of warmth, friendliness, and liking) or "distant."

In those laboratory simulations, teachers who displayed positive motivators and immediacy seemed to moderate student inclinations to CI. Teachers who did not show immediacies and prosocial motivators were seen as cold, uncaring, incompetent, and as deserving targets of incivilities by their students. So, according to Kearney and Plax (1992), power in classrooms is relational. Teachers have the power, if they have the skills, to use motivators and immediacies to moderate CI.

And students have the power, far more than most teachers appreciate, to effectively undermine teachers who seem not to care about them.

Why is this research important to new faculty? It identifies simple qualities of good teaching that have gone almost unnoticed in traditional, conjectural books of advice. And it raises the possibility that the most basic things effective teachers do, such as smiles and forward leans, can be taught and learned.

Field Studies of Why Classroom Incivility Matters in the Beginning

Because I knew of no documentation of classroom incivilities in real-life campuses when I set out to understand them, I did the research myself. I began inductively and atheoretically, just as I once did as an ethologist watching the social dynamics of box turtles and toads (they do have their moments). I had few expectations and so I took notes on almost everything and I looked for normative behavior patterns.

With a working taxonomy of CI in hand, I felt ready to undertake the first formal study (a near surfeit of details can be found in Boice, 1996a).

I usually sat near the rear of large, introductory classrooms so that I could come and go unobtrusively. And I quietly relocated myself during each visit so that I could see most students; with each move I observed a new foursome of them as notetakers. As I made my own notes and periodic ratings, I identified students randomly to interview after class. My interviews with faculty usually took place soon after, in their offices or by phone, because immediately after classes they were typically occupied with students asking questions or, in the case of teachers with low student ratings, rushing to something else. The latter reminded me of Mad Hatters. In their meetings with me, teachers answered questions, recalled experiences, and made ratings.

General Patterns of CI

Common Perceptions of CI

Some of the classroom incivilities I recorded resembled the kinds described in the traditional literature based on teachers' delayed recollections (e.g., both students and teachers were antagonized by late arrivals, late stopping, and each others' cutting or canceling). But these were neither most common nor most crucial. Novice teachers *and* their students agreed in ranking three other kinds of CI as most disturbing:

1. Students conversing so loudly that lecturers and student discussants could not be heard

2. Students confronting teachers with sarcastic comments or disapproving groans (e.g., the student remark, "You're kidding!" followed by sneers and the noises of notebooks slamming shut)
3. A "classroom terrorist" whose unpredictable and highly emotional outbursts, usually as insulting complaints or as intimidating disagreements, made the entire class tense

After listing these three most disturbing sorts of CI, students and teachers diverged in ordering the next most important kinds. Students, incidentally, perceived half-again as many incidents of CI as did their teachers. These are the next modal rank-orderings (positions 4–7) by students:

4. Teachers perceived as distant, cold, and uncaring (i.e., lacking in immediacy)
5. Teachers who surprised them with test items they had not prepared for or with grades they had not anticipated
6. Teachers who arrived five or more minutes late to class and/or who canceled classes without advance warning
7. Students who taunted and belittled fellow classmembers, with no corrective reaction from the teacher

Teachers, on the other hand, produced these rank-orderings after the first three:

4. Students reluctant to answer or ask questions, or to display interest
5. Students unprepared for class
6. Students demanding make-up exams or extended deadlines for projects
7. Students arriving late or leaving early, disruptively

A glance back at this second level of rankings reveals variations in how students and faculty experienced CI. Students were less likely than faculty to notice or care when students were not participating in class. But both wanted the other to be obviously caring and approving and, if they were not, blamed the other alone for the lack.

My own rankings of which CIs were most disruptive and common were an amalgam of sorts of those just listed. And, in their specificities, they were pleasingly congruent with studies such as those by Plax and Kearney (1992), even though I did not see those publications until after most of my data were collected:

1. Teachers alienating themselves from students with negative comments and nonimmediacies such as stiff, unsmiling nonverbals
2. Teachers distancing themselves from students by way of fast-paced, noninvolving lectures

3. Students conversing so noisily that lecturers and discussants could not be clearly heard
4. Students coming late and leaving early, obtrusively
5. Students making sarcastic remarks and gestures
6. Teachers surprising students with tests and grades
7. Intimidation and distraction by a classroom terrorist

Something that seemed more obvious to me than to teachers or students was the crucial nature of the patterning of CI over a semester. CI usually gets set in its course during the first few days of classes. Not until teachers' negativities confirmed students' skepticism did incivilities become salient and problematic.

All three perspectives on CI seem useful. Only when I presented all three vantages in a follow-up semester—where teachers were looking again at CI—was there understanding that translated into new classroom practices. Anon, I mention more about what happens in such interventions, but here I emphasize what struggling new faculty needed to appreciate before changing: Virtually all of them said they wanted to know more about the nature of CI, its generality among other teachers, the price it exacts, and its experience from a student vantage. They wanted a context for understanding CI and they needed to put their own context within a larger one.

Shared excerpts from my interview notes after classes seemed especially helpful to these teachers. The following are typical comments from students whose teachers had distanced themselves in the first or second class meeting:

"I got the feeling that he didn't really like students, not ones like me . . . that was pretty much when I gave up on him and decided to lag it. I closed my notebook."

"Who is he kidding? He doesn't want to teach us. He starts off by telling us that he won't be talking to us outside class, only his TAs will. He tells us that his lectures won't count on tests. Why bother?"

"I'll tell you what turned me off. He's a snob. So he went to school at Harvard. So? If he's so much better than us, what's he doing wasting his time here with us?"

And next are responses, made after class and on the walk back to their offices, from teachers seen as most distant:

"I couldn't really tell you that much [shrugs and walks even faster]. I was nervous and I just wanted to get through it."

"Who knows? I mean, there are definitely some in there who don't like me, or the class, or whatever. That's probably par with such poor students."

"Really? Who cares? This [i.e., teaching] isn't what matters. My chairman told me not to pay too much attention to this, just to get through it."

That same conversations about CI also helped *me* see things more clearly. I couldn't miss noticing that some teachers, almost always those rated as good performers beforehand on standardized student-rating instruments, were less affected by and less often involved in CI. And the same students I had seen exhibiting CI with other professors were more civil and involved in the classes with higher student ratings.

Telling Patterns of CI

I began sorting out those individual teachers who evidenced the most and least classroom incivilities. I looked more carefully at the roles of timing and teaching experience in CI. And I determined more systematically how CI levels related to other, more traditional ratings of teachers.

Some new faculty exhibited obviously frequent and maladaptive patterns of CI with surprising rapidity; those who treated their undergraduates with open disdain and obvious distance were associated with the worst levels of CI that I saw—comparable even to veteran teachers with the poorest records of student ratings and the most openly expressed disrespect from students. But even these most disrupted newcomers were not exposed to such severe CI as were struggling veterans. New teachers' students suggested the reason in my interviews with them: They could generally spot novice teachers and were easier on them (but not easy enough to make novices' beginnings encouraging).

The picture is quite different at the other end of the CI continuum. Exemplary novices experienced the lowest levels of student CI. They also, predictably, evidenced the most use of positive motivators and social immediacies among the new teachers I observed. Even so, these "quick starters" left room for improvement, compared to more senior teachers with high student ratings and teaching awards. Exemplary veterans reliably displayed more kinds of positive motivators than did the exemplary novices (e.g., in ways of coaching students to make better answers in class) and more depth of skill at expressing immediacies (e.g., ease at walking about the classroom and engaging eye contact with a variety of students). Evidently, complex skills such as teaching require many years, perhaps around 10, of regular and deliberate practice before full expertise is achieved (Simonton, 1994).

My ratings (confirmed for reliability by a trained research assistant) of how well these groups of teachers displayed immediacies such as eye contact and smiling, on a 1–10 scale, hint at a similar interaction between experience and student approval: Exemplary teachers of the seasoned kind scored at a mean of 7.6 for combined immediacies, exemplary novices at 6.2; poorly performing veterans scored 3.2, and their counterparts among beginners scored 3.7. The differences in this regard were statistically reliable and unmistakable. Still, teachers associated with high levels of CI seemed at least as knowledgeable about course materials as their counterparts.

How much do students contribute to these differences in CI? One answer relies on analyses of how CI develops over the course of semesters.

How Timing Affects CI

Consider how classes of new teachers in the study usually got underway. As a rule, students started semesters with reserve, respect, and optimism—so they told me as they entered classes for the first time. Yes, they were sometimes frisky and unruly as they assembled, often because they were greeting friends and testing classroom limits in playful ways. But on first and second days of class, they displayed generally moderate to low levels of CI; students evidently waited for teachers to make the first move, just as they predicted they would in preliminary conversations with me.

In classrooms where initial days were marked by conspicuously positive motivators and strong immediacies on the part of teachers, CI dropped off to low levels and generally remained there for the rest of the semester. In contrast, when the first few class meetings were marked by high levels of teachers' CI, the student level soon went up and then rarely went down.

Thus, as I indicated earlier, initial experiences with CI seem to generate lasting patterns, often before teachers realize what is going on. The following facts illustrate what differentiates poor starters from others:

- Novice teachers making good starts displayed less than three instances of blatant CI (e.g., strong guilt induction), on average, in their first three class meetings, well under half the rate of poor starters.
- Faux pas of poor starters were judged and reported by students as far more dramatic and offensive than those of good starters, perhaps because the former seemed more distant and disdainful (e.g., "Yup, yup, now we all know he went to a better school than this, that he must be called 'doctor,' that he doesn't have respect for us").
- As semesters proceeded, counts of CI for good starters decreased, whereas those for the worst starters did not.

Additional Turning Points

There were also, in most courses I observed, other points during semesters where CI was likely to occur in strong, episodic fashion. For example, students seemed primed to exhibit CI before and after first and second exams (especially big tests such as midterms), and near deadlines for major projects. When, on the other hand, teachers helped prepare students for tests and projects with approximations such as practice tests or intermediate deadlines for preliminary versions of projects, reactions were optimistic or quiet.

One other interaction proved important: When students talked with faculty outside class in friendly and immediate fashion, CI levels were lowered. Students explained it thusly: "When you get to know him, he's a pretty nice guy. Not so intimidating after all. . . . That was when I realized that he cares about students, that he wants me to do well in the course. No, now I wouldn't dream of giving him a hard time." The most exemplary of new teachers, it figures, arranged the earliest student meetings in semesters; many of these instructors made a visit to their office a firm but congenial course requirement.

Uncommonly Traumatic Kinds of CI

The most upsetting CIs were least visible to a classroom observer, least likely to be admitted by teachers in mail surveys. I began to appreciate them only after many conversations with novices (and veterans). The following were CIs that embarrassed and hurt in lasting ways:

- Personal comments by students on formal evaluations at ends of semesters (e.g., "She dresses badly"), even when the great majority of students' comments were positive
- Students who displayed seeming antagonism in class ("Did you notice him? He just sits there, arms folded, glaring at me, shaking his head in disapproval")
- Students complaining to departmental chairpeople, especially where faculty perceived that chairs then assumed them guilty until proven otherwise

In my experience, all three of these problems can be moderated by way of practices that exemplars, novice and veteran, model spontaneously—almost as if paid to illustrate the *nihil nimus* approach. Student evaluations can be screened by a neutral third party to exclude or edit personally hurtful, nonconstructive comments. Teachers can remind themselves that even the best of their kind do not please everyone, or want to, and that chairpeople can be coached to handle students' complaints in this order: First, by asking students to discuss concerns with professors; and second, by approaching the "defendant" in ways that do not put him or her on the defensive (e.g., "Can you help me think what we could do to make this student happier in our classes, less likely to complain to me?"). One of the surprising attributes of exemplary novices is their readiness to suppose that more senior colleagues, especially chairpeople, need occasional, diplomatic, almost undetectable, teaching about how to be helpful.

Student cheating also demoralized novice teachers to a surprising extent, especially when apparent culprits acted defensively and angrily. The tension in such confrontations distracted new faculty from their work and exacerbated their health problems. The way that exemplary novices handle such problems bears mentioning: In one case, the new teacher put some of the responsibility on his students to solve the dilemma. This is his direct report to me of a what he said to them: "Look, I need your help with this uncomfortable situation. The two of you turned in papers that seem very much alike. How can we figure out what happened and what to do?" Thereafter, the meeting focused on problem solving, not on prosecution, and it gave the miscreant a face-saving opportunity to suggest an appropriate solution.

How Classroom Incivility Relates to Other Behaviors of Teachers and Students

Teaching Ratings

In my initial study of classroom incivility (Boice, 1996a), student ratings of teaching were negatively related to levels of CI. Teachers with the lowest CI counts rated significantly higher on student ratings than did peers with the highest CI counts on dimensions, including the worth of the teaching for the day, the suitability of the teacher's pacing to student notetaking and understanding, the teacher's clarity/organization, and the students' own class involvement.

In the second study, heretofore unpublished, I used another kind of comparison to demonstrate the role of CI among teachers at opposite ends of student rating scales. My intent was to compare levels and consequences of classroom incivilities between the two groups of teachers, novice and expert. Directly observed distinctions between the skills of accomplished and struggling teachers have rarely been reported about college settings.

Participants

One study group consisted of 14 newcomers to tenure-track positions in their second or third semesters of teaching; none had taught a class of their own before coming to campus. All 14 of these novices had, in the semester prior, scored in the bottom quartile on a campuswide student evaluation of their teaching; all were considered by their chairs and/or deans to be in trouble as teachers; all had been encouraged by departmental colleagues to seek help. The second group of 14 was selected from faculty who had been on their campus at least five years and who had won teaching awards at the departmental level or above. All 14 "experts" had garnered student evaluations in the top quartile of campus norms for the preceding semester. All 28 participants volunteered.

There was another important commonality of the two groups in this follow-up study: All their members were regular teachers of undergraduate survey classes with more than 50 students in large lecture halls. I matched novices and exemplars within the social sciences or the hard sciences and for kinds of courses taught (e.g., mathematical/statistical, survey/conceptual, lecture/discussion, or laboratory-oriented).

Methods

I visited the classrooms of participants unobtrusively for 10 meetings distributed over the course of a semester, including the all three initial class meetings. In each such visit, I made four distributed ratings during a class and used a scoring system described in detail elsewhere (Boice, 1996a). These categories of classroom incivilities become clearer here as I move to the results of this second study.

Figure 8.1 depicts the dramatically different levels of classroom incivilities for the struggling novices, compared to the expert teachers, on four dimensions of failure at what I call *immediacies:* (1) teachers' negative communications (neg coms) to students (e.g., threats); (2) teachers' nonimmediacies (nonimmeds) in nonverbal expressions (e.g., immobile, unfriendly postures); (3) student disruptions (s disrupts) (e.g., coming late and leaving early, noisily); and (4) strong student incivilities (SSI) (e.g., cat calls).

The reliability of this general difference between struggling beginners and exemplary veterans can be seen in the MANOVA (multiple analysis of variance) of data in Figure 8.1: $F(5, 22) = 188.69$, $p < 001$. Here and in other instances where I had a second observer check the reliability of my ratings (in those 27 class meetings, agreement levels in all rating domains always exceeded 81 percent and usually averaged more than 90 percent), these were easily discerned items.

So, classrooms of the expert, highly rated teachers were comparatively quiet and their students appeared to be more positively involved. Students in these exemplary classrooms were far less likely to create the noisy din and other distrac-

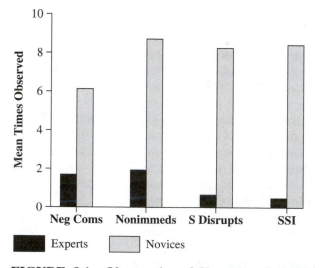

FIGURE 8.1   Observation of Classroom Incivilities

tions that made student involvement difficult in the other kind of courses—those taught by struggling novice teachers.

Figure 8.2 helps answer this question: Did the higher levels of incivilities in the classrooms of struggling novices really affect students? The graphed results indicate predictable differences in student notetaking (depicted as observed instances of "few notes") and in student ability to explain central concepts (observed instances where students could not explain [no explanation]).

To collect these data from the students of successful (expert) versus failing (novice) teachers, I observed four different students per class meeting and then individually observed/queried them after each of 10 class meetings. I compared students in terms of failures to take minimal notes or to recite and explain at least half of a list-like concept emphasized in class.

Students in classrooms of struggling novice teachers were far less likely to take useful notes or to comprehend central concepts from a class just ended. In contrast, students in the courses of expert teachers (where classroom incivilities were less prominent and where teachers' immediacies were more common) performed far better in terms of notetaking and comprehension. (In five cases, I was able to compare the notes of the same student with two teachers, one with a high level and one with a low level of incivilities; students' notes were always clearly better in the latter situation.)

The MANOVA for these two kinds of costs to students depicted in Figure 8.2 confirms the reliability of this difference: $F(2, 25) = 45.03, p < .001$.

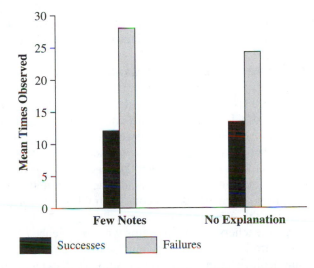

FIGURE 8.2   Students of Two Kinds of Teachers

Situations Where Near-Classroom Incivility Is Tolerable, Perhaps Even Helpful

Classroom incivilities can serve useful functions under the right conditions; this fact contradicted my expectations. It wasn't so much that better-rated, more "immediate" teachers didn't experience occasional, moderate incidents that could have grown into disruptive CI. Instead, it was more that when exemplary teachers noticed these interruptions as incivilities, they did not respond in kind. Expert teachers usually reacted respectfully, by listening carefully, as though the interruption had been offered up as a well-intentioned comment. These are typical excerpts from my notes of such interactions:

> A student in row 5 emits a loud "Ugh" and sinks in his chair. Teacher: "Oh no [laughs gently], I've worn you down, worn you out with all this. I do that sometimes. Ahh . . . thanks for alerting me. What do you think? Would it help if I stop and go through it again with you?"

> A student abruptly interrupts and challenges a point the teacher just made: "I know that's wrong." The teacher listens cheerfully and says: "Well, you might be right about that. I can always stand to be corrected; I can survive that. Can you come by my office and we'll share resources?"

> Teacher: "I'm seeing some big yawns and abandoned notetaking. Sorry. I'm losing you. Let's all stand and stretch for a minute and then we'll backtrack a bit."

These excerpts suggest one way in which teachers can sustain immediacy and its kin, optimism, in the midst of what could have become real CIs but did not.

Efforts to Moderate Teachers' Classroom Incivilities

Merely getting teachers to observe and comment on CI is a help. When participants in these studies of CI asked me, usually in our first discussion, about how often CI happened to their colleagues, my answers relieved them. Many had imagined their own experiences unique ("You never hear such things mentioned"). When I brought up incidents that they had not observed in their own classes, they tried harder to notice and understand CI. And when, eventually, they inquired about what exemplary colleagues did to cope with CI, they typically imagined themselves emulating the strategies I summarized.

A caution: Most teachers in my programs who experienced high CI wanted to bring it under control almost instantly, and when attempts at using positive motivators and immediacies went badly, they resumed old styles. Still, all of these teachers expressed an interest in trying new strategies again in future semesters.

A Formal Intervention via Coaching

Program and Participants

The study group consisted of 10 of the 14 novices from the study just abstracted. After my first semester of observing and discussing their CIs, they volunteered to participate in a second semester, where I coached them in the kinds of immediacy skills that expert veterans had displayed. They also agreed to a third semester of participation, where I again charted classroom incivilities and their student costs/ benefits during 10 of their class meetings in large undergraduate courses. This design provided me with baseline measures from the semester before and outcome measures from the semester after my coaching.

The other group in this experiment was a control and it consisted of 10 novices who had evidenced similarly poor teaching ratings. Control subjects were *not* formally coached in immediacy skills; they were, however, given similar amounts of attention and enthusiasm as were experimental subjects, but in more general ways such as encouragement to moderate CIs without specifics or practice. Each of the control subjects was picked to match an experimental participant in terms of general discipline and the type of course taught. Each control was followed as long as his or her matched experimental subject continued in the project.

Methods

The scheme for visiting and rating classes remained essentially the same as in my prior studies, except for two differences of note: I combined the measures of student notetaking and comprehension into one (because students in earlier studies who fared poorly in one sphere almost always performed similarly in the other). And here I took a general measure of students' classroom incivilities, one that combined the categories outlined in Figure 8.2.

The coaching scheme consisted of 10 individual sessions before classes in the second semester of participation, usually of about 10 minutes. In each, I modeled two simple skills of immediacy, based on deficiencies I had observed in the prior class of each subject (e.g., open postures with forward leans and smiles directed at students; positive comments given in response to potentially annoying student questions). After such modeling, the mentee rehearsed the posture/movement and restated the verbal response until we both agreed on their suitability. Then, during the class meeting that followed, I rated the success of each mentee in enacting the practices, and shared that information with her or him afterward—always in terms of what was done well and then as suggestions of how he or she could improve on approximations to effective immediacies. These immediacies, despite their simplicity and ease of practice before class, were mastered slowly in classroom use, with many regressions under duress. Not until the end of this semester of practice were most mentees and I pleased with their progress.

Results

In the final (third) semester of this intervention study, I stopped the coaching sessions and reverted to classroom visits like those of the first semester of participation in order to judge the enduring results of my intervention. The averaged outcomes, contrasted between the experimental and control groups, are graphed in Figure 8.3: Coached/mentored novices displayed fewer negative communications (neg coms) and nonimmediacies (nonimmeds), such as off-putting nonverbals, than did their peers without coaching. Moreover, the classrooms of coached novices evidenced fewer instances of problem noise levels (s noise). The students of coached teachers more often engaged in notetaking (graphed in the opposite perspective, as insufficient notetaking [INT]); more often demonstrated comprehension of essential points after class; and more often appeared to be more involved—obviously oriented, attending, listening, answering questions, and engaged in discussion. Note again that I represent findings in Figure 8.3 in the opposite view, as, for example, "S not involved."

These results suggest that a semester of coaching in simple skills of immediacy led to lower levels of problem behaviors in the classrooms of novice teachers who, prior, had suffered high levels of these negative and disruptive incidents.

The MANOVA for the data represented in Figure 8.3 suggests a reliable effect of coaching: $F(6, 13) = 38.53 \, p > .001$.

Student Ratings after Coaching

Students rated these two sets of courses, coached and uncoached, on a campus-wide instrument and awarded significantly higher scores for the novices coached

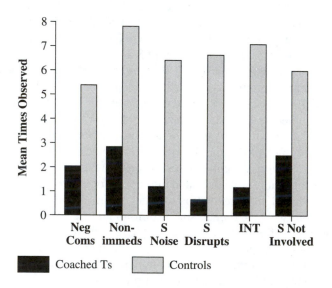

FIGURE 8.3   Results of Coaching

in immediacies than for controls: $\bar{x} = 1.98$ (SD = .50) for coached novices; $\bar{x} = 3.58$ (SD = .57) for uncoached novices (on a scale, adjusted across campuses, where 1 = excellent and 5 = poor; where there was one global score per teacher [based on the item, "likely to recommend this class to a close friend"]); in a one-way ANOVA $F(1, 18) = 44.31, p < 001$.

Conclusions about Classroom Incivility

Overall, CI was more common than uncommon in the classes of all novice teachers I observed; it occurred disruptively and dishearteninglys in over two-thirds of the courses of novices I tracked. In large survey courses, about half showed chronic and demoralizing patterns of CI; fewer were seen in smaller classes.

In all the courses with high CI, both students and faculty usually reported annoyance and demoralization. But whatever the setting, struggling novices noticed less CI than did their students.

General Faculty Awareness of Classroom Incivility

The faculty with the keenest appreciation of CI's nature and liabilities were, ironically, most unlikely to suffer it. They were the novice teachers of the four courses I observed where CI was virtually absent and where other indices of exemplary teaching—such as enthusiasm, pacing, and clarity of organization—rated highest. Exemplars, again, were likely to prevent CI by maintaining immediacies and social motivators, and, by converting the beginnings of CI into occasions for explanations, fresh starts, and good-natured humor.

Why, on the other hand, did struggling new faculty often overlook CI? Sometimes they were too tense and self-centered to see it. And they were, as usual, too fixated on content to attend to process. When they did perceive CI, their usual attitude was reminiscent of physicians' common reaction to resistant patients: What the teacher offers is undoubtedly valuable and when students frustrate the teacher, the loss is only theirs. Indeed, high CI professors, novice and veteran, often acted like specialized kinds of doctors, psychoanalysts who imagined that student resistance only proved the meaningful difficulty of the material under discussion. In their defense, though, these professors typically knew no better. Few of us have been told about the nature of CI or its preventives; most novice teachers I have tracked through first days of classes were simply puzzled by the ruckus in their classes (a typical comment: "These students are certainly not the kind of student I was").

Costs of Classroom Incivility

Another finding in these direct observational studies is that CI mattered, deeply. The differences between classrooms with a lot of CI and those without it were astonishing. With persistent CI, students generally grew more and more uninvolved, oppositional, combative. At the same time, their teachers found their own seemingly innocent remarks and gestures (often emitted without their conscious awareness) escalating into contentious battles with students. Even when the CI was largely limited to a single, disruptive individual, to what faculty and students often call a classroom terrorist, teachers were surprised to discover how much more difficult the teaching became—and that the other students held teachers responsible for not squelching the terror.

Among the hundreds of new faculty I have tracked closely, experiences of unmanaged and unsettling CI constitute a turning point that can ruin professorial careers (Boice, 1993a). Why? New faculty in their first two or three semesters tend to spend most of their time preparing for teaching (even at research universities), and when they fail at teaching, they lose the self-efficacy they need to meet challenges of research/scholarship and collegiality/professional networking. Promising newcomers overwhelmed by CI, especially women and other new faculty who start out feeling marginalized, too often decide to abandon professorial careers. One irony in this pattern is that people outside academe imagine pressures to publish are our only real problems. Another is that we, within the ivory tower, customarily imagine CI is either an impolite topic of discussion or an unavoidable symptom of ever poorer students.

Faculty Role in Classroom Incivility

The most important point in this study is the one most often overlooked. Teachers were the most crucial initiators of classroom incivilities. And, as a rule, their most telling provocations occurred during the first few days of courses, when everyone was most impressionable. Those initiatory CIs, incidentally, were no more common in courses reputed to be difficult; nor were longer-term reactions of students.

In the intervention project I just reported, teachers modeling a simple regimen of immediacies showed clear, reliable reductions in the CI levels of their classes and equally reliable increases in a variety of student ratings of their teaching.

What Have Classroom Incivilities to Do with You?

In the best of all worlds, perhaps at the most exclusive campuses, you may encounter only the most civil, tolerant students. Or perhaps you will be so attractive, sensitive, and entertaining in class that no one will dislike or discourage you. Even if you are, there is still reason to practice the things that moderate CI. Evidence suggests that your students will learn better if you display immediacies and positive motivators. And reality says that you will perform more comfortably and successfully, even when you do not encounter students who test the limits of your own civility. New challenges are being born every day.

Section I Summary and Extension of the Nihil Nimus *Approach to Teaching*

Recall, first, the eight rules of moderation presented in the eight preceding chapters of Section I:

1. Wait, reflect, and learn—rather than rush, impatiently and impulsively.
2. Begin early at truly important tasks, before feeling fully ready.
3. Work in brief, economical sessions.
4. Stop in timely fashion, before diminishing returns set in.
5. Moderate overattachments to what you prepare/present—and overreactions to criticism.
6. Moderate negative thoughts and excessive emotions.
7. Let others, even critics, do some of the work.
8. Teach with compassion, communicate with immediacy and comprehension, and thus decrease student (and faculty) incivilities.

Elsewhere (e.g., Boice, 1996b), I've labeled these guidelines as *first-order principles* (FOPs) because of their primary qualities. These first-order principles are such elementary ways of learning to work at teaching that teachers who fail to practice them usually struggle more than they need or want to. You've already seen the common ways that teaching without benefit of FOPs undermines teaching: Rushed presentations, off-putting overpreparations, impatient reactions to student confusion and frustration, exhaustion, and discouragement.

The curious thing about these simple failings is that college teachers are so rarely exposed to their correctives. Academe is, I suspect, far more accepting of FOPs applied to, say, distance runners being taught optimal pacing, efficient movements, and generally moderate emotions.

In my prior writings (e.g., Boice, 1996b), I've shown how FOPs help prime novice teachers for the more complex kinds of teaching improvements usually prescribed in books of advice for college teachers (e.g., McKeachie, 1994; Weimer, 1990), including the admonition to replace most lecturing with discussions.

Most graduates of this teaching program spontaneously read a variety of books and articles about teaching improvement, and experiment with alternative advice (more about this in Section III). Their usual (but not unanimous) and delayed shift to discussion-based teaching is one example. Other higher-order changes prompted by immersion in FOPs are judged equally essential to excellence in teaching, at least by program participants over the long run.

Generalizing First-Order Principles to Nonteaching Activities

The most valued projection of FOPs is to productive and comfortable ways of scholarly writing. The reason may surprise you: Once FOPs are experienced in both contexts, teaching and then writing, the act of writing reilluminates teaching to help make it even simpler and more educational.

In telling you about this, I get somewhat ahead of my story. But this opportunity to mention how teaching facilitates writing may keep you involved through another section of this book. Readers who apply the same essential FOPs to both teaching and to scholarly writing tend to fare better at both than do practitioners in just one domain or the other. It's a fact.

Evidence from Exemplars

How can I claim that the same kinds of FOPs (e.g., patience) advance both teaching and writing? In part, by way of extensive interviews and observations with exemplars (again, those new faculty who work with the greatest self-reported ease and who elicit the most student approval and learning). Virtually all of them can recall and demonstrate *how* they learned to rely on first-order principles as teachers *and* as writers:

- By noticing that both teaching and writing were slowed in the long run by impatient rushing and its fatigue
- That both were aided by avoiding bingeing and its high emotion in favor of brief, regular sessions of work
- That early preparations for both allowed more playfulness and reflectiveness
- That brief, regular sessions at both afforded more reflectiveness, revision, and clarity
- That both need strong, sensitive senses of audience to moderate meandering or offense

One other fact about exemplars, just implied, is particularly relevant. The quick starters who teach with high ratings and rates of comprehension also write/publish most productively and successfully during their first six years on campus.

Evidence that facility in one domain generalizes to the other, though, rests more instructively on the results of my programs where other new faculty model the FOPs of teaching and then apply them to writing (compared, of course, to proper control groups who did not participate in the program, even to new faculty who programmatically practiced *nihil nimus* approaches in only one domain or the other).

Evidence of Generality from Program Participants

In a long, involved study, I coached 20 struggling new faculty to apply the same essential first-order principles to both teaching and scholarly writing (Boice, 1995a). Half of them practiced FOPs for teaching in year 1 and similar FOPs for writing in year 2. Half followed the opposite pattern. I coached 20 more new faculty (over a decade-long collection of subjects), 10 with two years of programatic work at writing only, and 10 who had taught for two successive years.

Participants in their second mode of working (either teaching or writing) were clearly more involved, moderate, and satisfied than peers who continued in the same mode of practice during the second year. Measures of student comprehension were highest for teachers who had spent the prior year at writing. Measures of writing output and quality were highest for writers who had first practiced the FOPs of teaching. Even students' standardized ratings of teaching were clearly best for teachers who already wrote the *nihil nimus* way.

These results set the stage for the more general question here: Are traditional beliefs in the incompatibility of teaching and research excellence wrong? And for its terse answer: Clearly.

FOPs for writers lie just ahead, in Section II. You already know why I encourage you to at least scan its principles, even if you plan to stay at a campus that seemingly doesn't care if you write for publication. In actual practice, you'll find that the more clearly and easily you think and write, the more clearly and easily you'll think and teach.

Section II

Write in Mindful Ways

Rationale for a Mindful Approach to Writing

Why does usual advice for new faculty exclude writing? Tradition assumes that professors already know how to work as writers; new faculty, after all, have almost always written a thesis or dissertation. So, custom limits most advice for new faculty to teaching because teaching seems less sufficiently mastered (or less examined) than writing during graduate training. Academe further justifies this narrowness by claiming that writing grows at the expense of teaching (and vice-versa); it even assumes that advice about teaching and writing depend on very different and contrary kinds of expertise. Add to those another fact, that most books of advice for new faculty are written by academics who value teaching over research, and the conventional emphasis is understandable.

How well does that customary and one-sided approach—of help for teaching but not for writing—work for most new faculty? In my studies of hundreds of novice professors at a variety of campuses, the result is disastrous. According to resumés submitted periodically to departmental files, the great majority of new faculty struggle as scholarly writers; during years 1 and 2, over two-thirds of them produce virtually nothing that "counts," despite their earlier plans for substantial new output during that critical period (Boice, 1992). For many newcomers, especially those caught up in busyness, this silence continues into years 3 and 4, often well beyond. Meanwhile (as depicted in Chapter 8), most novice professors, even those who read traditional books of advice, make awkward and time-consuming starts as teachers.

Reasons Why Most New Faculty Struggled with Writing in My Studies

1. *They did not learn how to write with fluency and constancy in graduate school.* Instead, most worked on proposals and dissertations erratically and

painfully, often procrastinating their writing far longer than they imagined possible. The mean length of time for dissertation completion in most disciplines—once courses and qualifying exams are completed, once the research proposal is accepted and the data are collected/analyzed—stands now at 4 years, depending on discipline, and is ever growing. Shameful numbers of graduate students remain ABD (all but dissertation) for 10, even 20 years before finishing. Disproportionate numbers of nontraditional graduate students never finish.

2. *They too often learned to work in isolation.* In my own direct observational studies of graduate students during the dissertation stage of their careers, one reason stands paramount for the miseries and delays: Dissertation writers are traditionally left to work alone with little day-to-day direction, and with the expectation they will not bring written materials to committees until the work is essentially finished and perfect. For better and for worse, that pattern of working at writing alone and with high demands for perfectionism tends to persist into professorial careers.

3. *Writing, by nature, seems more difficult.* Its scheduling in academe is often left open ended, with few clear directives or deadlines in the short run (or, in the case of dissertations, in the long run). Not only is writing more easily put off than teaching but it is also, because of old associations with uncertainty and pain, more tempting to procrastinate. Writing—at least at first—cannot provide the quick relief from the feeling of not doing enough that teaching can.

4. *Writing usually remains mysterious.* Indeed, writing offers peculiar challenges that few of us have been helped to understand. Only a handful of scholars (e.g., Weissman, 1993) have usefully explained the roots of those difficulties, such as (a) expectations, apparently left over from the days of inspired poetry, that we should await Muses and the opportunity to produce the writing in a single, brilliant burst; and (b) brain mechanisms that commence the writing process by way of nonverbal images and that require either strong excitement or else profound calm (plus, ideally, some conceptual outlining or other prewriting on paper or screen) to help translate those images into linear prose. In the absence of that information, we all too easily suppose that writing works in magical ways, without explicit rules or understanding.

5. *Most of us were imprinted with mistaken ideas about the nature of writing, probably during our school years.* Dominant among those is the misbelief that writing is best done in large blocks of uninterrupted time, when writers are at last motivated and inspired, when production can be spontaneous and brilliant. The problem is that writers who wait for such ideal circumstances usually wait a long time. A second popular fallacy is that good writing needs no outlines or other careful preplanning, that it happens best in a single and spontaneous sitting.

6. *New faculty approach writing with all-or-none thinking.* Once we are rushed and stressed, we too often believe we can *either* master teaching *or* scholarly

writing during our first few years, but not both. So it is that some books of advice (e.g., Rheingold, 1994) counsel new faculty to put off writing until teaching is mastered. Without effective practices of working at teaching, that could take too long.

7. *New faculty who do little of the writing they had planned for years 1 through 3 have so ready and sincere a defense that they can see no alternative explanation.* They are, they almost always say, too busy to write. In the main, they feel too overloaded by teaching—preparing class materials, grading papers and tests, keeping office hours—to attend to writing in proper fashion. They complain that ongoing demands of teaching and committee work leave few of the large blocks of uninterrupted time they supposedly need for apt writing, or that when they've worked all day at other things, they have no energy or interest left for writing.

8. *New faculty often reject simple, efficient ways of writing as counterintuitive, even as insulting.* That is, they prefer to do what they imagine geniuses do as writers: Struggle and suffer but nonetheless do their best work without constraints such as rules. In fact, though, the simple efficiencies of constancy and moderation produce far more creativity and better writing than rule-free spontaneity. I present data to this effect in the chapters ahead.

What else happens when writers shun these efficiencies? They feel disappointed about not being able to develop and communicate exciting ideas, and about lost opportunities for professional visibility and portability (even at teaching campuses). Stress is associated with writing that is delayed and then forced under deadlines. And, eventually, dislike for scholarly writing evolves when we write because we must and without time for reflection or preparation. (Imagine sex under similar circumstances.)

How many new faculty in my observational studies found constant, creative output as writers while relying solely on mindless spontaneity? None. How many survived the tenure/reappointment process at campuses that require writing of publishable manuscripts and fundable grant proposals? Virtually none. No wonder that the number of us who actually write for publication is the square root of those who want and intend to (Boice, 1993c).

Exemplary new faculty, as in Section I on teaching, model better ways of working at writing: They get writing underway by learning to work in brief, daily sessions that seem impossibly brief at first. They learn ways to simplify and clarify writing, even to enjoy it. And their constancy and moderation produce more manuscript pages with more likelihood of publication in refereed and prestigious outlets.

One more thing distinguishes thriving new faculty from struggling peers. These quick starters work efficiently; they do it in an even deeper way than we have yet to discuss in this book. Exemplars are "mindful" about their work at writing.

What Mindfulness Has to Do with Writing

On first reflection, mindfulness and writing might seem worlds apart. Mindfulness means a calm attentiveness to the present moment. Its basics—of being here, now, with clear seeing and compassion—are commonly practiced in a meditative state. And mindfulness practice often aims consciousness away from thinking and external doing:

> *In practicing meditation, we're not just trying to live up to some kind of ideal—quite the opposite. We're just being with our experience, whatever it is. . . . Just seeing what's going on—that's the teaching of awakeness right there.—PEMA CHODRIN*

> *Mindfulness practice means that we commit fully in each moment to being present. There is no "performance." There is just this moment. We are not trying to improve or to get anywhere else . . . [but] to dwell in stillness and to observe without reacting and without judging.*
> *—JON KABAT-ZINN*

Writing, on the other hand, usually gets portrayed as hard work that strains the intellect and overstimulates the emotions. Even some of its most celebrated practitioners struggle and suffer at writing:

> *It was not an instant or easy process, and throughout [Charles] Dickens's writing life the symptoms at the beginning of a new novel are the same. "Violent restlessness, and vague ideas of going I don't know where . . ." Dickens becomes irritable, solitary, preoccupied. . . . At the close of each book he was almost as irritated as he was at its beginning, and he would go wandering once more in a "sorrowful mood."*
> *—PETER ACKROYD*

> *When things were not going well and the characters did not spring into being, [Joseph] Conrad became tormented by neurasthenia, which crippled his attempts to write: "My nervous disorder tortures me, makes me wretched, and paralyzes action, thought, everything! I ask myself why I exist. It is a frightful condition. Even in the intervals, when I am supposed to be well, I live in fear of the return of this tormenting malady . . . before the pen falls from my hand in the depression of a complete discouragement."—J. MEYERS*

Even less artful or renowned writers expect their practice of writing to be anything but the calm and patience of mindfulness. Why? Because they, like us, learned to write in mind*less* binges where our mania temporarily outraced our fears and doubts, and because most of us have associated writing with deadlines, exhaustion, and criticism.

Why haven't more of us found attractive and productive alternatives to writing in such mindless, joyless ways? The methods for writing in mind*ful* ways have not been obvious. But then, neither have ways of mindful living. So it is that too many of us live as we try to write: Amidst the constant busyness, anxiety, and fatigue of mindlessness. Mind*ful* ways are simpler, healthier, and more amiably rewarding.

You may already know mindful ways of working, in preliminary fashion, from practicing patient, reflective, and socially sensitive ways of teaching (Section I). How else can you learn about mindful ways, especially in regard to writing? As a first step, look to the extraordinarily fluent writers who have made mindfulness central to their work, and then to the intriguingly serene writers who explain mindful practice.

What Exceptional Writers Hint about Mindful Practice

Indications that mindfulness helps writers write are anything but new, just uncommon and usually unknown. One old insight about mindfulness is shared by writers who have managed both productivity and health in their work, the one by Adam Smith that we saw at the beginning of this book: Constancy and moderation lead to the most output and well-being in the long run. In effect, he argued that workers, including writers, would profit by being consciously present and patient in their efforts, by working regularly and enjoyably but without strong emotion.

The normal experience of writers is quite different, as typified by this comment from an author, Stanley Karnow, appearing on the television program for prominent writers, *Booknotes* (Lamb, 1997):

> *I don't know any writer who thinks that writing is fun.*

Indeed, folklore teems with macabre jokes about writing being no more difficult than opening a vein, submitting to torture, or contracting with the Devil.

Among the prolific and healthful novelists who practiced constancy and moderation was Anthony Trollope (1883). He not only found time to write during an innovative and full-time career with the post office (he invented the corner dropbox); his consistent and serene style made the writing relaxing, renewing, and voluminous.

Even some writers who don't quite find serenity and sanity in their work use writing to change and better themselves. E. B. White, for instance, surmised that we would do better to write mindfully as a means of organizing our "character" than to try to improve ourselves before writing (Elledge, 1984). Teddy Roosevelt, among others, wrote when depressed, to clear his mind of pessimistic thoughts and maladaptive emotions (Morris, 1979). Otto Rank, once a favorite disciple of

Freud, first wrote to find creative ways past his neuroses and then renounced public writing to put that creativity to work in the exclusive service of simplifying his
personality (Lieberman, 1993).

What Contemporary Writers Hint about Mindfulness

In her best-seller *Bird by Bird,* Anne Lamott (1994) describes how her father, by
coaching himself to work at writing each day, learned to "pay attention" (i.e., be
mindful) and take charge of his own life. Mindful ways of writing not only taught
her father (and presumably her) to finish things but to see how writing surprises,
enlivens, and educates the writer. How, exactly, can her readers achieve a similar
result? There are clues but no specifics—for example, Lamott's delightful sense
of humor and self-deprecation could be the result of mindfully distancing herself
from taking writing too seriously, too personally.

   Natalie Goldberg's (1994) *Long Quiet Highway* comes even closer to
explaining a mindful path for writers. She supposes that meditation and writing
complement each other because both depend on allowing ourselves to "let go" and
settle within our minds. Writing, in her experience, connects us with what we
really feel and think; staying with that connection, patiently and persistently,
could become our daily practice of mindfulness—in place of mindfulness practiced as meditation without external doing.

   There are still more clues. Consider just a few from popular books by experts
on mindfulness. In this preliminary look at how mindfulness and writing interact,
I draw most on three current favorites: Sylvia Boorstein's *Don't Just Do Something, Sit There* (HarperCollins, 1996); Pema Chodrin's *When Things Fall Apart:
Heart Advice for Difficult Times* (Shambhala, 1997); and Jon Kabat-Zinn's *Wherever You Go, There You Are* (Hyperion, 1994). Additionally, I rely on more scientific works such as *Mindfulness* by psychologist Ellen Langer (Addison-
Wesley, 1989). I've chosen to limit the categories of mindfulness to seven relatively uncomplicated and conventional practices. And in each I move boldly to
expand what these writers have said to suggest ways that mindfulness applies to
writing:

   1. *Mindfulness as being awake:* The experience of awakeness begins with the
elementary act of stopping to notice our customary reactions to ongoing experience. Awakeness alerts us when we are caught in blind thinking or impulsive
action, unaware of why we are doing what we are doing. Once awakened, we
become more aware and involved. We might even begin to sense that we ordinarily use the blind rushing of busyness to escape and avoid threatening tasks like
writing for public consumption.

   2. *Clear-seeing:* The more we stay awake by remaining in the present moment,
nonjudgmentally, the more clearly and objectively we see. With clear-seeing, we

begin to notice how our usual struggles lead to suffering. Perfectionistic myths about geniuses who create masterpieces in a single session are a good example, once we notice how these misbeliefs unnecessarily pressure and complicate work. This clear seeing of what matters in our work helps us unlearn dependencies on the short-term emotional relief of speeding or perfectionism and their kin, procrastination and blocking.

3. *Calm efficiency:* With wakefulness and its clear seeing comes an efficacy that does not need severe disciplines. Just by noticing when and where to focus mindfulness, we experience more freedom, more initiative, more resolve. By staying in the present and noticing the effects of our experience, we learn to spend less energy on needless struggling or on its equally inefficient opposite, impulsivity. As we aim our minds to see what needs doing and what can be done, we are less often trapped in mindless acts of panic, doubt, conflict, or misdirection. By calmly accepting the moment for what it reveals, we help make work like writing more contemplative and creative.

Restated, mindfulness in work is tantamount to a process orientation—the opposite of a product orientation where we work principally for productivity, public approval, external reward. A *process* mode of working centers on staying and learning in the moment, the only time we can work efficiently. Process awareness, with its calm, reflective centering in the present, enhances decisiveness and lessens dependence on moods or surrounds. Its efficiencies include a surprising sense of reality about timeliness (e.g., the realization that important practices like writing need to be addressed now, not at some vague point in the future when we hope for better circumstances such as more free time).

4. *Freedom from excessive emotions and busyness:* Mindfully slowing down to the present calms us by way of a moderate pace. Its clear seeing encourages contemplation and patience in decisions and actions that might otherwise be impelled, blind, exhausting. And as we notice the long-term costs of rushing and bingeing at tasks such as writing, we undo old addictions to speed, even to chronic hopes that a better circumstance or self must lie ahead if we just work harder and faster. Without the usual blindness and busyness in work (e.g., writing), we can replace impatience with loving kindness for ourselves, even for our critics.

Freedom from chronic extremes in emotions, from ceaseless haste and its disillusionment, means more serenity and cheerfulness in working. It means less dependence on the emotional rushes of near-mania for motivation, and less exposure to the debilitating depression and pessimism that follow the immoderation of bingeing. Most clearly, it means freedom to work at important, worthwhile tasks without having to fight off distracting moods and noisy self-doubts. Moderation of emotional reactivity also fosters a useful distancing from fear of criticism. And ironically, this same distancing from fear helps us connect with ourselves, our audiences, and our critics; the less we fear, the more patiently and tolerantly we listen and see.

5. *Connectedness and compassion:* When we practice the clear seeing of how others are hooked to mindless actions in patterns much like our own, we show more patience and understanding for their foibles and criticisms. And as we feel more connected, we let go of the pessimistic feelings of separateness and victimization so characteristic of mindlessness and of writing blocks. Connectedness helps us deal with rejection and criticism more compassionately because we less readily blame others when our communications do not bring immediate approval. The more connected we are, the sooner we see where we could be misunderstood.

6. *Letting go:* The clear seeing and compassion of mindful practice help us relax. They encourage letting go of blind obedience to ego and its process orientation—no small matter for writers, including me. Letting go of ego means distancing ourselves from its contentious demands for universal respect and affection; as we stop grasping for the certainty and predictability that ego wants, we work more easily and contentedly in the moment. Not trying to relive the past or to control the future frees us to work in a process mode. That, in turn, brings more confidence, more playfulness and involvement, more risk taking and creativity, more love of mastery in work, more consistent fluency. And all those, finally, teach us to enjoy the work for its own sake, the very root of healthy industriousness.

7. *Self-discipline:* We've just seen suggestions of mindful ways to create calm, patience, clear seeing, efficient actions, connectedness, and tolerance. These processes include the discipline of self-stopping to awaken ourselves from mindless rushing or stultifying inhibition. They include the will and compassion to pause and reflect, to stay in the present, even to stop work in timely fashion when diminishing returns or fatigue set in, or when something else important needs doing. So, discipline builds as we stay in the moment, patiently, with no intent but to experience what happens and to notice which actions meet or change goals. One of its results is a process style of working that helps us unlearn impulse-based compulsions to rushing, bingeing, and overattachment.

Fortunately, none of these disciplines demands the painful measures beloved by tradition (e.g., having oneself locked in a cool room, unclothed, until a daily quota of writing is met). The self-discipline of mindfulness is more gentle. It depends, in the main, on staying in the present to caution ourselves from reverting to blind thinking, loss of hope, impulsive action, or product orientation. Like all sorts of self-discipline, mindfulness needs regular practice to become effective and effortless. So does writing.

How can we gauge our own self-discipline as practitioners of mindfulness? By the readiness with which we return to awakeness once we notice ourselves caught in mindlessness. And by the constancy with which we work and live in a process mode (and, so, enjoy the work and the moment for their own sakes).

What's still missing in this list of seven mindful practices? We've yet to see more than hints of how these practices are mastered. And so far I've only asserted that such mindful practices help writers find fluency and comfort. To begin to move toward specificity and proof, I summarize the observations that awakened me to mindful ways of writing.

What Already Mindful Writers Do That Makes Them Distinctive

When I began helping new faculty as writers some three decades ago, I had no idea how widely and deeply they suffered in their work. I had read about the dramatic effects of writers' blocks and I knew that writing problems sometimes led to loss of careers and lives. But not until I studied new faculty who sought no help from me did I sense the general inefficiency and pain of writing. Writers with seeming success and clear acclaim were generally no less likely to agonize over writing than writers with spectacular blocks.

I was just as amazed to discover that almost all those hundreds of writers expected to suffer at writing. More so, that many of them supposed pain essential to good, creative writing. (I'll address the validity of this assumption, often labeled *creative madness,* later in Section II.) But I was relieved to find writers, some 3 to 5 percent of the total, who already worked with comfort and productivity. I soon concluded that the key to their success is mindfulness. See if you agree, at least in a working way:

1. These exemplary writers (and teachers) *work patiently.* As writers, they don't rush impulsively into prose writing; instead, they calmly prepare and rearrange preliminary materials until the accumulation of ideas compels prose writing. As a result, they generate more healthy motivation and useful imagination for writing than do normal new faculty.
2. Exemplars *work regularly and constantly* at writing but with moderation. They spend far less time and energy, overall, than do normal writers who work in great binges and under deadlines. Exemplars also produce more and better writing than do others in the long run.
3. Exemplars' *emotions while writing tend to be gentle and stable,* punctuated by occasional bouts of peaceful "not-doing" or of mild euphoria; their writing outputs are similarly stable, even though the process mode in which they work creates little anxiety about productivity.
4. These mindful writers, compared to others, *suffer far less uncertainty and pain at writing.* Indeed, exemplars like to note how much they revel in its fun, discovery, and mastery.
5. These quick starters are rather unique in *welcoming criticism.* They even let other readers and writers, especially critics, do some of the hard work of writ-

ing, by getting them to specify places where it does not communicate completely, plainly, compassionately.

6. Most distinctively, these exemplars concentrate on aspects of mindfulness that could be called *efficiencies*—such as getting to work in timely fashion and doing more and better writing in less time overall. While mindful writers display a sense of good-humored detachment from their writing, they strive to write simply and unpretentiously. Why? Apparently because their love for writing brings enjoyment in its mastery.

I didn't quite make sense of these exemplary styles of working until I compared them to the similar messages in writings about mindfulness. When I juxtapose the two lists—the first of mindful practices, the second of exemplary writing habits—you may begin to see the resemblances as I do:

Seven Simple Practices of Mindfulness

- Awakeness and staying in the moment
- Clear seeing of what needs doing and can be done
- Calm efficiency in doing it, including timeliness
- Freedom from destructive emotions
- Connectedness and compassion with self and others
- Letting go
- Gentle self-discipline

Exemplary Writing Styles Restated

- Awareness of the need for preliminaries before rushing to prose
- Patience for timely stopping (and, in turn, for timely starting)
- Seeing what needs doing and doing it with constancy/moderation
- Calm emotions and low levels of suffering
- More compassion for self and critics
- Self-disciplines focused on pleasant efficiencies

In the chapters of Section II, just ahead, I translate mindful ways of working at writing into simple, memorable rules and practices. Why do I make explicit this usually tacit knowledge about writing—what some of my critics suppose should be self-evident to those of us who "deserve to write" (those few of us who, as a favorite censor of mine put it when she was president of the American Psychological Association, have something worth saying)? First, because I've found that too many writers with things to say, especially nontraditional new faculty, learn to work as writers amid pain, by way of trial and error—if at all. Second, because I continue to notice that few teachers of writing make explicit the prescriptions for working at writing with comfort and fluency. And, third, because I've learned that almost all new faculty as writers, even the advantaged, can employ mindfulness to find more ease, joy, and productivity than they had imagined possible.

Ten Mindful Ways of Writing

The 10 chapters in Section II (Chapters 9 through 18) outline what I've learned and applied from exemplary writers. In each chapter I present some mindful ways of writing, such as calming and slowing for awakeness. I also depict the struggles and successes that lie along the way for normal writers who follow this path. Just above, I overviewed some of the reasons why I see these simple but effective methods as mindful; as we move along, I'll link mindfulness with healthy and productive writing by way of experiential and experimental results. The benefits include life and work without busyness, rushing, and never quite catching-up. That, in my experience, is what new faculty need most.

9

Wait

Most of us already know how to wait as writers, in much the same way we once waited for teaching improvement—passively, mindlessly. We put off writing in favor of something easier while awaiting Muses and hoping for magic. And we try to delay efforts to write until the sudden appearance of brilliant ideas and compelling inspirations will make writing spontaneous. Sometimes these marvelous things happen, but not frequently enough to sustain most writers. More often, passive waiting is spent doing things that postpone the real work of writing. Passive waiting is the child of mindlessness and the parent of procrastination.

Passive waiting works unreliably because it operates blindly and depends on mysterious, irrational, unpredictable forces such as spontaneity. Passivity misleads with its short-term relief from reality because it eventually leaves writers feeling hopelessly behind, incompetent, and trapped. In the long run, passive waiting exposes writers to a pair of cruel and inefficient oppressions—the forcing of deadlines and the discomfort of contritions. Passive waiting undermines writing by occasioning too many poor starts (e.g., prolonged procrastination followed by rushed beginnings under deadlines) and troubling outcomes (e.g., writing that is blocked and hindered by pain and doubt; writing that remains superficial or unfinished because its goals were not clearly and realistically outlined beforehand).

What Makes **Active** *Waiting Different?*

At first glance, active waiting seems much the same as the passive kind. Active waiting, too, means putting off prose writing when we might feel pressured to begin and finish now. But active waiting is more than avoidance. It does things to set the stage for planned work in the meanwhile (much as efficient sleepers quiet themselves well before bedtime). With active/mindful waiting, things like writing and sleep come painlessly, almost effortlessly.

Said another way, mindless waiting often amounts to *doing nothing,* whereas mindful waiting is *not doing* (as in not keeping busy, externally). So it is that Sylvia Boorstein, a foremost teacher of mindfulness, entitled her book *Don't Just Do Something, Sit There.*

Active waiting requires patience. This is another crucial difference between passive and active waiting: Active waiting, at least until you are used to it, seems to require more work. Foremost, it involves that most difficult skill of writing skills: patience.

That patience is necessary for slowing and preparing for writing while we would rather do other, more immediately comforting things (like first cleaning our offices). We need it to work largely in the present moment, to hold back from the hurrying that owes to worries about finishing quickly enough, to let go of the distractions that come in dwelling on past disappointments.

Active waiting requires suspending disbeliefs. Active waiting, for most writers, is a new and counterintuitive stance: "It's hard to imagine that I will get more done eventually if I start out so slowly, patiently, planfully . . . by kind of waiting around. That doesn't seem possible." So to begin to benefit from it, you may need to question your usual ways of doing things: Said one of my program participants, right on cue, "My old methods haven't worked all that well and I might as well give this a try."

Active waiting means pausing reflectively. Reflective pausing is the opposite of plunging impulsively into firm decisions and formal prose. Active waiting and its awakeness temper impatience by putting off pressures for quick results. Active waiting brings an observant and wakeful tentativeness, often of a playful sort, while we get the writing organized. Its clear seeing helps make sure that the right question will be answered once the formal writing is underway, and its patient compassion helps writers forgive themselves for inevitable missteps. At its best, writing is first a process of discovery, then a communication of discoveries. Finally, if necessary, it demonstrates a writer's brilliance. When we put the last goal first, we court writing problems.

More gradual, planful beginnings prove enjoyable because of their calm, reflective, and engaging nature. They also bring a reassuring sense of having something worth saying before trying to write it formally. Stated another way, active waiting helps make writing an act of broad self-education; it proves to be so much fun that it hooks writers on writing. Moreover, motivation based on active waiting and its patience/readiness works far more reliably than drive rooted in impulsive impatience, in anxious shame, in looming deadlines. It's a fact.

Experimental Evidence for the Benefits of Waiting

Something else helps make active waiting attractive—examination of what typically happens to writers who work with and without it. The most impatient writers in my studies not only rushed into prose, they made it a chore of trying to do several things simultaneously. All at once, they struggled to devise a significant plan, to conjure motivation, and to write fluidly, coherently. The result is called *cognitive overload* and it is a common reason why writers suffer, procrastinate, and block (Hayes & Flower, 1986). Here are some of my data to support the merit of active waiting.

Ten dissertation writers evidenced the highest levels of impatience in, first, their comments (e.g., "I've got to get moving here and get the thing finished as soon as possible; I'm very busy and I usually don't have enough time to write") and in, second, their actions (e.g., they more often attempted to begin formal prose writing almost immediately after seating themselves in their writing sites). They, compared to 10 highly patient writers of dissertations, were far more likely to display external evidence of long hesitations and blocks while writing (i.e., periods of staring at screen or paper for 15 minutes or longer with no writing, or periods of an hour at the writing site with no more than one sentence of output). These most impatient writers were also more likely to put off scheduled writing in lieu of something easier (e.g., making phone calls or answering electronic mail) that consumed the time set aside for writing. And these "impatient" writers far more often described themselves as blocked and miserable when asked how soon they planned to resume writing.

More specifically, impatient writers were about five times more likely to block/procrastinate and suffer in the first three months after they began writing their dissertation proposals than were patient writers. The 10 patient writers, in contrast, were nearly unique in both waiting actively (i.e., spent time patiently thinking about writing and making notes/diagrams before beginning) and in prewriting before prose writing. Perhaps because of that, they were:

- Almost two times more likely to express confidence about the worth of the writing before they undertook it
- Over three times better able to specify useful creative ideas once writing
- About three times as likely as their impatient counterparts to mention experiences of joy and self-discovery during the first few weeks of writing dissertations

Why Isn't Practical Information Like This Presented More Commonly?

We already know part of the reason: Mindful ways of working at writing have gone unnoticed, unappreciated in a culture that encourages rushing at writing; tradition supposes the best and brightest writers work quickly, spontaneously, enchantedly. It's a lovely romantic idea that genius manifests in a flash, without much effort or preparation, but it's simply untrue (see Perkins, 1981; Simonton, 1994), except, perhaps, for the truly inspired poets of past centuries (Weissman,

1993). The facts, like them or not, link genius with constancy and moderation—and with the same old rule of this book: *Nihil nimus.*

[I apologize for sounding a bit like Thomas Gradgrind, the man who loved facts in Dickens's book *Hard Times* but, as the little circus girl could have told you, Mr. Gradgrind was also little given to explanation or repentance.]

Something else makes it hard to give up passive waiting: Many writers, even successful sorts whose writing I admire, commend it:

> *The first thing a writer should be is—excited. He should be a thing of fevers and enthusiasm.—RAY BRADBURY*

But what if you, the writer relying on such expertise, are not ready, not already excited? You could wait for exhilaration, not quite sure how to summon it except by bingeing. You might, if the waiting for inspiration seems interminable, decide you lack the gift of writing. (If so, you would help confirm that already familiar fact about traditional ways of teaching writers how to work at writing: Only the square root of those who could write and who want to, do.)

You would fare better to listen to writers who counsel more *active,* mindful forms of waiting, who model patient ways to motivate themselves effectively before getting into prose. Here is a reasonably well-known example of such advice:

> *As for my next book, I am going to hold myself from writing it till I have it impending in me: grown heavy in my mind like a ripe pear; pendant, gravid, asking to cut or it will fall.—VIRGINIA WOOLF*

The key is holding oneself back from the actual writing. It means "not doing" in explicit ways while getting prepared anyway. The action is simple but uncommon because of the same old problem: Impatience.

An even better way to learn about active waiting may be to observe what exemplars (as I defined them in the introductions to Sections I and II) do that makes them distinctive. And to check which of their ways are most readily and beneficially modeled by other, more normal writers. That approach is the basis for the proven exercises that follow here and in ensuing chapters.

Writing Rule 1: Wait, Actively.

Informal Exercises for Writing Rule 1

The first exercise is beginning almost every writing session by pausing for calm and reflection. It means waiting and "not doing" (externally), even arbitrarily at first, instead of rushing, impulsively, into formal writing. Its pause for awakeness (the first step to mindfulness, you might recall) is one of the least complicated but hardest practices. Impatience is, once again, the culprit.

As you might expect, I advise a bit of active waiting *now*—before you launch into the exercises that follow. Try spending a whole minute in mindfulness simply by staying here in the moment and seeing how you react to a respite from doing. [Surely, I say—in the wonderful style of guilt-induction I learned as a psychotherapist—you can spare a mere minute for the sake of experimenting with new practices in writing. Eh?]

How should you do it as part of writing? Sit comfortably at your writing site, at ease but with awakeness (i.e., awareness of being in the moment, without, say, blind and impatient thinking about the future). For now, attempt little more than attending to your breathing as it moves in and out. Let your exhalations take as long as they need. Watch for tendencies toward "breath grabbing" that keep exhalations from reaching full completions (and that discourage a mere, brief pause at the end of each expiration). Look out for breath stopping. And ask yourself if your need to hurry is real or imagined. (See Farhi, 1996, for more yogic exercises on breathing—arguably, you write as well as you breathe.)

Then notice that the act of attending and noticing slows, calms, and frees your mind for clear seeing. Whether you're novice or expert at this exercise, you'll sense the patience that mindfulness requires and forges. With practice at this clear seeing, you may begin to understand the wisdom of patience, of letting your thoughts collect, of first seeing what you want to do and what can be done realistically.

> *To find our way, we will need to pay more attention to this moment. It is the only time that we have in which to live, grow, feel, and change. . . . There is nothing passive about it. And when you decide to go [after waiting and attending to the moment], it's a different kind of going because you stopped. The stopping actually makes the going more vivid, richer, more textured.—JON KABAT-ZINN*

Mindfulness practices can seem difficult in the short run. You, like me, might get locked into the impatient product orientation of an almost irrepressible ego ("If I'm as smart as I think, I'll breeze through this"). Slowing down enough to simply stay in a process mode—in the moment, without immediate concerns for external results or rewards—can seem overwhelming and unpalatable at first.

How do the writers who learn mindfulness usually manage this beginning? They merge acts of mindfulness meditation with acts of writing. This is a typical sequence:

- First, mindful writers pause in getting off the edge of their beds to plan to write that day. Psychologists call this *precommitment* (Logue, 1994) and it consists of little more than a calm, clear decision about what to write that day

—along with a lucid visualization of how and when it will occur. Mindful writers like to point out its value in reassuring them that at least something worthwhile will be accomplished that day, whatever else. They also note that this habit—of clear seeing what needs doing and what can be done—often generalizes to other plans for the day. Once in the process mode of simply doing the necessary, they end up with more free time for other things, including play. My dog, Wiley the Basenji, favors this move.

• Second, mindful writers pause for a moment of meditation at the beginning of writing sessions, almost, as many like to term it, prayerfully. They follow their breathing, they settle into a comfortable but alert posture, they calm and slow themselves while almost getting to work. Some even ask for a bit of divine guidance.

• Third, mindful writers keep these bouts of mindful meditation brief—and, too, as a rule, the writing (or its preparation) for now. The most mindful writers work in brief, daily sessions that neither fatigue them nor keep them from other important activities. And when they're getting underway on a project, they commonly suppose that, say, 5 minutes a day are better than no practice at all. They've already precommitted to the notion that no matter how busy they feel during the day, they can afford at least 5 minutes for some mindfulness about writing. As they begin a daily session, they usually do something else to help let go of inhibitions and inertia. They calmly allow themselves to be content, at least for awhile, with these slow, imperfect, and playful preliminaries.

Still, writers on this path sometimes see such starts as frighteningly small. Spending a week or two, often more, doing little more than 5 or 10 minutes a day of active waiting can seem, as one of them put it, "about as weak a solution as homeopathic soup." But with lots of practice and a bit of coaching, they come up with a crucial insight. This very struggle and its patient resolution are the essence of this first writing exercise.

What do writers who become mindful find most helpful in that struggle? Appreciating that they can afford a week or two with small outputs (indeed, most confess to many weeks with no product or progress in their recent pasts) and seeing that the long-term effects of active waiting are what matter. How do they confirm this optimism? By way of less blocking and procrastination at starting times; by way of accumulating more ideas, confidence, and themes for writing; and by seeing that mindfulness practice costs little time and effort in relation to its benefits.

> *Using the breath to bring us back to the present moment takes no time at all, only a shift in attention. But great adventures await you if you give yourself a little time to string moments of awareness together, breath by breath, moment to moment.—JON KABAT-ZINN*

The more formal exercise for writers, just ahead, needs only regular, brief practice. Even here, I'll ask you to wait before launching into external action. Patience, patience, patience!

For the moment, make a mindful commitment to look for two things as you begin practicing:

- First, notice that active waiting is less a matter of time management than of emotional management. The demand in this exercise on your time is minimal; the changes in how you emote while spending that time are large. So instead of supposing you must set up a new, comprehensive rescheduling of your life to manage enough writing (the sort of time-charting that time management experts cherish), look instead for benefits of simple, mindful practices of slowing and calming during the brief openings for writing you squeeze into your days. And expect your dark side to continue to tell you that you are too busy, too overscheduled to write. May the force be with you!

  These are ways you can see how the process of emotional management works: In the slowing and calming for more reliable, comfortable starts on writing days (compared to the moodiness and hurry that might previously have been customary), and in the letting go of the need for feelings of control that impatient rushing brings in the short run. Again, mindfulness isn't so much about finding lots of time for writing as it is about working more patiently, calmly, and wisely.

- Second, notice that you need *not* be tense or hurried to be in control. You will be more in control if you learn to wait, actively, mindfully. (Any Zen practitioner could have told you that; you probably already knew it yourself.)

A Formal Exercise for Writing Rule 1

Schedule a week or two, starting now, for doing *nothing else* as a writer but *pausing, holding back from writing*. Schedule brief, daily sessions of this active waiting each weekday, for perhaps 5 to 10 minutes, no more. Find this time, preferably, amid an otherwise busy morning; remember, it only needs to be 5 to 10 minutes— not a whole hour of your schedule. Spend this brief time at your writing site, with materials—such as notes, references, and old manuscript pages—already on hand. (Writing sites can be portable so long as they become somewhat constant.)

  Begin with a moment of meditative mindfulness by just staying in the present moment, following your breathing in and out. This might last a minute or two, for now. Then use the remaining minutes, without hurrying and without leaving the present, to mentally sketch ideas about your intended writing.

Suggested Goals
You might aim, consciously and gently (i.e., mindfully), for the following:

- Patience: Calm yourself so that you increasingly experience beginnings of writing projects (and of daily writing sessions) with the *patience* of feeling content to stay in the moment. That, according to mindful writers I've studied, needs a few minutes of not doing, of just sitting with your experiences, nonjudgmentally, and not trying to accomplish anything in particular as a writer—for now. And it means tolerating frequent "slips" into impatience and mindlessness, including worries about whether the writing will be good enough. In particular, it means forgiving ourselves for slips while learning from them.

This very moment is the perfect teacher. Generally speaking, we regard discomfort in any form as bad... but feelings like disappointment, jealously, anger are actually very clear moments that teach us where it is that we're holding back.—PEMA CHODRIN

- Slowing and clear seeing: Congratulate yourself about becoming more patient, no matter how small your progress. Pause to notice how the constant and regular practice of patiently waiting (as opposed to blindly, impatiently rushing) begins to foster a readiness to write every day. Then deliberately use pauses to slow down, calm down, and induce a nonfatiguing pace of working, one that persists from the earliest involvements in a writing project.

    You might look for something related to happen now: Generation of clear plans and of interesting ideas for the writing, without really trying. This is where the real magic of writing enters the picture—by way of patient discipline, not via Muses or inborn genius.

- Look for generality: Remember that you have (if you've read Section I first) already practiced and learned from similar ways of working at teaching, such as the holding back of patience and the reflection basic to discovery and readiness. And then reconsider a fact I presented at the end of Section I: New faculty in my programs who practiced constancy/moderation with teaching *and* writing fared better at both than did peers who immersed themselves in just one (Boice, 1995). Why? That generalization of mindfulness to a new context revealed more about basics, such as working largely in the moment, in a process mode.

- Be patient with yourself: If you are like most writers I've known, at this point, you may still feel vaguely unready to write. Participants in my programs say something like this: "OK, I'm slowing down. I may have some good ideas for writing; I'm not sure. I am sure that I still don't feel fully ready to write. What next?"

I refer them, as I do you, to the next chapter.

Begin Writing Early (Before Feeling Ready)

How does this second rule for writing (begin early) jibe with the first rule (wait)? The active waiting of Rule 1 is a process for getting on task early.

To get on task here early, consider the ways that active waiting sets it up. First, active waiting not only calms a writer, patiently and mindfully, but it loosens inhibitions such as blocking. Second, active waiting lends itself to daily repetition because it gets you started at writing effortlessly, before you realize you're working.

The next step follows naturally from active waiting. You'll see the ideas and images you've begun to generate as meaningful starts at writing. For now, though, the writing remains mostly imperfect and preliminary; composition teachers call it *prewriting* (Murray, 1995). Writers who rely on it before moving to formal writing fare much better than writers who rush ahead with few preliminaries (Hayes & Flower, 1986). I first appreciated the importance of patient, playful preliminaries when I worked in a sex clinic; most of the male patients I saw were impatient practitioners of foreplay.

Prewriting is a kind of foreplay, of taking time for preliminaries that prime the best results. In writing, it often begins with getting some of what you are thinking about your writing project out into speech or onto paper, well before you consider it a final product. The crucial step is getting started before you feel at all confident about the worth of your actions.

Even some famous writers lend credence to preliminaries (but without being as specific about how to manage them as I'd like):

When inspiration does not come to me, I go halfway to meet it.
—SIGMUND FREUD

Work brings inspiration if inspiration is not discernable in the begin-
ning.—IGOR STRAVINSKY

Beginning Early Can Be Difficult
Until It Becomes a Habit

Beginning early—well before you usually do or want to—requires constant, patient practice. It benefits from mindfulness meditation that keeps you in the moment, ready to work and supplied with ideas. But even with those supports, its practice demands a great leap of faith. Only trust allows us enough patience to experience these preliminaries called *prewriting*. Trust helps us wait and see how prewriting generates ideas and momentum as we:

1. Talk aloud what we *might* write.
2. Read aloud what we've begun to write.
3. Take notes about what else we might write.
4. Begin to see the project more wholistically.

Moreover, trust (i.e., active waiting) metes out enough tolerance to abide the tentativeness, imperfection, and slow, seemingly wasteful, pace of preliminary work. Patience begets tolerance, and vice versa.

Problems of trust are so common that society has a host of labels for their varieties of mindlessness:

- *Procrastination:* "I'm way behind on lots of other pressing things and I can't afford the time to deal with this project at all until the deadline forces me to work on it."
- *Perfectionism:* "I don't want to be in the habit of producing a lot of second-rate material, not even as so-called preliminary writing; I want to write well or not at all."
- *Elitism:* "I believe that really brilliant writers write quickly, in a single draft, without much of a struggle or a plan; they are born-writers and I doubt that they need to waste much time on preliminaries."
- *Blocking:* "Want to know why the begin-early rule won't work for me? I'm the kind of writer who can't write at all until I am in the mood and then I write as much as I can and try to finish in one sitting because I may never write again."
- *Oppositional:* "I don't like rules; I need to be myself, unfettered, to be a good writer; rules are for robots."

Notice the similarities among resistances to beginning early. Struggling writers of all sorts wish for spontaneity and quick, easy results. They base their hopes in blind thinking that can help them escape reality for the moment (e.g., by assuming that forcing under deadlines and with binges will work well-enough in the end). And they mistakenly equate freedom and brilliance with working in rule-free fashion. What typically happens to writers who maintain these beliefs and habits? They don't begin early, if at all. They wait passively. They work sporadically. They struggle to begin and to stay with it. They continue to see writing as difficult, perhaps even as something mastered only by a gifted, pained few.

An analogue provides another way to appreciate writers' usual reluctances to begin early. People who display the most resistance to being hypnotized display obvious commonalities; they are most unwilling to go along with suggestions, to suspend suspicion and disbelief, to trust themselves and the hypnotist. These 'low-susceptibles' also struggle the most as writers. Why? They have not learned to trust general images and rough wordings that could be put on paper or screen in advance of formal writing. Instead they work cautiously, looking for perfect sentences to begin with, listening too soon to internal editors (those voices of authority figures who remind us of rigid rules and standards about writing), and doubting too readily (Hilgard, 1977).

In contrast, highly trusting, suggestible (and hypnotizable) writers are more fluent. They tolerate ambiguity because they welcome vague images as a useful first step, because they most readily appreciate the lowered pressure of beginning early and informally, because they produce more and better writing in the long run. Moreover, they are less stressed in their work because they begin early to put some of cognitive load of planning what to write outside their heads.

> *Our knowledge is not just in our heads...but in accessible notes, knowing how to consult references, in having friends to call for a steer.*
> —*DAVID PERKINS*

Writing Rule 2: Begin Early.

Exercises for Writing Rule 2

A caution: These are the most extensive and demanding exercises in the book—as well as the most productive. They, more than most exercises, reward pauses from daily activities to practice.

As usual, take a moment of holding back to anticipate by way of review (in the chapters on teaching, I called this *setting and resetting context*):

- Early starts mean practice at launching a project without quite having figured out what you will say (much as in mindful teaching preparations).

- Early starts mean letting things happen, including surprises, by experimenting and playing instead of rushing into deathless prose (or lecturing).
- Early starts rely on process orientations that keep you in the moment, mindfully seeing what needs doing, and focused on what can be done now (in contrast to a product mode that focuses your attention, impatiently and perfectionistically, on the eventual outcome of your work).
- Early starts mean letting go of mindless inhibitions or impulses and allowing calm motivation, inspiration, and ideas to appear in their stead. In my own experiences of coaching writers in this mindful way, such things actually do happen. Commonly.

When they are distributed (rather than bunched), the mindful practices for Rule 2 are easier than you might suppose. The basic habits and attitudes are already in place, more or less, from the practices of Writing Rule 1—just reviewed in the preceding list. I'll rely on a hero of mine to remind you of just one more specific:

> *Don't hurry to breathe the next breath in—the next breath will arise on its own whenever it is ready. There's a sense of ease that comes from letting the breath just happen.—SYLVIA BOORSTEIN*

Now, with that gentle caution in mind, we'll restart from something else in Writing Rule 1.

Exercise 1. Slightly Extend the Holding Back.

After the week or two of simple "waiting exercises" in the practices of Rule 1, try expanding your mindfulness (and even your productivity) a bit. Now, perhaps before you feel ready, spend about two weeks adding related practices that help keep you centered but actually writing (well, prewriting). I suggest you schedule at least 10- to 15-minute sessions for every weekday. Find the time by way of two or three sessions per day if necessary.

Start each session with a minute or two of mindfulness meditation about what you might write. Precommit to begin writing (i.e., prewriting) in just a few minutes. Then, after staying in the present with your writing ideas, talk aloud some of what you've been thinking about writing. Listen patiently, without rushing to judgment. Listen compassionately, as though you are a coach helping someone else find what they have to say. Then take notes or draw diagrams, unhurriedly, about what you *could* write if you decide to use the material. Notice something: Ready or not, you're writing.

As a rule, but not always, this note writing is a revision of what you've just imaged or thought and then said. Sometimes this earliest form of prewriting condenses and clarifies. Sometimes it expands and connects.

Exercise 2. Begin Writing Projects Early, with Informal Outlines.

Exemplars provide another annoying example for normal writers: They like to outline. They use outlines—despite the aversive ways outlining is often taught during school years—to organize and clarify their images and thoughts about writing, and to stimulate ideas about what needs adding or subtracting. They do it as a warm-up for writing and they rely on it while writing from the directions of the outline.

In each of the weekdays where they talk and write out their preliminary thoughts about writing, exemplars end the session with a minute or two on a related task. At that moment, often before feeling ready, they organize even the most tentative ideas into one or a few points they hope to make in the next day's writing.

Don't be surprised if this directive about outlining doesn't work well for you in the short run. It will, eventually. Exemplars usually say that they, too, struggle with this easy but difficult bit of discipline but they are quick to note the reason why: Impatience.

Now try it yourself. Please. (You see, Mr. Gradgrind would never ask nicely.) For a while, make those sorts of outlining your main task in sessions. A model may help you understand how successful participants began to manage this task:

Example from Real Life

Scenario: A sociology professor is dangerously near the campus reappointment-decision deadline for one new manuscript to be submitted to a refereed outlet.

Suppose you, like this professor, want to write about the neglected role of women in marital abuse, compared to men, a topic you had researched before your dissertation project. Imagine that you, too, as a means of getting new writing underway at your new campus, agreed to analyze and write up the part of an ongoing study by colleagues with a funded project on that topic. One more thing helps set the context: The professor had only recently renewed her reading on this topic, and her first attempt to master the newest books and articles left her feeling overwhelmed by the amount of relevant material, unclear about what theme she might draw from it all, and uncertain about when to actually stop the notetaking and begin the writing.

Then, picture yourself in this professor's position of taking up a stance of active waiting, of beginning early even while feeling adrift and alienated. Imagine yourself beginning, as she did, by mindfully listening to yourself reviewing the points that stand out from your reading notes and from your data analyses (neither of which need be perfectly complete now). Be patient and reflective. Take time to consider the theme of the large project you joined.

Calmly ask and re-ask yourself what the point of your data is and how you could portray your message most simply.

But what if you, the professor, at this point, begin to panic and lose your mindfulness? Get back to it by pausing and following your breathing in and out. Even by adding what she did, a yoga posture of breathing calmly while standing and stretching until you calm and resee what you need to do now.

With the patient mindfulness of staying in the moment and of just talking aloud and then outlining, you (as she) might begin to notice a few main ideas that appeal to you. (In the case of the sociology professor:

1. Until recently, marital violence was underreported and underemphasized for women.
2. The low profile of women as violent may be due to a sexist tendency to suppose that men alone would initiate such interactions in physical fashion.
3. More objective reporting of womens' role in marital violence may help provide a more realistic basis for treating violence in couples.)

How might you have drawn out two or three main points if you began, as she did, by feeling blocked? By imagining yourself just telling someone like me about the things that impress you most as you look back at what you have read and noted. By actually saying it aloud to someone else (to me, in the case of the sociologist). By tolerating its initial imperfection (as in the excerpt from an early outline, above). And by jotting it down again and again, until it clears and reassures. By this point, as you grow more excited and confident about what you have to say, your outline will probably compel more writing in list-like or diagrammatic format.

But what if you, like her, want to continue revising your compact outline until it is perfect? Practice the holding back of mindfulness that can moderate temptations to excessiveness. And what if you, too, find my insistence on saying what you will write aversive to tolerate? Practice tolerance and just do it. The doing will get you past one of the most challenging points of beginning: Clarifying what you can say, aloud, before you write it.

Or what if you worry that you are beginning without having completed your scholarly searches? Tell yourself that one purpose of early outlining is the clarification of places where you need more searching of a specific sort, as opposed to the general and often wasteful sort that precedes most writing projects.

Then, like the professor, use the next sessions to revise and expand your outline by adding supporting materials to each main point. Some of these additions you will have already spoken aloud; they may be most apparent when you pause and reflect, remember, and, in particular, talk about what you might have said. Others additions are cued by perusals of your notes. If your notes are too comprehensive, too detailed to make this latter move easy, set aside brief periods for nothing more than drawing out the essentials that pertain to your plan, perhaps in the margins of your notes. As you begin to arrange these most memorable subpoints alongside (or under) your main points, write them as you would talk them, informally but to the point.

When you build more conceptual statements into your outline, see if there is a logical flow in your scheme by asking yourself questions like these:

- Does it make sense to begin with *this* point? Am I answering the right question?
- Do the next main points follow from the first and each other; do they say all that I need to say?
- Am I trying to do too much; could I make my essential message clearer by abbreviating or removing some of the points around it?
- Do the same subpoints appear in two or more places?
- Are some essential subpoints missing or underdeveloped?

Carry out these things with patience and tolerance, not with impatience and perfectionism.

But what, for example, if you suppose your initial versions do not cover everything you want to say? Congratulate yourself; this is, after all, just an early, informal beginning. Wait before trying for comprehensiveness, before worrying much about having missed something vital, even before fretting about someone else having already said what you've just put on paper or screen. Remind yourself that every writer essentially rewrites things written some where, some time, before; exemplary writers aim less for novelty of topic than for new and better ways of connecting and presenting ideas. Yes, I know there are exceptions where writers conjure new theories or clever proofs, but they are just that, exceptions. And let go of customary objections and focus on making sense of the two main points (or three or four, but probably not more) for now.

Then decide, somewhat playfully, that you will limit yourself to developing your initial points, and little else, as you participate in this scheme for the day and week. Mindful writers almost always look to simplify/clarify their work here more than anywhere else—at the outset, when plans might otherwise become grandiose or confusing. Procrastinators and blockers, in contrast, tend to try to do too much too soon (Boice, 1996c). So it is that they struggle and complain when asked to state their plan for a manuscript simply.

Finally, ready or not, assume you now have a working sense about what, specifically, to look for as you scan to make marginal notes as possibilities for expanding your main points. Pause to make sure you are being economical and clear while reminding yourself of your mission (e.g., write, "I only need to write a brief but useful review/rationale to which I'll add some new data I've collected, not another dissertation. The point I have to make is worth making and I can make it best with directness and brevity").

As you let go and trust yourself, notice again what to look at in filling out your main points in the outline: Your notes. Just as important, begin to see what you can neglect and omit in your reading. Good writing is as much a matter of figuring what not to say as of what to say. That's why it needs so much awakeness and clear seeing about what communicates most clearly, helpfully—and what doesn't.

Pause, at least every 5 minutes, to see where you are in this second exercise (generating and organizing tentative ideas/directions) of Writing Rule 2 (begin early). Writers profit, in my experience, by staying here for a while, by continuing to revise their expanded and conceptualized outlines until the result impels them to prose-write what they've already prewritten.

This patient strategy of beginning early works nicely for making early starts at all the kinds of prose writing I've encountered: Formulating dissertation problems or storylines for novels; starting complete revisions of short stories and other pieces once or more rejected; reviving abandoned ideas for a funding proposal; and, of course, getting scholarly writing underway in timely, imaginative ways.

Exercise 3. Throttle Down, into the Moment.

Throughout these preliminaries called prewriting, pause to return to your breathing. Remind yourself to be calm and relaxed, to deliberately slow your pace and lower your tensions from what they might be if you were impatient. And notice that, for now, no harm comes in struggling at writing without much apparent product.

Many writers at this point in my programs are writing and rewriting just a page or two; some soon switch to prose. Others turn to formal prose only when their conceptual outline is as long as the manuscript will be. "I'm leaving it up to you," as Dale and Grace sang it in their R&B classic.

Other things matter more than traditional measures of productivity for now: Clear seeing of what can happen, confidence that it will, and returning again to work at writing the next day.

Goals for This Exercise 3

- *Use brief pauses to comfort and reassure yourself as you make your task harder.* For example, mindfully notice whether you can sit and work with nearly effortless grace, without much strain. That may require looking at yourself, almost from outside yourself, at times. And aim to acquire the habit of sitting (as mindfulness meditators call it) with yourself and with your writing each weekday, not only in the beginning but during pauses throughout the writing. This simple but difficult accomplishment will turn out to be as important as anything else you do as a writer—even if it only approaches the ideal.

Energies which formerly were squandered in compulsive drives and pur-
poseless actions are reserved and channeled into a unity through correct
Zen sitting.—PHILIP KAPLEAU

- *Use some prewriting to do one thing at a time and to do it well—but not per-*
  fectly, for now.
- *Get at least some of your thoughts about what you can/will write out onto*
  paper each day. Write something, anything—even that you can think of nothing to write. Talk aloud, no matter how silly it may seem at first, to generate
  material that can be transcribed into prewriting. Employ this useful exercise
  of prewriting (i.e., first talking and then writing what you have to say) as a
  warm-up for another one.

Exercise 4. Extend Patient Beginnings
and Discovery via Freewriting.

Oddly, this seemingly automatic, mindless task can help make you a mindful
observer of yourself at work. You'll need that attentiveness just to manage the
usual instruction for freewriting:

- Write whatever comes to mind; better yet, write whatever appears on paper
  or screen without judgment.
- Don't correct or edit; ignore ongoing and anticipated criticisms.
- Push ahead, patiently and with tolerance, for *im*perfect writing—without
  rushing.
- Don't apologize for the product, not even to yourself.

Freewriting is just as easy and substantive as something you already know
how to do—freetalking. (Freud started by having his patients freewrite but found
freetalking easier to elicit and sustain.)

If you find your impatient, perfectionistic ego demanding immediate correc-
tions, or pushing for a fast and productive pace, remind yourself of a pair of relevant truths, one familiar and one not. First, you'll have time later—in the revision
stage after the prose draft has been written—to manage thorough revisions and
near-perfection. Second, you'll work less painfully in the meanwhile if you tolerate a modicum of mistakes in prewriting stages. That means leaving flaws on the
page or screen, and not letting their continuing presence bother you for now; this
is, after all, early and informal work.

Begin by interspersing bouts of freewriting among routines you are already
practicing—to help transform what you could say into approximations of writing.

Return to the Real-Life Example

The sociologist writing on the role of women in marital abuse next tried free-
writng the two subpoints under the first main point this way:

1. Until recently, marital violence was underreported and underempha-sized by women.
   a. Here are the studies and reviews that make that point.

No, wait, I don't like that. Too unimaginative. It misses the point I want to make up front. What I might really need to say here, now that I notice that what I just wrote is all-too-well-known in the field, is that the real proble [sic] in the oversight lies in prior research, because of that limitation, not having generated useful treatments/interventions. The poor outcome record of exist-ing interventions supports that idea.

So, I'm going to revise the outline of the three main points, like this:

1. Usual oversight about women's role marital violence has led to inef-fective & one sided treatments of spousal abuse.
   a. Very brief review/reminder of the studies that note the oversight and the reasons for it; I may just describe just three recent reviews, beginning with _____, which may be the best known because it has the first solid data base to draw on. . . .
   b. Beginnings of realizations in the literature, some as yet unpub-lished (e.g., _____) on how this imbalance in reporting under-mines treatments. One thing I want to say for sure here is. . . .
2. Existing theories of how a more balanced appreciation of marital vio-lence will turn into more effective treatment plans.
   a. The usual suspects, put in order of their apparent usefulness, begin-ning with _____. . . .
   b. My own superior (ha!) theory and supports for it in my pilot research.
      — What makes my approach different is (what?) its weighting and sequencing of how violence typically occurs in abusive couples. The essential patterns, three of them, suggest an intervention that reflects the basic interactive problems in each escalation. . . .

What did this writer and I conclude about the more written-out version abstracted above? That it was suitably imperfect but directive. That it regen-erated initial main points into a tighter, more manageable and meaningful scheme. And that the expansion of those focal points into conceptual state-ments helped her stay on track as she generated more prewriting.

In the next session, those subpoints were freewritten again (re-freewrit-ten?) after a brief revisit to her notes (some of them new) to clarify and sim-plify them. Why did I not encourage her to move more quickly to real prose? Because soon enough the revisions become real prose without having to struggle.

Consider how writers of 18 pages (typed) of journal articles usually worked at this aspect of prewriting: They spent 2 to 3 weeks adding briefly and freely written concepts to their outlines before moving to more complete and freewritten approximations of prose writing. As they completed that transition, they retained outline points only as headings and subheadings. Yet, not until beginning to write the first prose version, did they edit after writing (even then, casually). They put off serious editing during writing until final revisions, much later on.

The following things, in particular, are worth keeping in mind about this exemplary way of working at writing: It keeps the work simple, mostly by having the writer do one thing at a time (e.g., just adding freely written concepts) instead of many (e.g., trying to approximate conceptual points while editing them). And it makes the work painless by way of patient revisions where each reordering or rewrite is a little more complete. In these ways, the hard work of writing gets done before the writer fully realizes it. Donald Murray, one of the heroes I keep refer- ring to, likes to cite the instance of a writer who took meticulous but focused notes and who kept rewriting/rearranging those notes on a huge expanse of floor until, at last, the manuscript had written itself, without struggle.

Exercise 5. Add Mindfulness to Freewriting.

By itself, freewriting is simple to practice but narrowly limited and given to excess; conventional advice directs freewriters to work hurriedly and in binges, without pauses to keep writing on track. Uninterrupted freewriting can even be dangerous when its mania of rushing leaves writers drained, dysphoric, and dis- sociated from work that needs doing now (Boice & Myers, 1986).

What makes freewriting so potentially productive but underutilized? Free- writing, compared to usual writing, relies less on conscious verbal thinking and more on mental images. So it is that freewriters like to say, "How do I know what I think, until I see what I write?" And so it is that freewriters develop a striking tolerance for surprises and ambiguity.

Freewriting has the potential to conjure powerful images—and to frighten conservative writers; its imagery is a form of altered consciousness that can seem uncontrollable. But reliance on calm mental images helps make the freewriting comfortable and containable. The more deliberately and reflectively you use wholistic images to direct writing, the better you can represent their affective overtones, the more compelled you will feel to write regularly, and the more imag- inatively you will write.

Why does image-influenced freewriting work best with mindful moderation? Regular pauses to switch back and forth, from the generation of writing to reflec- tion on the imaged pattern behind it, foster the clear seeing that underlies clear writing. That clear writing, in turn, helps clarify the image. New faculty who prac- tice those shifts—from the generation of writing back to thoughtful analysis and revision of what is being generated—demonstrate impressive results, including:

- More succinct but interconnected writing, even in the freewriting stage
- Quicker realization of what needs saying and what doesn't

- Better/faster completion of both prewriting and writing
- More direct translation of images into writing, without as much verbal mediation

There is, as you might expect, an initial difficulty among writers unaccustomed to working with awareness of writing images. They've rarely noticed them and they doubt their value. One corrective is somewhat familiar; recall our exercise amid the teaching chapters to pause and notice the self-talk that may earlier have gone largely unheard. Here, in noticing the initially faint images that accompany and, ideally, direct writing, you may need to add more direct practice of imagining a thing and writing about it solely from the image. Another corrective is, of course, the practice of mindful freewriting to encourage more and clearer imagery.

Or you may choose not to develop your imaging now, while you simply need to write enough to survive in academe. A problem in delaying is that the absence of an image for writing leaves more room for telling yourself other, often negative, stories.

How Exemplars Experience Mindful Freewriting.   They eventually model the very procedures I've been mentioning, often not with proficiency until their sixth through tenth years on campus. And when they describe mastering this more complex form of freewriting, exemplars like to note two things about the experience: First, mindful freewriting slows the pace enough to optimize the rich material in images. Second, the unexpected joy of slowing for clear seeing stimulates contemplative ways of working, including temporary returns to handwriting. Some of the most mindful writers I have known occasionally write with a calligraphy pen to keep their work reflective, clear, and attractive; authors such as James Michener type with only two fingers to keep the work slowed and mindful.

More specifically, exemplars report alternating between:

Periods of letting mental images find expression within and then without onto paper or screen

and

Bouts of conscious attention to what has been written, in part to further clarify it on screen or paper, in part to put more order and usefulness back into the mental images that direct writing at its deepest level.

How, in their experience, does the verbal thinking represented in writing find its way back into images? Automatically. Visual images can not only anticipate, organize, and direct outward actions but they can also reflect what is learned in ongoing, outer acts.

isn't this part of drafting?

What do exemplars do when they have no ready, helpful image? Again, they coax it by talking it aloud until it makes sense, so much that they can say it implicitly and even begin to visualize the action it could induce. They also work patiently. While this circular process of shifting between (1) image and generation and (2) reflection and revision brings immediate benefits, hoped-for improvements in ability to produce/clarify images can take longer.

Why, if mindful freewriting takes so long to master, bring it up now? Because new faculty in my programs have said they like to keep some long-term goals in mind. Also, because this information helps shortcut the path to fluent writing. Imagery can be put to use early and with little extra time; indeed, you are probably using more of it now than you realize.

Exercise 6. Broaden Prewriting the C. Wright Mills Way.

This step could have come earlier, like almost everything else in this book. Exercise 6 takes us back to processes of generating motivation and imagination. I've put it here because it helps cultivate the initial images we need for fluent and enjoyable writing.

Here, for a change, I got the idea from someone other than an exemplary new faculty member: C. Wright Mills (1959), the pioneering sociologist, was one of the first writers to share this mindful way of working. We saw him earlier, in Section I, in regard to collecting and filing ideas for teaching in order to draw out and organize their implications. Because the same first-order principles of collecting and filing apply just as well to finding imagination and organization for writing, I'll remind you of them here:

- Rearrange files to look for general themes, then for interconnections.
- Maintain an attitude of playfulness by casting ideas into categories and types to help make sense of them.
- Consider extremes or opposites of important ideas.
- Find comparable cases by way of brief revisits to the literature.
- Arrange the materials for public presentation as a way of bringing closure to prewriting.

Working the C. Wright Mills way is the epitome of prewriting. It has you constantly collecting and organizing ideas amidst daily life, using freewriting to shape themes into linear copy, reexamining core ideas to rework writing creatively and succinctly, and doing most of the hard work of writing before you get to formal prose. It, once again, gets you started early, before you feel fully ready.

A Pause to Set Up an Ending

I trust that you've found prewriting interesting, but I wonder if you believe it worth your while. So I end this chapter with a brief account of a study that proves prewriting beneficial. At this point in so long a chapter, these data might be a dessert or a soporific.

Experimental Evidence for Benefits in Beginning Writing Early

In a study of 14 writers about to attempt their first completely new manuscripts at their new campus, 7 followed Writing Rules 1 and 2 (in Chapters 9 and 10), including the Mills approach. The other 7 new faculty worked in their own support groups and without exposure to those rules. By the end of the first month, the 7 "prewriters" in the program were working 1 to 2 hours a day at prewriting their manuscripts. At the end of 3 months, 6 of those 7 had produced at least 18 new pages of conceptual outlines intermixed with revised freewriting and arranged the C. Wright Mills way. Those writers expressed confidence that the writing ahead would consist largely of rewriting what they had already collected, arranged, and simplified. They were correct. All 7 of these prewriters finished first drafts that they submitted to refereed outlets within the next four months. I verified these outcomes directly, by examining parts of manuscripts as written, and by seeing letters of manuscript receipt from editors.

Of the 7 other writers, all of whom wanted to rely on nothing more than weekly meetings with each other to somehow impel writing, none displayed the kinds of prewriting practiced in the program they shunned. And none had come close to completing a rough first draft of their manuscripts after 7 months (1 had done virtually nothing; 2 writers still had little more than 10 pages of new notes and analyses that had not been transformed into prose; and of the other 4 writers, none had more than 12 pages of any kind of writing). Instead, they reported spending much of their time for writing feeling discouraged or blocked, waiting for better writing times, looking again at the literature and data for new directions and overlooked details, or trying to begin anew by writing or rewriting a single, isolated section of their manuscripts to near perfection. So, in a way, they were trying to prewrite, but only in spurts and not until they were mired in premature prose.

Prewriters, again, not only waited actively and began well before feeling ready but they also emphasized working with constancy and moderation far more than did the other writers. And prewriters, like exemplary/mindful writers I've studied, anticipated the next rule (in the next chapter).

11

Work with Constancy and Moderation

What else, besides prewriting, distinguishes the most fluent and successful writers from the rest of us? They work at their craft daily. Donald Murray, the most mindful writing teacher I know, states the principle in his usual, deceptively simple, way:

Writers write.

Jerry Leiber and Mike Stoller, the most mindful (and soulful) song writers I know, make the point in a more explicit way:

The more you write, the better you write.

Recent studies of expertise and greatness confirm the importance of constancy. Outstanding writers, scientists, and artists work regularly, day in and day out, at their craft—for years and years of constant practice. They rely on coaches and on social networks (even critics and detractors) to direct and hone their patterning of skills. And they learn to limit practice sessions to periods brief enough to minimize fatigue. They know that long, exhausting practice sessions not only persist beyond the point of diminishing returns but that those excesses associate working and performing with mindless rushing and sloppy habits (Simonton, 1994).

Constant writers simply produce more output, overall, than most other people. They also demonstrate clear benefits in this great fertility: They generally work with modest perfectionism. They open themselves to risks, to criticism, to discovery. And they produce far more products of value than do less prolific writers. Why? Their failures inform them as much as their successes and their successes carry them past their failures.

Writers who manage this sort of fruitfulness are surprised that other writers do not do the same:

Nine out of ten writers, I am sure, could write more. I think they should and, if they did, they would find their work improving even beyond their own, their agent's and their editor's highest hopes.—JOHN CREASY

Most academic writers don't write enough to get up to speed... they don't know the craft.—DONALD MURRAY

The seeming contradiction in this prolific output is the moderation with which it is produced. Exemplary writers, as we have seen, work a lot, typically every day, but in brief, daily sessions (BDSs). Consider their own explanations for this moderation:

- When writers work daily on projects—even very briefly—the ideas stay fresh in mind from day to day; so, less warm-up time is needed before writing the next day.
- Brief, daily sessions allow time and energy for interludes of "near-writing" at other times of the day—for noticing things that relate to writing, for collecting and noting things that induce more imaginativeness and clearer organization.
- The habit of writing every day helps make the work more welcome, less a struggle.
- Brief, daily sessions mean shorter, less fatiguing sessions of work.
- Because they eventually provide a realistic sense of doing enough and of progressing fast enough, BDSs help reduce pressures to write quickly and perfectly in first drafts.
- Brief, daily sessions help writers learn how to work proficiently, like real writers, and to feel like real writers.
- Because they are brief, BDSs fit into already busy schedules.
- Brief, daily sessions are more productive, creative, and successful in the long run than writing in spurts and binges.

Said simply, moderation allows for optimal persistence and joy. And for more mindfulness.

Writing Rule 3: Work with Constancy and Moderation.

Exercises for Writing Rule 3

The following practices for establishing and maintaining BDSs (brief, daily sessions) are new but they were presaged in the initial chapters of Section I, on teaching—and in the first two rules here, in Section II on writing:

Exercise 1. Arrange a Regular Time for Writing and Do It in the Same Facilitating Location.

The most fluent, healthy writers not only work every day but they generally put great value on doing it at the same time every day. The most efficient writers I've known choose to write in the mornings, when they are most awake and clear. They also work in surrounds that encourage writing. They set aside a room or location where *nothing but writing* is done (i.e., with few distractions such as magazines or televisions nearby, often not even phones or electronic mail). And they unashamedly, unapologetically, close their office doors and post a sign that asks potential visitors to limit interruptions to true emergencies. They'll tell you that this posting does not offend most people; instead, it enlists them as collaborators in keeping writing times sacred. (The same happens with periods set aside for meditation and/or prayer.)

Equally important, exemplary writers make their writing spots comfortable and comforting. They display favorite artwork and other decorations and mementoes. They most often work facing a window—which not only allows an occasional glance at pleasant things like the sky but also affords distance focusing, an important preventive of eye strain. Or, if they have no window, they gaze on something pleasant during pauses (e.g., a large scenic poster). And, most shocking of all, they often work in comfortable chairs that allow back, neck, arm, and leg support. (Yes, it is possible to write competently on paper or a keyboard while sitting decadently in a Barcolounger! John Updike is among those who do.)

Incidentally, no exemplar I have yet discovered writes much with music in the background. Although no exemplars felt strongly about keeping it out of their writing sites, all of them supposed that music took space and attention away from their nonverbal systems of imaging for writing. The essential thing, they told me, was to keep the writing context as simple and serene as possible.

Exemplary new faculty in my studies also displayed the most comfort at writing. They evidenced the most changes in seating posture and the fewest complaints about stiffness or pain. And they talked about why working in an easy chair, even reclining in bed, doesn't induce sleep: Work done mindfully is comfortable and calm but also alert and focused. It is wakeful and clear-seeing. In that mindful state, sleep is about the last thing that will happen. (Incidentally, mindfulness meditators say much the same thing: If you're drowsy during meditation, you're not doing it mindfully, wakefully.)

Exercise 2. Make Time for Regular Writing

If you fret about how and where you'll find, say, an hour a day for regular writing sessions, let go of so intrusive a demand. Start small and flexibly, during brief openings already available on busy days. Struggling writers who suddenly schedule a whole hour a day for writing usually find themselves too busy to give up that much time in already busy lifestyles; instead, they suppose they must wait for a day that magically offers a whole and free hour, or else a day where they feel strong enough to arise at 5:00 A.M. to suffer a bout of writing.

Every newcomer to the professoriate I've tracked could find at least 5- to 10-minutes a day, no matter how seemingly busy. And everyone I coached found ways, gradually, to add more and more time for writing, usually by utilizing several brief openings during workdays. Why hadn't they already put those 5 to 10 minute periods to work? They supposed writing could not be done well in them.

Something related helps writers find time for writing. They notice that many routine activities can be compressed or eliminated, without loss of quality of life or loss of enough work at other important things. One of them put it this way: "It all began when I noticed that I normally laid abed after awakening for about 15 minutes. Before, it had seemed essential, nonnegotiable, until I simply got by with less and less. I'm content with a few minutes. Then I noticed that I spent 20 to 30 minutes sipping coffee and reading a newspaper. And that I often took time to run errands on my way to work in the morning. Those, too, I could see, took away time for writing in the morning." In response to my question about whether this was a hardship, this person answered, "Not really. No. What little comfort I thought I missed at first was soon made up by spending that time having fun at writing, feeling I was getting the most essential work of the day done before the usual problems arose. Now I read the papers in the evenings when I'm tired and little good for more."

Said another participant at this point: "It sounds self-righteous, I know, but I feel good now about getting my writing done before I go to campus. It puts me in a bright mood for the day and I've needed that."

This is the main message: Don't give up if you cannot manage hour-long BDSs with constancy in the short run, even the 5- to 10-minute variety. Settle for approximations. Try writing at times when you might suppose you could not, perhaps during commercial breaks on television, to do simple prewriting like making notes and filing/organizing them. If you distract yourself from the TV programs, what's the loss? Expect something else worthwhile as you free up time from unnecessary things—more occasions for family life and exercising.

Exercise 3. Force the New Habit of Brief, Daily Sessions, but Only in the Short Run.

To make brief, daily sessions a regular habit, try the proven strategy of what psychologists call *contingency management*. That means making something you would rather do (e.g., reading newspapers and e-mail) contingent on first doing your daily ration of writing. Stated more operationally: No writing for the day, then no reward, except in extraordinary circumstances.

You will see your contingency is strong enough when it induces you to write regularly, regardless of mood. You will know your contingency is too strong when it always makes you write and you hate it (e.g., having to sit, unclothed, in a cold room until you finish your daily quota). How long should writers employ the forcing of contingencies? Only in the short run, perhaps for a few months, until the habit of BDSs becomes automatic and welcome. Why not extend the contingencies indefinitely? Writers work better and more creatively, in the long run, without oppressive external constraints. Drop-dead contingencies such as writing to avoid punishment or to make a major deadline risk the association of forced and unpleasant work with the act of writing.

Social Contingencies.   A related kind of contingency management may seem less constraining, more comfortable: Find someone with whom to share writing schedules, someone you will meet at a specified place and regular time. As a rule, you should work together, quietly, but on separate projects. You might make daily contacts via phone or electronic messages to your partner. Social contracts work because they make us feel guilty if we fail to meet or call our partner. And once we see our counterpart already writing, we are more likely to write.

Other kinds of social contracts also help. If you set appointments for showing others your ongoing work, even in its most preliminary forms, you help make writing something you do in more timely fashion. When you interest others in what you are doing, they help impel you to keep working at it because they expect to see progress, often. And when you show others your ongoing work, you are less likely to continue writing (or prewriting) past the point of diminishing returns. Why? Because readers/listeners are far better able than we to tell when enough is enough.

Exercise 4. Start without Inspiration.

Learn that even brief sessions generate momentum, motivation, and substantial amounts of output. Inspiration and motivation come far more reliably in the wake of working than in advance of it. The BDS principle works for all kinds of writers, including literary types, scholars, and pulpsters:

> *Authors like [Louis] L'Amour didn't wait for inspiration.... L'Amour wrote five pages every day. To the nonwriter this might seem like few—*

but the computation is simple—it multiplies out to 600 pages every four months, two or three books a year.—RUSSELL JACOBY

Why else are BDSs so productive? We have already seen some of the answer: Brief, daily sessions help keep projects fresh in mind; they lessen the fatigue often associated with writing; they establish a discipline of working regularly and productively through variations in mood. The rest of the answer is just as vital. BDSs help us break large tasks of writing into a series of small, manageable bits and, thus to moderate problems of cognitive overload. When all the sequential components of a project—the first, the last, and even the next to last—seem doable, we are more likely to undertake it and stay with it (Rachlin, 1995).

Exercise 5. Chart Your Progress.

This practice, too, is as essential as it is brief. It is also uncommon despite its proven value. The more a writer struggles, in my experience, the more he or she resists keeping logs and graphs of progress. One way that records can help is by reminding and chiding:

I started keeping a more detailed chart which also showed how many pages I had written by the end of every working day. I am not sure why I started keeping such records. I suspect that it was because, as a free-lance writer, entirely on my own, without employer or deadline, I wanted to create disciplines for myself, ones that were guilt-making when ignored. A chart on the wall served me as such a discipline, its figures scolding me or encouraging me.—IRVING WALLACE

Many other great writers, Hemingway among them, kept charts of their progress posted on their walls. But how did they tolerate this intrusion on freedom and spontaneity? Did the discipline repay the effort? Irving Wallace again:

How can a writer adhere to such rigid hours? Once, long ago, deceived by the instructors, professors, by an old romantic tradition, I had believed that a writer writes only when he feels like it, only when he is touched by mystic inspiration. But then, after studying the work habits of novelists of the past, I realized that most successful writers invest their work with professionalism.... These authors were uniformly industrious, and when they were once launched on a book they wrote regularly, day in and day out.

Charts and graphs also give feedback about how well we are progressing toward our goals, short and long term. Sometimes they indicate a need to readjust self-assigned outputs upward or downward. And, if we post them publicly, they usually elicit curiosity in other people who then monitor and reward our diligence. Always, in my experience, writers come to value their records as signs of accomplishment; visitors to their offices are often met with a smiling comment about their writing chart: "See this!?"

Charts and graphs, in combination with brief, daily sessions, encourage something else crucial to mindful ways of working: A greater awareness of time and of controlling it calmly. This experience is, whatever else, surprisingly new and effective:

> *Time is like a language and without mastery of the new vocabulary and grammar of time, no persuasion is going to change behavior.*
> *—E. T. HALL*

Structuring time without being tense about it helps writers stay mindful, and therefore find extra opportunities to work and play. When they work with a sense of structured routine, with a present orientation (rather than dwelling on missed opportunities), with effective organization, and with persistence, writers are more likely to display higher self-esteem, better health, more optimism, and more efficient work habits. It's a fact.

When they do not learn mindful ways of dealing with time, writers rush and risk depression. Then they doubt they have enough time and they induce psychological distress, anxiety, neuroticism, and physical symptoms of "time-illness" (Dorsey, 1982).

> *Neither willpower nor motivation will help students who don't know strategies including scheduling.—LINDA FLOWER*

Evidence for the Efficacy of Brief, Daily Sessions

In an ambitious attempt to document the effects of BDS, I measured the writing habits and outputs of newly hired professors over six continuous years. I tracked two groups, each with 16 new faculty. The first group began and persisted with clear habits of binge writing. The second group started and continued as regular writers who worked mostly in BDSs. Figure 11.1 shows that self-described binge writers evidenced (1) more binges of writing in long, euphoric, fatiguing sessions; (2) fewer hours spent writing on average per week; (3) fewer manuscript pages produced overall; and (4) fewer total manuscripts submitted and accepted in refereed outlets through year 6 on campus.

Two output measures, pages of scholarly prose and hours of work at writing, were taken weekly; two measures, manuscripts submitted and manuscripts accepted, represent totals over the first six study years. Differences in these outputs between the two kinds of writers were highly significant statistically—and otherwise. All 16 binge writers failed to write enough to gain retention and tenure;

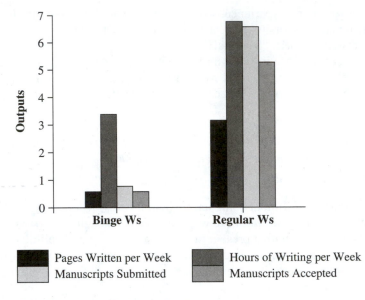

FIGURE 11.1 Effects of BDS

all 16 regular writers were awarded retention and tenure on schedule. So, the constancy and moderation of BDS associated with productivity and success at scholarly writing, while spontaneity and rushing did not. BDS also led to far less suffering (i.e., observable bouts of painful procrastinating and blocking). And its process was less often angry (e.g., comments about being victimized by writing pressures during writing times).

I've demonstrated this sort of effect for BDS in a series of published studies since 1981. Nonetheless, writers outside my programs seemed reluctant to adopt this sort of constancy and moderation until I combined its methods with mindful approaches to writing. Nothing characterizes the sort of thing better than the next writing rule.

12

Stop

Stopping is even more difficult and important than starting, as the massive literature on problems of impulse control shows all too well (Baumeister, Heatherton, & Tice, 1994). Chief among the causes for difficulties of stopping in timely fashion is a society that does little to teach patience and tolerance.

That same oversight applies to writing. So long as writers cannot hold back and stop on time, they do not become productive and healthful workers. Why, exactly? When they fail to hold back from busyness and avoidance, writers rarely end writing before diminishing returns set in, and so make the work aversive and the writing superficial. And so long as they run overtime at writing, other important things get put off and eventually supplant writing.

Failures to stop in timely fashion fortify that self-righteous enemy of fluent and comfortable writing: Busyness. When we cannot stop because of the short-term rewards of continuing, we binge. And when we binge, we usually get only one major task done per day. That often means that the next day or two must be devoted to work other than writing, or maybe a needed rest.

You might recognize the problem more readily among the teachers we saw earlier (Section I) who hadn't learned timely stopping. They waited too long to set off for class. They rushed to the podium and lectured at a rapid pace that left many students detached from the class. And, by running their classes past the bell, they tired themselves and their audiences. They got less from more.

What makes timely stopping so difficult in tasks like teaching and writing? When we have impetus in hand (especially when it was difficult to find in the first place), we dislike interrupting it; momentum can become a uniquely attractive state. Momentum seems to provide the chance to at last catch up when we are behind schedule. It tempts us to add that extra point or two that comes to mind. It brings a seeming decisiveness and fluency that we are loathe to abandon; after all, we might wonder, what if momentum like this never comes again?

> *One of the laws of composition is that a pen in motion, like matter in New-ton's first law, continues in motion unless it is compelled to change that state by forces imposed from without.—WILL AND ARIEL DURANT*

What really makes stopping difficult are the same old things that make all the efficiencies in the *nihil nimus* approach onerous at first: Deficits in patience and tolerance. Timely stopping requires the patience to put aside an uncompleted activity for another—as opposed to succumbing to the impatience that entices us to do more, preferably the whole thing, once we have momentum in the task at hand. And timely stopping needs the tolerance to overcome the temptation that otherwise inveigles us into supposing that having to stop and begin something else will squelch our genius and cause too much discomfort.

Learning to stop in timely fashion is basic to another essential skill of working at writing: Acts of omission. The practice of not saying everything you could, of not displaying all your expertise or imagination is no easy thing. Recall Jack London's comment about omission being the hardest to learn, and add this related bit of wisdom to your store of bon mots:

> *When I was twenty I was in love with words, a wordsmith. I didn't know enough to know when people were letting words get in their way. Now I like the words to disappear, like a transparent curtain.*
> *—WALLACE STEGNER*

Writing Rule 4: Stop, in Timely Fashion.

Exercises for Writing Rule 4

Exercise 1. Begin to Prepare Early for Stopping, Before Feeling the Need.

Here, early means really early! At its best, the habit of calming and slowing extends throughout whole days, beginning with awakening with awakeness. In the section on teaching, I overviewed ways to hold back from leaping out of bed and launching into old patterns of mindless rushing. More mindful ways of start-ing the day include stretching out and getting in touch with your breathing while still in bed, and then sitting, meditatively, on the edge of bed before moving on to other things. All this takes only a few minutes and it helps both teachers and writ-ers set a calm pace that includes holding back and encourages stopping. This time for early planning also helps us visualize what needs doing and how much will be enough.

Exercise 2. Start on Time, but Patiently.

The most efficient and effective writers take care to begin writing sessions on time, even when not in the mood or when busy doing something else beforehand. This, again, needs precommitting, mentally, to stopping the prior task on time, perhaps even a minute or two early.

Keep this in mind, too, when talking yourself into stopping early: Once writing sessions are brief, and once regular progress is being made, you will make great headway.

Exercise 3. Continue to Prewrite Briefly, Planfully Before Moving to Prose.

This now customary bit of warming-up not only helps generate imaginative ideas and approximations to what can be written formally but it also brings more ease in beginning daily sessions. And when brief prewriting clarifies what needs doing for the day, it reinforces earlier commitments about how much will be enough and when it will be time to stop.

Exercise 4. Continue to Pause Regularly during the Writing.

Pausing is itself a kind of stopping. It, too, falls prey to impatience and mindlessness when we imagine ourselves too busy, too far behind, too inspired to hesitate for rest and reflection.

Pausing also demands the same basic components of mindful practice as does stopping in order to be useful: (1) regular practice until the habit becomes strong, automatic, and welcome; (2) external reminders like timers and partners to cue us when to pause; and (3) ongoing mindfulness of internal signs that help prompt pausing :

- Bodily tensions and discomforts, especially in locations where you commonly symptomize stress (e.g., neck and forehead, stomach, back)
- Eye strain
- Rushed, unreflective pacing
- Fatigue, evidenced not only in a sense of tiredness but also, externally, in errors such as mistyping

Exercise 5. Stop Most Sessions Early.

This act not only combats impatience and intolerance—neither of which condone stopping on time for ourselves, let alone early—but it also leaves time to prepare writing sites and materials for the next session.

One effective way to practice Exercise 5 is to make a habit of always stopping your writing for the day just as you did for teaching, in the middle of a sentence and a paragraph. That way, resumption of the sentence and paragraph will be easier when you get back to work—even on the next day—because uncompleted tasks tend to remain fresh in mind and impel us to finish them. A related way is to stop while you still have momentum and sense of direction left over:

> *Hemingway said a long time ago—and I subscribe to it—that a smart writer quits for the day when he's really steaming, when he knows it's good and knows where it's going. If you can do that, you've fought half the next day's battle.—JAMES MICHENER*

Exercise 6. Record Your Successes at Stopping Early.

Not only should you chart, log, or graph your daily productivity (in terms of time spent and/or pages completed) but also record your progress at pausing and stopping in a timely fashion. Some of the justifications for this charting are familiar: It takes only a moment; the record can chide us to do better and it rewards us when we do; and, better yet, this act gets us to pause for a bit of mindful reflection about why timely stopping is both difficult and important. What may be surprising in this reflection is the special joy in seeing the effects of self-control that allow stopping on time; this is where writers in my programs report the realization that they can write enough without having their work interfere with other important activities.

And that bit of progress, writers tell me, brings a fresh realization about the nature of freedom: It depends on efficient use of time and resolve—including a growing ability to say no to things they don't really want to do. Stopping and saying no are much the same. Freedom depends on getting enough done on the things they want to do to permit time for leisure and rest. And it requires clear seeing that they are doing enough for now: "Before," said one writer, "I always felt the nagging pressure of being behind, of almost never putting in sufficient efforts. I thought I was free because I did things when I wanted to, but I really wasn't. I was constantly frustrated and unhappy."

One more thing bears mentioning, just the sort of thing that should appear toward the end of this chapter on timely stopping. Knowing how to stop allows time to indulge something that works best just after writing for the day: Judging your work to see if it will meet your standards. Why then and not earlier? Judging too soon and too harshly can prevent you from getting to the end.

> *Finish, then evaluate. Perfect is the enemy of good.*
> *—DONALD MURRAY*

When you've practiced early stopping for awhile on a session-to-session basis, you may be ready to try two of its more extended applications.

Exercise 7. Finish Conceptual Outlining (COL).

A peril in the ease and joy of conceptual outlining is that it can become functionally autonomous (i.e., an end in itself). So stopping COL to move to the next mode of writing can be a difficult matter; but then, everything about holding back in the right places is.

The most mindful writers I've studied pause to remind themselves about the balance involved in deciding when to stop COL. First, they guard against premature ends to the prewriting of COL, sometimes by citing the experts who advise this move. This leader of composition research speaks succinctly to benefits of keeping plans simple and clear:

We respond to the problems we pose.—LINDA FLOWER

Then, as exemplars proceed through revisions of what seem, increasingly, like enough of COL, they attend to the other side of the balance, turning to prose. Donald Murray specifies the gradual process that tells writers when it is time to turn to formal prose; each of his steps to that point is mindful, each could be already familiar from your practice of the teaching rules:

- You see possibilities for writing on something you have studied, noted, and filed.
- You have a definite, perhaps distinctive, point of view on the writing topic.
- You have listened to yourself prepare until you sense a "voice" in how you might present it; the writing will sound distinctively like you. (One writer put it this way, "I knew I had sounded too stuffy and remote before, but now I sound more natural, like I'm not straining and like I'm at ease.")
- What you have to says is news (e.g., somewhat novel information or a novel way of presenting it).
- You have a single line to begin the manuscript, one that informs and entices readers while giving you more sense of control as the writer (a modest example is "Call me Ishmael" from *Moby Dick*).
- You see a pattern in the subject, one that begins to suggest a shape for the entire piece of writing.
- You begin to see and hear images that will help guide that whole.
- You know, with some clarity, what problem you are going to solve in your manuscript and you are confident you can get it said in prose. You are, at last, ready to stop COL and start prose writing!

Now that you are, or will soon be, writing in prose, how will you know how much time to spend on it in the grand scheme of working? The answer is matter of mindfulness, specifically about moderation and balance.

13

Work with Balance

This rule, too, is based on the ways that mindful writers work. Compared to peers, exemplary new faculty spend moderate amounts of time preparing (i.e., prewriting); these mindful writers portion about the same amount of time for preliminaries as for more formal acts of writing over the course of a project. They exhibit this balance not only in obvious ways, such as investing as much time and effort overall in the COL (conceptual outline) as in the prose that mirrors it, but they also continue to intermix preliminaries and writing throughout the project. That is, mindful writers start with a dominance of prewriting and gradually reduce its role into the latter stages of working where they use it only to prime final drafting and revising. Prose writing, on the other hand, plays a small part at first but grows paramount as the writing project nears its end.

In a curious way, a reminder about struggling novice teachers (Section I) helps make the point. Beginning teachers too often spend many, many more hours preparing than in class—so long, that is, as they work inefficiently, somewhat mindlessly. The surprise in that general observation, you might recall, lay with the exemplary teachers who balanced time spent between preparing and teaching: Students rated them more highly in all dimensions of teaching. Students themselves evidenced better notetaking, more comprehension, and more civility in the classes of such teachers. And these uncommonly balanced teachers self-rated the following things more highly than did unbalanced teachers: (1) their teaching, (2) their enjoyment at doing it, and (3) their commitment to improving it. It seems inevitable, don't you agree, for a psychologist to label some people as unbalanced?

What about Balance Is So Valuable?

Balance, because it helps avoid excessivism, helps writers prepare only what needs saying and displaying (just as exemplary teachers tend to present fewer main concepts but more examples of each). And, because it makes room for preliminaries, balance frees writers to get underway while still less than perfectly prepared. It even eases the usually difficult transition from planning to prose because its gradualness of working through increasingly closer approximations to prose engages the writer in prose before she or he is aware of it. This patience in preparing also means that once in prose, writers can be more imaginative and spontaneous in writing. Why? They don't need to plan what to say and write it formally at the same time.

Constant but moderate practice of balance also means that writers are almost always doing preliminary work for new writing projects. While they finish one, balanced writers think of another project and begin to notice and collect, even to take notes and COL. Before they quite know it, they are already writing the next manuscript and are farther along than they realize:

> *If you're immersed in a project, by the time you sit down to write, you almost know the whole story.—PHILIP TAUBMAN*

Here, too, the balance of always keeping some prewriting in motion helps ease the writers past a common blocking point, the transition from ending one manuscript (with its post-partum doldrums) and starting another.

What Keeps Most Writers from Adopting Balance?

They're normal. They, like unbalanced teachers, are only following old customs. Moreover, the balance rule often seem incredible to them at first (e.g., "I would *never* believe it. I wouldn't have enough time for all that").

Mindful writers (and those on the path to becoming so) emphasize two ways of getting past this skepticism. First, they remind themselves that the evidence contradicts their doubts: The most productive, successful authors over the long run not only work in moderation but they also balance prose writing with preliminaries, including COL and mindful freewriting. Their second way of moderating skepticism amounts to practicing balance before it seems worthwhile—by trusting it (i.e., by actively waiting).

Balance Brings Harmony

This is how mindful writers describe the experience: Balance blends *excitement* with *patience* as the writing moves between focus on *discovery* to *resaying* things more clearly (i.e., what was described in Chapter 10 as the mindful interplay of imagery-based generation and of verbally-based revision). Intermixture of those two working moods and modes suggests new connections between ideas and themes for writing. And, as you know, it impels writing but in moderation.

When they at last find this deep sort of balance, writers in my programs talk about flow and its kin, mindfulness. Sometimes they cite experts with similar ideas:

> *Although flow appears effortless, it requires highly disciplined mental activity.... Jobs are easier to enjoy than free time because, like flow activities, they have built-in goals, feedback, rules, and challenges ... all of which encourage concentration and losing oneself in work.*
> *—MIHALY CSIKSZENTMIHALY*

And sometimes they generate their own parallels: "Balance grows with mindfulness, and vice versa."

Writing Rule 5: Work with Balance.

Exercises for Writing Rule 5

While the experience of flow and mindfulness remain somewhat indescribable for most writers at this point, the urge it generates is expressed concretely. Writers seek more balance between time spent on prewriting and prose writing. They even want to balance writing, gradually, with time for sitting at mindfulness meditation or in other "not doing." Their busyness has, by now, decreased to the extent that daily schedules typically allow this luxury.

Exercise 1. Approximate the Time Spent Meditating to That Spent Writing.

This sort of balance works best when acquired patiently and gradually. It works well enough when the time for meditating is kept far briefer than writing—but still constant. Still, the more you practice the calm, focused attention of mindfulness meditation, the easier it becomes to stay mindful while writing. Similarly, the more you remain mindful while working, the more readily you regain mindfulness when you've regressed to mindlessness. Most important, mindfulness meditation helps you make your writing your "practice" of mindfulness because as the two become more balanced, they grow more alike. And this balance, perhaps because its combination brings strength and depth to mental action, helps build resilience:

Equanimity doesn't mean keeping things even; it is the capacity to return to balance in the midst of an alert, responsive life. I don't want to be constantly calm.... What I value is the capacity to be balanced between times.... Meditators in research studies show quicker return to calm, focused attention after a startle response.—SYLVIA BOORSTEIN

How does mindfulness meditation begin to teach/implant this sort of balance? The most fundamental way starts with the awakeness and clear-seeing of imbalances, then of how they detach what we do from our true selves:

Many of us are so alienated from our basic needs, so programmed to run after what the ego wants, that we have to relearn the basic mechanics of how attention and intention actually work. This is hard to realize when the mind sets up its own separate agenda for fulfilling other kinds of desires, ones that are loveless, without joy or satisfaction.
—DEEPAK CHOPRA

This potential for relieving the self-estrangement that lies within is so important that it has been a constant theme of psychotherapy (usually without quite being called mindfulness):

If aspects of the person remain undigested—cut off, denied, projected, rejected, indulged, otherwise unassimilated—they become the points around which the core forces of greed, hatred, and delusion attach themselves.... As Wilhelm Reich demonstrated in his groundbreaking work on the formation of character, the personality is built on these points of self-estrangement; the paradox is that what we take to be so real, our selves, is constructed out of a reaction against just what we do not wish to acknowledge. We tense up around that which we are denying, and we experience ourselves through our tensions.—MARK EPSTEIN

When we no longer rely on our hidden thoughts and their tensions to generate writing, we not only come to know ourselves better but we also write more directly and simply, in our own voice. Why? The mindfulness that keeps most interfering and irrational thoughts away also allows us to work with unified motivations and needs. Blocked writers struggle against themselves; exemplars connect with their healthy selves and thus fare better at writing what they know and feel.

When we integrate mindfulness with our work, a wonderful thing happens: Less interference between thinking and doing (and between intention and action) because mindfulness can put thinking out into the moment and to work in rational fashion—or else it lets the thought go for now. As mindful writers, we think about what needs doing and can be done now, while doing it (e.g., clarifying preliminary images and thoughts by stating them aloud and putting them in COL).

Hypomania. But what, some participants have asked me at this point, about rushing, bingeing, and euphoria as ways of generating writing, acts beloved by writers for their immoderation, imbalance, and genius? I agree that a similar transfiguration of image-into-writing can be managed with immoderation—but not in so reliable or heathy a way over the long run as with the calm and clear seeing of mindfulness.

Indeed, both mindful and frenzied writers occasionally report a remarkable juxtaposition of nonverbal imaging and writing, with no apparent intermediate actions. But only mindful writers, so far as I can tell, manage this congruence with calm and broad understanding of why it works, of how to make it work better, and of how to induce it during brief work sessions.

And while both kinds of writers report seeing themselves writing, even seeing what they write as though taking dictation, only mindful writers can reproduce that state with constant health and high output over the long run. Frenzied and hypomanic writers, as we will see in the next chapter, relish the experience of frenzy, excuse its general unproductiveness, and often avoid it for its aftereffects.

Exercise 2. Use Balance to Keep a Second
Writing Project Going.

If, for example, you've begun your ongoing writing project with less than balance between the prewriting and prose than you now want, start another writing project with more deliberation, more mindfulness. Don't abandon your present project; just make brief openings each weekday for the patient, unrushed beginnings of a new one. If you set aside your current project, do so with moderation; the longer it sits idly, unseen and untouched, the harder it will be to resume. Constancy fosters finishing; inconstancy risks procrastinating.

Commitment to a second writing assignment, often a third (but no more, according to exemplary writers in academe), suffices. Among other things, it helps reduce the sameness of writing at just one project and it leads to interplay of ideas and working styles.

Exercise 3. Continue Preliminaries Once in Prose.

Prewrite, at least briefly, before almost any daily bout of writing, even once well into prose. One exemplary strategy consists of retyping the last half-page (or less) from the prior day's output. Do it mindfully, deliberately, patiently. Revise only if the changes can be made quickly, decisively. But do it even if you have to recopy everything without change. This helps you retain the two main rewards of prewriting: (1) momentum, and (2) awareness of what you were writing before and where you will probably go next.

As a rule, this exercise of rewriting a bit of what you've written the session before leads to painless starts and almost unnoticeable extension into the new writing for the day.

Exercise 4. Balance Prime-Time and Off-Time Work.
Don't let less important things such as writing of e-mail or remodeling your living quarters take more time than writing (or teaching). Do them in brief, daily sessions where possible.

Exercise 5. Balance Work and Play.
In case you suppose this point is obvious, I warn you that another distinctive quality of poor starters in my studies is an almost complete lack of hobbies put into action or of playing in ways that are unpressured and fun. Who was it who wrote, "All work and no play make Jack a dull boy"? That blocked and rather angry writer in *The Shining*.

14

<hr>

Let Go of Negative Thoughts

The imbalances we've seen so far—including the usual dominance of generation over reflection in freewriting—amount to mindlessness. The imbalance we confront in this chapter is no exception. When we work mindlessly, we encourage an excess of tense and negative thinking that distracts and undermines our writing.

One of the first writers to describe this insight clearly and publicly was Joanna Field, a young psychologist in the 1930s struggling to find mindfulness on her own. She, sensibly, wanted to rid herself of the confusion and distress that dominated her days. Because she could locate few usefully directive books about finding happiness, she set her own course. She began by patiently observing her mind in action:

> *I was eventually able to gain a fair idea of how my thought behaved when left to itself. One of the first things that struck me was its inconsequence and irresponsibility. . . . I could never predict what would be in my mind the next moment, and I was often amazed at the way these thoughts completely ignored what I felt to be important occasions. . . . This chattering mind was an unreasonable mind: it seemed unable to escape from the narrow circle of its own interests; it recognized only itself and it was always trying to force the rest of the world to do the same.*

To lessen what she called her blind and mean-spirited thinking, she relaxed and lowered herself below the rising clouds of her chattering thoughts, to focus on the direct experience of being alive (what we might call mindfulness).

Even though Joanna Field never got much notice in a psychology then ruled by masculine demands for laboratory experimentalism, strategies similar to hers—of noticing, then calmly evaluating, and then replacing negative thoughts—eventually became widespread. Albert Ellis's methods of rational-emotive therapy may be the best known of those; he coaches patients to calmly notice irrational thoughts and to dispute them by staying in the moment, realistically. This cognitive approach, now so common in psychology, has at last grown popular because it works.

Consider one reason why: Ordinarily, negative thinking is far, far more common than the positive sort. Perhaps this imbalance owes to our evolutionary past or to contemporary deficits in society. Just as likely, it reflects a general lack of education about mindful ways of living and working. Whatever their origins, our internal critics and other negative self-talk can easily overwhelm and block writing. These are the dominant patterns of thinking about writing revealed in my earliest studies amongst new faculty who struggled and disappointed:

- They thought perfectionistically and so they prematurely concluded they could not write well enough.
- They dwelt on prospects of criticism or rejection and they wanted to avoid writing.
- Internal censors haunted their thinking as they wrote and inhibited them from proceeding beyond narrow, premature attention to things like spelling, grammar, and style.
- They thought of writing as unbearably difficult and unrewarding and so they opted for things easier and quicker.
- They thought they knew enough about what they would write to excuse rushing into prose (without conceptual outlining and other prewriting) and so found themselves stumbling and lost.
- As they got farther behind in their writing, thoughts about it emphasized product over process. With that imbalance came another: A tendency to consider the process of working at writing mysterious, one better left unexamined.

But there is more, much more.

Negative Thinking Has Broad Effects

Pessimism and helplessness bring depression and inaction. Anxieties make us inefficient, impatient problem solvers; writing is, whatever else, a problem-solving task. Its excessive self-focus keeps us isolated and shy and unlikely to solicit social support—and then overreactive to public criticism. Its self-criticism inclines us to despair and, at least for awhile, to indecision. And its impulsivity makes us prefer other activities that offer immediate rewards and relief. The more we come to rely on quick and easy escape, the more likely our minds will object by way of negative thinking when we attempt to write anything more than a quick memo.

Positive thinking, as we will see, is far more efficient. To head us in that direction, I begin with this question:

How can you tell if your thinking is getting in the way of your writing?

Mindfully. First, by noticing when your thoughts delay and discourage, particularly when their discomfort makes you turn to a less threatening activity. Second, by clearly, calmly seeing when you are worrying about correctness and perfection too early. And, third, by keeping in mind the costs of negative thinking.

Experimental Evidence about Commonality and Costs

In a study (Boice, 1985a), I collected "talking-aloud" protocols from two kinds of academic writers as they began writing projects: one group with documented records as blocked writers and another group who wrote with occasional fluency. The blockers were most afflicted with negativism but even their more fluent colleagues depicted surprisingly high levels of negative thinking (see Table 14.1). These data can tell you a couple things worth remembering. First, the most common and problematic of negative thoughts were more about the hard work of writing (and about why something more emotionally pleasing in the short run might be done in its stead) than about criticism and perfectionism. Second, even the relatively fluent writers reported surprisingly high levels of aversive thinking when

TABLE 14.1   Percentage of 10-Minute Bouts of Talking Aloud in Which the Thought Was Salient

Type of Cognition/Thought	Blockers ($N = 40$)	Nonblockers ($N = 20$)
1. "Writing is too fatiguing, unpleasant"	65%	43%
2. "It's OK to wait for now and procrastinate"	30%	10%
3. "I'm too upset, depressed to write"	23%	5%
4. "I feel impatient about what I'm getting done"	20%	13%
5. "My writing needs to be superior"	13%	3%
6. "My writing will be unfairly criticized"	8%	18%
7. "Good writing follows rigid rules"	3%	0%

TABLE 14.2   Type of Self-Talk Reported

Group of Writers	Maladaptive	Neutral	Psych-Up	None
Blockers	74%	8%	7%	11%
Nonblockers	42%	6%	49%	3%

getting projects underway; they eventually managed writing but they suffered while resisting it

A different look at these data in Table 14.2 reveals an advantage for the non-blockers. Semi-fluent writers, more often than their usually blocked counterparts, spent comparatively more of their thinking on positive statements that helped psych them up to write (e.g., "This will be pleasant enough once I get going") and about the same small amount of thinking on neutral thoughts (e.g., "It's snowy outside"). But the semi-fluent writers evidenced many more bouts with no discursive/reflective thinking. I judged a period of time as "unthinking" when writers accustomed to talking their writing process aloud (1) ceased commenting; (2) seemed more immersed and efficient at writing and pausing; and (3) afterward, told they could remember the writing but no thoughts while doing it. During such bouts, writers were most fluent and pleased in their work.

Still, semi-fluent writers most often said aloud what they were writing as they wrote it and they hesitated until they could say it clearly. Blockers, in contrast, spent more time with me relating their self-talk, less at talking about writing or doing it; as a rule, they told themselves how unreasonable their task was, that it's OK to procrastinate, and so on—the usual kinds of negative thinking we saw in Table 14.1. And when they were not thinking, blockers most often engaged in strong emotions such as panic or in related behaviors like off-task busyness (e.g., arranging their desktops). All this fits with what is known about mindfulness: Expert practitioners of mindfulness meditation not only revel, calmly, in their release from most negative thinking and strong emotion; they also like to mention their freedom from discursive thinking. When they write, that means they no longer need to say or hear whole sentences, even approximations, to generate writing; instead, they simply let go and allow images to generate writing for the moment. Said another way, they work without having to carry on a story or a chronic discourse; they just do it.

These most mindful writers employ other useful clues about the most basic methods for moderating the role of thought:

> *Sit, focus, and be alert to the periodic presence of these thoughts [that leap ahead in planning, anticipating, and worrying] . . . [realize that] the*

thoughts themselves are not the problem; they are natural. Mindfulness of these thoughts will enable you to notice them without getting involved.—SYLVIA BOORSTEIN

So when we encounter thoughts that hang on and sweep us away, label it all thinking with as much openness and kindness as we can muster, and let it dissolve.—PEMA CHODRIN

The most mindful writers I've studied emphasize the shift away from thinking of any kind to working in the present (with balance from occasional thinking/reflection about what they are doing, of course). They talk about having learned to let go, calmly and nonjudgmentally, of most thoughts during writing sessions, especially those of no use in the moment. In particular, they mention something like this: "It's simpler and more direct. I don't really think so much now; that's wasteful, tiring, you know. Instead, what I'm doing is just letting images turn into writing, almost like an interested observer who needs to pay attention but not interfere very much."

And yet, when I've had mindful writers talk with groups of struggling writers, these experts put far more weight on the basic practices that precede direct writing. "First things first," they like to say.

Writing Rule 6: Moderate Negative Thinking.

Exercises for Writing Rule 6

Correctives for negative thinking grow easier, mindful writers (and mindful teachers) point out, once you are already practicing mindfulness. The best strategies, in my programs for writers and teachers are the simplest of these. (They are also so redundant with Section I, on teaching, that they may try your patience. I hope not.)

Exercise 1. Notice Your Thinking at Writing Times.
This is difficult in the short run because most of us are unpracticed at noticing much of our nearly constant self-talk. Most of it ordinarily goes unheard (particularly so long as we are mindless), but all of it is potentially powerful and problematic. The key solutions are all too familiar—patience and tolerance. Patience by way of pauses to listen, even when nothing seems to be happening in the nether regions of our minds. Tolerance to calmly hear the amazingly negative, depressing, irrational things we often say to ourselves.

Begin by noticing (and noting) your self-talk at just one critical time, the few minutes that precede the beginning of a writing session. Look for signs of blind, mindless thinking like the ones I listed earlier in this chapter (Table 14.1).

Exercise 2. Dispute Negative Thinking.
This act amounts to noticing and challenging the usual absurdity and deceptive-ness of negative thinking by consciously listening to how rational the thought is when repeated slowly and calmly. If, for instance, you find yourself thinking that your writing assignment is unfair and that the assigner doesn't deserve your work done well or on time, practice a pause to look for irrationalities. For example, you may realize that you have the right to change the assignment, you might even come to like it as much as you did when you agreed to accept it, or you might decide that fairness is not so much the issue for the moment as simply getting to work.

Another kind of awakeness and clear seeing is just as important: Appreciating that part of the reason we engage in too much thinking and story-telling (espe-cially of the negative kind) is the perverse pleasure they provide; the stories we constantly tell ourselves entertain and excite, explain and excuse, and distract or exaggerate. What are we trying to escape in the short run? What really stands between us and our best writing?

> *A restlessness and fear . . . a level of experience that requires making*
> *friends with ourselves at the most profound level possible . . . and the*
> *fears that the fears have no power if you do not need them.*
> *—PEMA CHODRIN*

Exercise 3. Replace Negativities with More
Constructive, Optimistic Thinking.
Once you have disputed and exposed an irrationality, turn your thinking to getting on with the task—and, eventually, to getting past much reliance on thinking-at-all-once writing. With practice at this kind of letting go, images for writing replace much of your usual thinking.

> *You can't think and hit at the same time.—YOGI BERRA*

An essence of this third exercise is moving away from *product* orientations to *process* modes of working; the former are more about thinking, especially of the worrisome sort, than the latter. Because product orientations rely on thinking outside the moment, they aim too soon at outcomes and induce unnecessary pres-sures about working fast enough. Process styles, in contrast, focus attention on the present and not on regrets about the past or anxieties about the future With regular practice at process modes of noticing and replacing irrational thoughts—in the present moment—writers learn to get themselves on track with a simple and bor-rowed reminder like this: "Just do it."

Remember, too, what makes the transition away from old habits of mindless-ness and its negative thinking so difficult at first:

*One reason mindfulness may seem effortful is because of the pain of neg-
ative thoughts. When thoughts are uncomfortable, people often struggle
to erase them. The pain, however, does not come from mindful awareness
of these thoughts, but from a single-minded understanding of the painful
event.—ELLEN LANGER*

What works better than single-mindedness? Mindfulness.

In the longer run, this mindful letting go of negative thinking leads to deeper
changes. First, writers see the inefficiency of pessimism and the efficiency of optimism. That is, they learn to reinterpret the things that happen in a more positive
light (e.g., by supposing that failures do not reflect a personal weakness so much
as a correctable problem, such as having prepared insufficiently or needing to find
a new audience). Second, writers freed from constant thinking as they write attend
more to pacing and to levels of quality, even to objective information about rates
of output.

Other Experimental Evidence

Ellen Langer (1989), the most prominent researcher on mindfulness, finds that the
demonstrable costs of mindlessness and its negativity include:

- A narrow self-image that encourages unreasonable social comparisons about
  our work, as when we look only at a productive person's accomplishments,
  rather than at the processes he or she went through to get there. Then we
  mindlessly label ourselves as failures by comparison.
- An unintended meanness toward ourselves and others because we or they
  have fallen into routines of blind thinking that go unquestioned. So, for example, we might make impatient and reflexive self-statements about a lack of
  intelligence when others (or ourselves) do not display immediate brilliance.
- A blind compartmentalization of our thoughts (e.g., so that people from blue-
  collar backgrounds must have less inborn natural talent as writers than do the
  upper classes).
- A readier loss of feeling in control when we limit intelligent choices (e.g., by
  blaming our failures on others) and so we see fewer ways we could work
  against a background of chronic frustration and anger.
- An inclination to learned helplessness because we remain mindlessly passive
  in situations that could be easily handled with awakeness and its decisiveness.
- A stunted potential in our work because mindlessness (by diminishing self-
  image and self-esteem with its constant and negative chatter) narrows our
  choices and weds us to single-minded attitudes.

Langer's evidence also suggests that mindful alternatives are easier and better than staying with mindless negativity:

> *While some people think that mindfulness takes a lot of work, research discussed in my book shows that mindfulness leads to feelings of control, greater freedom of action, and less burnout.—ELLEN LANGER*

15

$$Moderate\ Emotions$$

This seventh rule for mindful practice of writing, like the six before it, is about self-control. Here, though, awareness shifts to something even less often considered by writers, modulating emotions while working. Why strive for moderation? Writing with too little emotion results in dull experience, weak motivation, and mundane output. Writing with too much emotion exhausts the writer and makes the work aversive. Rule 7 aims to avoid both extremes.

The hardest part is reining in emotion and we already know some of the reasons why:

- Impatience and its impulsivity
- Mindlessness and its love of extremes
- Momentum and its short-term rewards

One other difficulty in moderating emotions may be most problematic for writers:

- States of high emotion are addictive.

High emotion in writing usually takes the form of hypomania.

Hypomania

This near-state of mania, with its intense rushing and prolonged emotional escalation, is pathological (American Psychiatric Association, 1994); although hypomania's short-term benefits are tempting (and addictive), its long-term costs far outweigh them. The problem with hypomania goes beyond the superficial and disorganized writing it often produces—even beyond the lingering exhaustion that makes restarting difficult. Hypomania commonly leads to dysphoria (just as mania begets depression) and to its sad inaction or angry impulsivity. With this cycle of ups and downs in place, writers work only sporadically. When they at last break out of their dysphoria, they need the emotional state that ensures the opposite experience: hypomania. And when they have drained themselves in a rushed and emotional binge necessary for hypomania, they face another bout of dysphoria. In fact, hypomania co-relates with:

- A measurable wake of depression after its manicky bingeing
- Less output and quality of writing in the long run
- More long-term difficulties in writing, including blocking

Hypomania also undermines the general health and social life of writers. Consider the case of a devoted binge writer, Ayn Rand:

> *Ayn suffered both physical and mental agonies in her struggle. Sometimes Frank [her husband] would find her slumped over her desk as if she were unable to rise again; she would emerge from her study with new deep lines on her brow and her body sagging with weariness. At other times she projected an emotional tension that was painful to see; she could not eat or sleep, or even talk. . . . As the last of her powers of endurance were spent, as her nervous state grew more jagged and fragile, the bitterness and pain in her personality began to take the ascendancy.*
> —*BARBARA BRANDON*

All this doesn't mean that hypomania has no place in writing. Although writers with the most fluency and happiness typically keep emotions at low to midrange levels, they also know the value of changing their pace. Sometimes they use a burst of excitement to work past their internal censors or to convey the appropriate voice in their writing. Other times they write dispassionately (just to get ideas down on screen or paper), knowing they can wait to find more imagination in revising it later. Best of all, in their opinion, they work with a rhythm based in mild happiness, one punctuated by occasional swings in mood that do not persist to the point that impedes returning to moderation (and mindfulness).

Why Moderation of Emotions in Writing Is Generally Unmentioned

The reasons are, of course, much the same as for the neglect of mindfulness practice in our society. While moderation of emotions sounds like common sense, it seems impractical in real life. And where the idea has been tried, it has lost favor.

Early psychotherapists, for example, particularly those with an interest in Eastern philosophies, made a clear case for its value:

> *Poets and philosophers of all times have known that it is never the serene, well-balanced person who falls victim to psychic disorders, but the one torn by inner conflicts.—KAREN HORNEY*

Some of those pioneers were even more direct: Pierre Janet, Freud's predecessor, found that work with too fast a pace and too high a level of tension caused neuroses marked by emotional instability (Ellenberger, 1970). Nowadays, only a few psychologists continue to document the costs of working under extreme conditions of emotion. Baumeister, Heatherton, and Tice (1994) currently lead this dissident movement and they promote generally unappreciated findings like these:

- When people rush mindlessly, they respond so exclusively to their emotional needs that they are unlikely to solve more important problems.
- High emotion elicits high arousal, which consumes the very energy needed for self-stopping; states of high emotion are therefore self-sustaining beyond the point of diminishing returns.
- High emotions invite thoughts with broadly meaningful understandings (e.g., concerns about the worth of one's writing and of oneself) and these, in turn, risk the inhibitions, such as blocking, that exist at similarly high levels.

This information not only remains generally unknown and unimplemented in psychology, but also in composition teaching and other disciplines that educate writers. The reason, simply, is that most writers and teachers of writing aren't interested. They place writing into its own isolated category of behaving (a sign of mindlessness, as we saw in the prior chapter), with its own special rules that cannot be examined like ordinary phenomena (see Boice, 1996c). So, for example, writers often resist empirically based information about the counterproductivity of writing in hypomanic binges; even the "hardest" scientists in academe have insisted to me that they simply know, with a confidence not dependent on evidence, that high emotion produces the most brilliant writing.

Recall some of the reasons why this mindless tradition may be changing: (1) newly popular directives from expert practitioners of mindfulness meditation about slowing down and working in the moment, with calm and clear seeing; and (2) similar advice from mindfully-oriented writing teachers:

> *So try to calm down, get quiet, breathe, and listen. . . . If you stop trying to control your mind so much, you'll have intuitive hunches about what this or that character is all about.—ANNE LAMOTT*

We also have (3) the mindful habits and attitudes of exemplary writers to model after.

Writing Rule 7: Moderate Emotions.

Exercises for Writing Rule 7

Writers on the way to mindfulness, at about this point in my programs, typically become close observers of their moods; they notice which emotions impede or impel writing. And here the most mindful of them become patient experimenters who compare the effects of working with hypomania versus moderation. This is the usual progression:

Exercise 1. Monitor and Record Mood Levels and Types during Writing Sessions.

Begin by rating emotions on a scale measuring, for example, high nervous tension versus calm patience. That emotional continuum might have endpoints labeled as *anxiety–serenity*. With practice at noticing affective states as simple as happiness while working (something most writers have not been educated to do), other, more elusive emotions such as anger and fear become more discernible. The importance of recognizing anger and fear is that their narrowness maintains a status quo contrary to mild happiness and confidence.

Aim first for ongoing awareness of how emotions affect your writing. If you have trouble feeling emotions while you write, try awakening to emotions that occur during your regular bouts of "not doing," in practice of mindfulness meditation while sitting or walking.

[handwritten margin note: be aware / Mindful]

Exercise 2. Set Reasonable Goals for Emotional Moderation.

At the least, try to maintain the calm pacing you already know about as you begin daily sessions of writing. Then, add the occasional emotion of mild happiness to it. Why? To optimize the kinds of problem solving essential to writing. To make writing more enjoyable and rewarding.

How can you tell if you are mildly happy while writing? Pause and observe; compare your feelings and expressions with other experiences. How can you induce this state if it's not already there? Scan for negative thinking, supplant it with positive thoughts—better yet, let it go. Then, plant a faint smile that helps relax your face and your mind (this grows easier with practice, even for New Yorkers). And notice moments when your writing is calm but joyful.

Expect to struggle, at least at first, in the absence of usual tension. You might suppose, mistakenly and mindlessly, that you are not working hard enough (or suffering enough). In the longer run, anticipate something else I've already mentioned. While most mindful writers commonly work with a low but noticeable level of emotions, they also rely on changes of pace and perspective to keep themselves awake and interested.

The two major positive emotions are: 1) Interest-excitement generated by a moderate level of novel stimulation or complexity and ambiguity in one's environment; and 2) the joy experienced in matching or assimilating such novel or complex information with previously established schemata. . . . Reflective awareness and long processing may slow reactivity, lead to some loss of information (but most of our environments are highly redundant anyway), and establish a sense of control over input that maintains an emotional stance of interest and excitement or joy.
—JEROME SINGER

Exercise 3. Work and Write with a Sense of Rhythm.
This seemingly mysterious skill begins with pausing to shift emotions in timely fashion. Its basis, holding back, is the hardest part of mindfulness. But holding back brings more awareness about when to slow down to get ready to stop, and a greater appreciation that writing can be done at differing tempos. Sometimes, you might find benefit in writing as deliberately as though you are doing calligraphy and crafting succinct, clear sentences. Sometimes you might look to add elements of repetition or of parallel. Sometimes you might ensure a steady pace by working in concert with your breathing, even a metronome. Other times you might make a contrasting point or add a short sentence to change the pace. All this helps establish a pattern and a voice as a writer:

> *Vary your discourse; a style too equal and uniform puts us to sleep. . . .*
> *Keep a sharp ear for the cadence of your words.—BOILEAU*

Exercise 4. Accept Difficult Emotions.
Because mindful writing brings you face to face with real problems in your life, it also occasions pain. What then? Don't avoid or escape the pain by turning to procrastination or bingeing. Instead, slow down and embrace it, mindfully but briefly:

> *Putting your attention on your feelings gets you closer to the state of witnessing: you observe the pain without getting all wrapped up in all the secondary blame, avoidance, and denial that usually follow. . . . It takes detachment to bring understanding, and if you get caught up in your hurt, you won't see the reason behind it.—DEEPAK CHOPRA.*

Exercise 5. Work without Sustained High Emotion.
In the research brief that follows, I show how rushing, bingeing, and immoderate emotion (compared to writing with more constancy and moderation) lower productivity in the long run and bring unnecessary suffering and depression to writers.

Evidence for the Benefits of Working with Moderate Emotions.
From longitudinal studies of hundreds of writers new to professorial careers (Boice, 1992c), I selected 16 new faculty members who came to campus with the most extreme attitudes about the role of emotion in writing. During my visits to their offices as they wrote (or tried to), 8 of them stood out as self-described romantics who claimed that their best writing needed high emotions and strong suffering, and 8 valued calm and moderate happiness as writers.

Group 1.   The eight highly emotional writers worked at a hurried pace and said that they deliberately maintained it until they felt euphoric, brilliant, and frenzied. During our discussions they expressed strong disdain for their peers who planned to write with moderate emotion: Those "mechanical writers," the romantics assured me, would produce less overall, write with less creativity, and find less acceptance for their writing in prestigious outlets. The particular advantage of working amid crazed emotions, romantics assured me, was its creative madness and its special genius.

Group 2.   The eight writers working with moderation of emotion were also in their second year on campus when I began studying them more formally. They, too, had demonstrated unmistakable patterns, but of constant and unhurried writing during their first years on campus. They, unlike the first group, never mentioned needing Muses, sudden inspiration, or heated emotions to write. Nor did these constantly moderate writers express much concern for brilliance, creativity, or perfection—at least in the present. And, finally, these moderates could not be coaxed into strong judgments about the writers in Group 1 (e.g., "If it works for them, fine").

Data Collection.   All 16 writers agreed, without coercion or pressure, to endure even more of my scrutiny through their sixth years on campus (all were at research universities with clear requirements of writing and publishing for retention/tenure). All 16 writers soon learned to ignore my presence as they worked, even to disregard the appearances of my graduate assistant who periodically checked the reliability of my ratings of work habits and my notes of comments.

Results.   My first task, given challenges from critics of my earlier work, was to document the extent to which romantic writers displayed rushing and euphoria, compared to their moderate counterparts. In fact, as Figure 15.1 shows, the romantics displayed far higher frequencies of hypomanic behavior: (1) They had more sessions, once underway, with distinctively high rates of words per minute, (2) more spontaneous reports of euphoria while writing, (3) more sessions where they worked impulsively and without resort to notes/outlines/plans, and (4) more errors in typing/writing that interfered with their fluency.

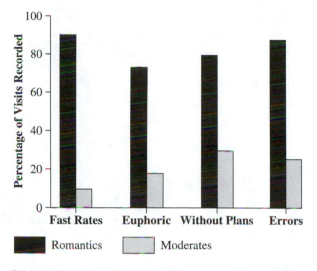

FIGURE 15.1   Hypomania

Differences between the romantics' levels of hypomania from those of writers in Group 2 were highly reliable statistically. Thus, the romantic writers had been correct in describing their writing styles as highly emotional, rushed, impulsive, and spontaneous—even in supposing their style carried some small disadvantages of higher error rates while composing and keyboarding in what they called a fine frenzy.

Figure 15.2 shows that these romantic writers resemble the binge writers of Chapter 11 in terms of work habits and long-term productivity. That is, writers who professed romantic beliefs of creative madness produced the same disappointing result as writers who worked in binges because deadlines forced them to. Here, as there, binges (intense, fast-paced, and rarely uninterrupted bouts of writing for at least 2 hours per session) documented per month were more frequent in romantic than for moderate writers. Moderates, in contrast, excelled in *all* long-term measures of output they needed for tenure/promotion (e.g., 1.8 vs. 0.2 manuscripts a year over their first 2 years on campus—a difference that continued until at least year 5).

Moderates, writers who wrote with deliberately calm emotions, worked with more brief, daily sessions (BDSs). Moreover, their BDSs were far more often marked by a calm pace (at least 4 pauses an hour) and short duration (no more than 90 minutes a day). And moderates, contrary to the expectations of their more romantic colleagues, managed far higher levels of output, both in terms of pages written per month and manuscripts finished and submitted to refereed outlets per year over the five years of formal observation and recording. (Recall that the formal study began after participants had displayed consistent patterns of high or moderate emotion during year 1 on campus.)

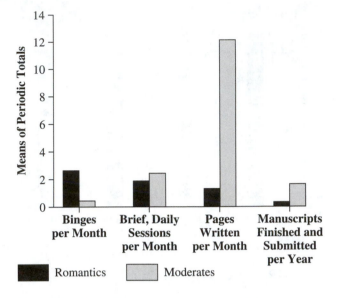

FIGURE 15.2   Bingeing and Productivity

Not until romantics were confronted with evidence about how their working style related to levels of creativity did they begin to admit their approach might not be ideal. They had assumed that creativity was a sure benefit of working with hypomania (e.g., "That's what divine madness means"). Here, too, I had data to test their assumption (Figure 15.3).

From the outset of formal observations and recordings, I enlisted all 16 writers to note their thoughts of innovative and useful ideas for writing on notecards. (Apparently this index, based on self-reporting of creative ideas as they occur, is more meaningful than typical systems of estimating creativity during writing.) In my weekly visits and calls I had writers restate and explain their entries for me. I counted only those I judged as original and potentially useful for her or his writing project. (Here, too, I used a second observer to check for agreement.)

Mindfulness, of sorts, may explain that difference in creativity. Romantics, for whom ideal writing meant suffering, excused their low levels of creativity as a result of keeping writing out of mind between sessions. Romantics were also observed to pause and reflect less often during writing, apparently because they were working at full speed or not at all. Moderates, on the other hand, reported thinking about their writing as a routine, enjoyable habit; they emphasized a fondness for coming to writing sessions with novel ideas and new directions in mind. When they talked aloud their writing for me, they, unlike romantics, used pauses to generate even more creative ideas.

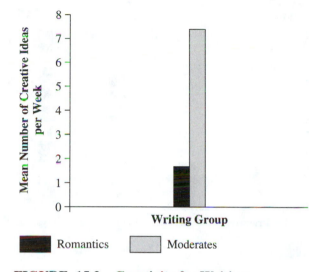

FIGURE 15.3   Creativity for Writing

Faced with these data and reflections about them, three of the binge writers began to question their writing habits and attitudes. The other five remained adamant, concluding that academic writing allowed them too little outlet for their creativity. All eight of the bingers, though, wondered if they had worked in ways that induced too much suffering. Indeed, binge writers did evidence far more discomfort connected with writing than did moderates, so much so that it seemed to interfere with their planned resumptions of writing.

To measure their misery objectively, I subjected all 16 writers to the Beck Depression Inventory (BDI) during times just after beginnings of semesters where all of them reported feeling especially overdue as writers. I administered this brief self-inventory of depressive symptoms just prior to the first writing session (prewrite), just after (postwrite), one day after (day later), and two days later. Bingers far more often scored BDI levels considered significant in terms of depression at each of those testing intervals (Figure 15.4).

Note that the difference between percentages of writers with problematically high levels of depressive symptoms grew most dramatically by the day after the first writing session of the semester (a session in which bingers invariably binged and moderates performed with moderation). The individual BDI levels usually reached by individual romantics in the days following their emotional binge at writing are those that typically interfere with fluency in writing in my other studies of depressed writers.

Moderate writers, finally, displayed higher levels of interest in activities such as meditation and spirituality even as they came to campus. Their romantic coun-

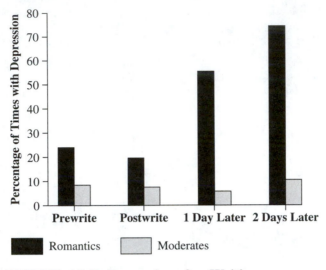

FIGURE 15.4   Depression after Writing

terparts, in contrast, evidenced higher levels of busyness and unhappiness in relation to tasks like writing.

Literary Evidence for an Advantage of Working in Brief, Daily Sessions

The kinds of data just presented don't appeal to all writers, I've discovered. Some novice professors prefer examples from "real" writers, not academics. One of the most informative cases comes from a biography of the novelist Joseph Conrad (Meyers, 1991).

It was Conrad who, when binging and depressed, suffered terribly from a crippling neurasthenia that paralyzed his writing arm and depressed his spirit. No wonder, given the writing habits of his early career: He often spent whole days struggling to get his writing started. If he got underway at all, it was usually in the evening and in binges. Despite these prolonged struggles, Conrad's outputs were small, often no more than 300 words a day; Conrad's editors also suffered over his slow, unpredictable pace. Despite its drawbacks, Conrad defended his style of waiting for crisis and frenzy before writing as one of "exquisite agony."

But during the middle stage of his career as a writer, Conrad was forced, more or less, into a mindful style of working when the novelist Ford Madox Ford became his close friend, benefactor, mentor, and amanuensis. This is how Meyers (1991) put it:

like a writing coach

Ford's literary help was even more significant [than renting him his house cheaply and advancing him money]. He listened as Conrad read aloud what he had written, suggesting words, phrases, and forgotten incidents. Ford proof-read and corrected Conrad's manuscripts. He even took dictation as Conrad talked aloud what he would like to write.

Ford also stimulated Conrad to write when he would otherwise have been overcome by depression and other forms of debilitating illness. In the main, Ford managed this coaching by structuring Conrad's writing days with planning and on-task work, always in a context of mindfulness about what could be written, always with an emphasis on staying in the moment and writing according to plan. The result for Conrad was a remarkable increase in both his writing output and his health. Conrad could, while talking aloud the writing process with Ford, write a thousand or more words day after day. During this period he made significant progress on *Nostromo* and finished *One Day More.* And over that time, Ford's moderation of Conrad's emotions during writing sessions removed the madness from his work, even while its productivity and publishability went up.

The problem with that arrangement was that Conrad never became more than a passive and skeptical recipient of Ford's mindful coaching. So, as Conrad's resentment of Ford's interventions grew, the two had a falling-out and Conrad resumed his old ways of tormented, maddened writing. His productivity and his quality of writing dropped as his hypomania reappeared; the creative struggle he suffered while writing *Under Western Eyes* was so intense that it led to Conrad's complete nervous breakdown (Meyers, 1991):

Conrad [again] suffered recurring pain from chronic gout and the ever-present anxiety about money. He often started his novels without a clear plan and had no idea where the book would end—or when. . . . In the sum-mer of 1909 Pinker [his publisher], dissatisfied with Conrad's failure to deliver the long-awaited manuscript, threatened to sever their business connection. In December they reached a crisis when Pinker refused to advance any more funds and Conrad [vowed] to throw the manuscript into the fire.

Here, as in my more direct and extensive studies of academic writers, this romantic approach to writing—amid high and sustained passions—was far less productive and healthy than working with the moderation of generally calm emotions. I know of no exceptions in other accounts of how writers worked.

Still, beliefs in creative madness are as popular as ever. Witness the admiration directed by scholarly reviewers to recent books such as Kay Jamison's (1993) *Touched with Fire,* an unsubstantiated glamorization of working amid hypomania. (She herself, as she proudly admits, is a well-diagnosed manic.) Why are her ideas so attractive to many other writers?

- First, writers who write, especially those who review, are far more often bingers and near-manics than are the exemplars I've mentioned throughout my book. Exemplars, recall, constitute a small minority of those of us who write. More to the point, exemplars are more likely to keep at their priority work than to judge and review, especially about manuscripts with an emotional or political edge; they tell me they prefer to work, even read, in contexts that foster calm and clear seeing.
- Second, mindless rushing amid high emotion has the enormous power of a well-entrenched habit. Its strength is increased each time it helps us get past difficult, discomfiting tasks like writing with a frenzy of blind emotion and driving euphoria.
- Third, the generally unexamined premise that fine writing requires strong pain makes a good excuse to oneself for not writing. (Recall the tables from Chapter 14 that showed blocked writers using the supposed aversiveness of writing as their most common reason for excusing themselves from writing.)
- Fourth, its culturally approved reputation as a madness available to only creatives born to their genius elicits mindless admiration and sympathy that reinforce the eccentric and unhealthy behaviors of writers. (Much the same romantic belief once applied to writers as consumptives, as they were then known; they, too, were presumably paying the price of their genius; they, too, sometimes made no attempt to cure the disease for fear its absence would drain them of their creative powers.)

Perhaps, then, the problem with mindfulness is that it offers too little romance and martyrdom. Or perhaps it offers too much practicality, too ready a success to all manner of writers (even those without the proper pedigrees). The real problems, it seems to me, are these: Too few of us who want and need to write have been shown this more democratic, humane alternative to mindless rushing and emotion as writers. And too many of us who already write want to keep the spoils to ourselves, by assuming that most other people should or cannot write.

Or immediate gratification / consumerism, we want the product now w/out thinking about how we got it

16

Moderate Attachments

The eighth writing rule follows from the prior two—both of them about mindful letting go. In effect, Rule 6 said: When we let go of negative thinking, we help disconnect writing from usual anxieties and conflicts. Rule 7 said: When we let go of rushing and euphoria, we no longer depend on binges for productivity. Rule 8 deals even more directly with letting go of habitual immoderations by at last facing that formidable opponent of mindfulness called ego. Ego, as we know from Johanna Field, can operate blindly, with contentiousness and meanness, and with an unthinking attachment to the status quo. Unless we moderate ego, it blocks the free and generous spirit of mindfulness.

> *Know the difference between ego and spirit. Spirit exists to give and not to take. It wants to bring joy, it has no hunger for approval. It does not crave the obedience or agreement of another person and lives beyond all demands.—DEEPAK CHOPRA*

This eighth step in the *nihil nimus* approach means easing off blind needs for perfectionism and its overidentification with our work. It means keeping some emotional and intellectual distance from our writing, particularly in its formative stages. It means working patiently and tolerantly, with a sense of playfulness and humor. It means letting go to allow more openness to alternatives, even to criticism.

A bit of reflection reveals why we get so attached to the things, like writing, we present for public scrutiny. We want them to elicit admiration and affection, to be seen as acts of brilliance. We dislike disapproval, more so indifference.

You might sense the usual result of overattachment, given what you're learning about mindlessness: We try too hard and we strive too eagerly. We work intensely and self-consciously, straining from the outset to work with genius, and we invoke all the risks of a product orientation (some of which are listed here):

- Rushing and premature editing
- Narrowness that excludes both playfulness and seeing alternatives
- Tension that causes fatigue, doubts, struggles, and blocking
- Hypomania and grandiose expectations of having locked into a dazzling plan—and then a driving desire to produce deathless prose
- Dysphoria/depression with its overreactiveness to criticism
- An equation of writing success with self-worth

Overattachment is so important that I explain it another way: When we set our expectations, mindlessly, to say a particular thing, we may not notice alternatives.

So, to communicate effectively with our intended audiences, we need to keep some distance from our work—at least enough to imagine how listeners or readers will react; enough to benefit from suggestions for change; enough to ensure some compassion for ourselves and our audience.

Mindful writers such as Pema Chodron offer the most direct interpretation of the problem and solution: Overattachment builds when we grasp for short-term relief from doubt; it moderates as we let go of needs for certainty. This means more than nonattachment from blind hopes for comfortable experience at every moment. It also means giving up false expectations that insecurity and pain can be eliminated. And it demands relaxing amid the unpredictability and uncontrollability of real life. Specifically, it requires clearly seeing that panic and embarrassment are of little lasting help when things don't work out. Other mindful acts that help overcome this mindless attachment are insight and compassion—insight about the costs of indulging addictions to immediate relief; compassion in replacing those frenzied hopes with direct, honest relationships, even with our own selves.

The results of practicing this kind of mindfulness are things I saw first in those most fluent and healthy writers I keep referring to:

- Calm and gentle letting go of concern about always gaining the approval of everyone else
- Contentment with staying and working in the moment, mainly for the discovery
- A sense of humor about their own foibles as writers

Thus, exemplars don't pressure themselves to be perfect, just to be awake, clear seeing, compassionate, and insightful.

Writing Rule 8: Moderate Attachments and Reactions.

Exercises for Writing Rule 8

Please don't underestimate the difficulty of mastering this stage—or its importance. All of us as writers are, I think, inclined to overattachment with our creative, public presentations. So it is that most of us suffer stage fright and blocking at times, and that we have found criticism difficult to accept in calm, agreeable fashion. The following exercises demand an acceptance of disapproval that can be more painful than any other step in mindful ways of writing.

Exercise 1. Monitor for Overattachment.
During pauses from writing, look for signs that you are not keeping your distance, and carry out the noticing calmly and playfully:

- A pronounced reluctance to pause or stop because the prose seems too splendid to interrupt or reexamine
- A belief, early in the project, that the work is going to be superior to that of most writers and that it must therefore be all the more impeccable and radiant
- A reluctance to share preliminary versions of plans or text for fear that ideas and phrasings will be stolen
- A growing anticipation that the writing is so special that it will necessarily be undervalued, even rejected, by the establishment
- A diminishing sense of humor about the work (i.e., can you joke about it; more important, do you tolerate humor about it from others?)

All those feelings *could,* of course, be based in reality. But in considering the possibility they are real, you might do well to keep three other realities in mind: First, most writing (even by idolized writers) is not great until revised. Second, we can make our writing less likely to face criticism by working with the mindful standing back for clear seeing that ensures clarity and simplicity. Third, the roots of overattachment lie in pride and suspiciousness. One good way to exorcize them is with moderation and modesty. Better yet, replace them with bits of gentle self-effacement, such as this favorite saying of mindful writers in my programs:

I'm not much of a writer, but I'm a great rewriter.

Exercise 2. Encourage Criticism, the Earlier the Better.
This remarkable feat begins with making early writing less private and less self-centered. It means working with other people occasionally. It means letting others look at what you are doing, from the initial stages onward. It means working with a compassionate sense of audience in mind (e.g., reading what you have just done

to hear how it sounds, to imagine how readers might respond). It means abandoning that favorite pattern of writers, working alone, somewhat secretively, and not showing the product until it is seemingly finished and worthy of unqualified praise.

Mindful ways of writing not only bring order and action. They are also more public and more open and more responsive. In the long run, this relative "nonattachment" while working makes the writing more palatable for editors, teachers, advisors, and all manner of readers. Why? Because writing in the broader and more compassionate context of nonattachment helps make readers feel more involved. Did you know that success in writing is often measured by the extent to which readers feel like writers who would like to have discovered and said similar things? Darwin's patient and good-natured writing in *Origin of Species,* for instance, stimulated some readers to say, "I wish I had thought of that." (But not *all* readers, as I recall.)

Exemplars, again, let go of overattachment to their writing in order to see a broader, more involving context for communicating. And they apply that same sort of good-humored nonattachment to utilize criticism more productively. These exemplary strategies can help you progress somewhat gradually through the most difficult parts of that stance:

1. Ask critics to limit their comments to only a few things that you yourself wonder about (e.g., "Do you see anything missing from this list?"), inquiries where you know you will not be overly hurt by the response. With practice, move to slightly riskier questions (e.g., "Can you think of a better beginning than this?"). Like any other kind of phobia, avoidance of criticism is best moderated by way of what psychologists call exposure therapy (e.g., becoming less anxious about heights by gradually working yourself higher, each time letting go of tensions and growing more tolerant). Don't expect the pain of criticism to go away; rather, face it objectively and calmly. You'll learn that the pain is, like everything else, only temporary—even that you can learn something by not trying to change or avoid the experience in its moment.

2. Ask critics to make specific, constructive comments. This means not accepting vague criticisms (e.g., "This is unclear"; "I don't like your writing style") but instead calmly asking for more specifics ("OK, please tell me what I should do to make it clearer"). And, as you muster more bravery, ask critics to begin with specific and positive comments about at least one thing you have done well. In actual practice, few critics refuse this request or even see it as an imposition; they may simply be unaccustomed to doing it.

3. Practice mindful ways of staying relatively calm and nonreactive while learning about your criticism. You already know the basics: Returning to your breathing while listening to or reading the critic and clearly seeing what is useful in the criticism. If you expect yourself to overrespond, get it by way of an intermediary

who restates the critic's remarks or written comments in gradual, tactful fashion. In that manner, you will be better able to sort the useful message from what might have seemed intolerably personal and hurtful.

4. Then, when you are ready to hear or read critics directly, maintain your focus and distance by taking careful notes on what you might consider doing differently. Stop your critic, calmly and compassionately, for clarification if necessary. (Doing this usually defuses what would otherwise be a tense situation.) Don't forget the reasons why critics need compassion: Theirs is a task that usually goes unrewarded, unappreciated. And they may feel obliged to demonstrate their smartness (writing is a context likely to do just that). They may not, you know, have been taught to make positive comments about writing; most college educations encourage criticism, not praise, of what is read and evaluated.

5. Practice ways of agreeing with criticism, at least *some* aspect of it. Begin by recognizing a basic truth about writing efficiently: All critics, even the harshest and most ill-informed, have something worthwhile to teach us. If the critic hasn't even read your manuscript carefully, find out what put him or her off from a closer and more patient look. If your critic has misunderstood your message, investigate to see where the confusion occurs. If your reader is offended, inquire about the stimulus (it may be something minor that you hadn't noticed; it may be something major, like a racist attitude). Whatever the problem, it is (in the view of mindfulness meditators) just a problem to be solved. Or you may decide, after calm reflection, that there is no problem (e.g., because your critic wants you to write the paper as she or he would).

An especially effective strategy for practicing these counterintuitive, unfamiliar things is this: Begin your spoken or written response, by finding something with which you can honestly agree (e.g., I can understand how some people might not find this interesting, but ...).

6. Thank your reviewer for his or her work. You may encounter the same critic again.

7. Exercise your sense of humor about your usual reactions to criticism.

> *My first response if they have a lot of suggestions is never profound relief that I have found someone in my life who will be honest with me and help me do the very best work of which I am capable. No, my first thought is, "Well, I'm sorry, but I can't be friends with you anymore, because you have too many problems. And you have a bad personality. And a bad character."—ANN LAMOTT*

17

*Let Others Do
Some of the Work*

This ninth rule may be the most surprising of all the mindful ways of letting go. Not until exemplary writers told me they practiced this strategy deliberately, did I begin to appreciate its worth. They not only had learned to excel at allowing other people do some of the work of writing, but they were overcoming two very ingrained, blind beliefs in doing so: That asking others to help with writing is an imposition on them, and that accepting help lessens the originality and worth of your own writing.

The other aspects of this mindful pattern are not surprising. Compared to others, exemplars:

- Encourage more observation and criticism of their work, especially early in the planning process. (When readers mention overlooked sources and confusing transitions in our plans, they do some of our work for us.)
- Collaborate more often and are quick to explain reasons for doing so (e.g., collaborators share the work and thus improve the product; they also help reduce the chances of fatal mistakes in manuscripts).
- Acquire a sense of audience that includes awareness of social conventions and ongoing conversations:

If thought is internalized public and social talk, then writing is internalized social talk made public and social again. Communities agree on sets of conventions and values for writers; not to have mastered the normal discourse of a discipline is not to be knowledgeable in that discipline and not to be accepted into that community.... We write in order to be accepted, to join, to be accepted as another member of the culture or community that constitutes the writer's audience. —KENNETH BRUFEE

How readily do writers accept this stance of letting others do some of the work for them? Even exemplars say they struggle at it and that they often fail to practice it whole-heartedly. Normal writers resist heroically. We already know the reasons why:

- Mindless tradition credits the most genius to artists, inventors, and writers who seem to work alone and without help.
- Custom commends writers who apparently produce finished, flawless work in a flash of brilliance (but not those aided by patient coaching and priming that, say, a Ford Madox Ford might provide).
- Conventional beliefs hold that writing shared early, while still imperfect, will create irreversibly negative images of our intelligence in those preliminary readers.
- Folklore perpetuates the tragic misbelief that fine writing is completely original.

New faculty who get caught up in these convictions also suppose that letting others do some of the work is tantamount to weakness or manipulation. The best counterargument is this: The most mindful, exemplary writers (and teachers) not only delegate some of the responsibility (as any good manager does) they also admit the truth: Virtually all writing (and teaching) is borrowing and restating of old ideas.

Writing Rule 9: Let Others Do Some of the Work.

Exercises for Writing Rule 9

Involving others in the work means letting go of some of the control—and of the credit. This delegation of responsibility is a difficult social skill for writers, one commonly overlooked and underappreciated.

Exercise 1. Broaden Social Contracts.

You may know these contracts in a preliminary way from Writing Rule 3 (Chapter 11), as part of setting contingencies to make the habit of writing more constant. Here, you not only enlist a writing partner to assure your presence at a mutual writing site each day but you also set aside times at the ends of sessions for exchanges of samples of what you've just written. This sharing helps bring focus and clarity to your work as you prepare it with your listener in mind. And actually reading/hearing it suggests even better ways of writing as you are stopped for clarifications and other comments.

The most common problem revealed in this social way of working, in listeners' opinion, is a failure to set a clear context for the writing, one that helps the listener know where you are going and why. The second-most frequent complaint is similar: A lack of useful transitions from one idea to the next.

Such a commitment to work in each other's presence and to check for real progress helps ensure timely completion of projects and it hints at the kinds of criticisms and misunderstandings likely from more formal critics later.

Exercise 2. Collaborate, at Least Occasionally.

I begin by anticipating a very common objection: Yes, some coauthorships are disappointing because one person does most of the work or because the partners don't communicate well. But other collaborations provide worthwhile educational experiences. Close, interactive planning and writing offer a rare opportunity to discover how other writers think and work. Collaboration can bring a richness of combined styles and ideas that neither author could have summoned alone. It can, again, reduce the kinds of mindless mistakes that undermine editorial acceptance. And it often produces a completed manuscript in less time than if done solo.

But collaboration, like anything else about writing, benefits from some awakeness and clear seeing—and from consulting with experts like this one (who doesn't mind doing some of the work for you):

> *You may want to consider the following questions before deciding to coauthor a project: 1. Do I like the prospective colleague? Do I want to spend time with this person? 2. Can the colleague and I establish an equitable work schedule? Are we going to divide the work into equal units or will one author assume the senior pattern? How will this judgement determine who is first, second, or third author? 3. If the colleague is senior in rank to me, will he or she perceive his or her role as a boss? 4. How will gender roles affect work assignments? Will male authors expect female authors to take orders and do the typing and secretarial work? 5. Can I trust the coauthor to complete his or her tasks on time? 6. Will ego taint the collaborative process? Is the colleague flexible or rigid in perceiving how the work should be completed? 7. Does the author pay close attention to detail? 8. Does the coauthor share a similar perspective? 9. Does the coauthor possess skills that I don't have that are necessary to the research?—JOSEPH MOXLEY*

Exercise 3. Critique and Review Other People's Manuscripts.

When you commend, critique, and edit the writing of others, you learn a lot about becoming a better writer, reader, and editor for your own work. And you acquire compassion for others as writers and as critics.

Exercise 4. Join the Conversation.
The three exercises before this one are about letting others do some of the work—
and, so, about moving away from the solitude that traditional writers have claimed
to prefer. These exercises, practiced mindfully, amount to making writing more
outgoing, connected, and social. That doesn't just mean sharing what you write.
It also means socializing with other writers working on problems like your own.
It means recognizing that when you write in a new area, you will save yourself
unnecessary pain by becoming a useful part of an ongoing conversation.

If you clearly see how others are posing problems, you can reshape your contribution to fit the mode while making sure you have something relatively new and
interesting to add. To the extent that you learn from the conversation (e.g., how to
state problems; how to present arguments), you let others do some of the work. To
the degree you allow others (even teachers and editors) to help you, the more
socially skilled and responsible you will become. Successful writing is in part a
social skill of accepting help from others, even competitors and critics.

A Caution Near the End of These Writing Rules

Some writers proceed through these 10 rules about writing more slowly and hes-
itantly than others. Why? Writing is one of the most personal, individual things
we can do. And one that seems to demand extraordinary care.

Publication—is the auction of the Mind of Man.—EMILY DICKINSON

18

Limit Wasted Effort

This last rule in Section II is about resilience in writing, about persisting through obstacles, about recovering from setbacks. A simple way to appreciate resilience is by way of an old maxim amongst efficiency experts:

The less the wasted effort, the greater the resilience.

Modern-day facts confirm this saying for writers in several ways. First, academics who write with constancy and moderation get the most writing done in the least time spent working and work with the least interruption through crises (defined as the aftereffects of traumas—such as a speeding citation—that stop the majority of writers from writing during the rest of the day). Second, these most mindful writers simplify their work (and so waste less effort) in ways now familiar:

- They devote only moderate amounts of time to writing each day (and so they continue to write amid unusually busy or distracting days because the writing takes little time).
- They write in brief sessions that require little warm-up time (and so the writing is not as difficult to get underway as it is for others).
- Their writing habits include acts of pausing and slowing that keep the writing on track, more succinct, and more satisfying.
- Their pauses also encourage stopping in time to permit other daily activities such as socializing and exercising (thus, with time to do other things, there are fewer excuses for not writing that day).
- They've prewritten, planned, and approximated enough so that prose writing goes quickly (thus, they work with comfort and happiness that minimize associations between writing and pain/exhaustion).
- They routinely practice ways of treating inevitable interruptions with calm and tolerance, either by returning to the present moment and its process ori-

entation of working, or, when that is impractical, as by taking breaks and gaining perspective on what they were writing.

- These resilient writers welcome criticism, learn and grow with it, and moderate reactions to it; they let other people, including critics, do some of the work of writing, even as agents of discipline (e.g., with partners waiting for their appearance at joint writing sessions, writers take fewer days off).
- They work, mindfully, toward mastery but they tolerate failures and mediocrities along the way with patience and humor (and so remain more process-oriented in the moment, while experiencing—and letting go of—distractions and pain).
- They produce more writing in less time because they work with an economy of action, a style uncovered early in this century by psychologists since forgotten:

[Jules] Amar...found that the accomplished journeyman normally adopted an efficient economy of motion that starkly contrasted with those of an apprentice, whose "chief defects are irregular and spasmodic action leading to unduly rapid fatigue."—ANSON RABINBACH

Said another way, resilience depends on the constancy and moderation I've harped on throughout this book. As BDSs become stronger habits, so does the likelihood they will persist through distractions, traumas, and sicknesses. Moreover, regular habits of work translate into faith:

Students' perceptions of their growth as writers centered [in this study of students practicing BDSs] on a sense of increased confidence and power. Student's perceptions of success and failure centered on self-discipline ...liking to write and getting readers' responses, finding the time to write, subduing external constraints such as fear of failure, and being able to find the right topics.—ROBERT TREMMEL

So, none of these foundations for resiliency is new. What changes here is the emphasis on seeing the efficiencies interactively, systematically, mindfully. It isn't so demanding and complex as it sounds.

Writing Rule 10: Moderate Wasted Effort.

Exercises For Writing Rule 10

The key to resilience lies in mindfully noticing the difference between efficient and wasteful actions in writing. Examples of the latter include the chronically negative thoughts and excessive emotions of writing we examined earlier; inefficiencies may be invisible or elusive at first.

Exercise 1. Monitor for Inefficiencies.

Make a brief, daily habit (perhaps at the ends of writing sessions) of noting inefficiencies in working for that day. The doing takes but a minute or two. These are common examples of inefficiencies that writers in the program have noted in their journals:

- Allowing too much distraction and interruption during writing times (e.g., an interloper to your office stays and chats well beyond the brief message he or she intended to deliver)
- Overreacting to unavoidable distractions (e.g., quitting a writing session, angrily, after having to stop for the noise of a leaf blower outside the window)
- Working to fatigue, even in BDSs (because of failing to pause, calm, slow down, even to do compassionate things for oneself like readjusting a cramped seating posture or looking out a window for a restful bit of distance focusing)
- Working off-track, on an aside that isn't necessary
- Rushing (and thus reflecting too little) to keep the writing direct, clear, and succinct
- Shifting too soon, too blindly, to product orientations, including interruptions to worry about meeting deadlines or pleasing reviewers
- Working beyond preset stopping points, supplanting the time for other important things like socializing and exercising
- Working euphorically, hurriedly, and moving completely away from conceptual outlines and other plans
- Trying to work at writing in the evening, when tired and when writing will take needed time away from sleep
- Putting off completions of project components like conceptual outlining while doing less needful things (or else continuing to redo COL beyond the point of diminishing returns)

I could continue the list but I suspect you get the point. Besides, these are things best discovered for yourself.

Exercise 2. Use Social Contracts to Discover and Appreciate Wasted Efforts.

Brief, regular discussions with a kindred writer about wasted efforts make the discovery process more economical. They impel you to do the noticing of your own inefficiencies so that you will have something to report at the next meeting. And as you listen to the reports of someone else's inefficiencies, you will notice wasted efforts you had overlooked in your own writing.

Exercise 3. Put Increasing Emphasis on Efficiencies (Not on Inefficiencies).

There are limitations in looking too closely or too long at inefficiencies. They can demoralize, especially if they seem to dominate your actions. They can confuse;

sometimes, for example, it is hard to distinguish between inefficiency and play. And they don't always tell you what to do in their place. So in the long run, resilient writers tend to emphasize what they do well and then add more and more economies. Examples are:

- Add more mindful practices of prewriting to further abbreviate the writing process while bringing added motivation, clarity, and imagination (e.g., "I'm learning how to make good use of that back-and-forth freewriting and it's helping me getting to the point more quickly").
- Make more pauses, stretches, and refocuses that refresh and enhance mindfulness about what needs doing now and how it can be done directly but imaginatively (e.g., "I'll say that briefly and then explain and enliven it with a good anecdote that just came to mind").
- Find enjoyable ways of doing BDSs (e.g., "My bigger chair and computer screen almost make me look forward to writing").
- Post reminders at the writing site to stay in a process orientation, in part by looking out for mindless negative thinking. (Franz Kafka had a sign over his desk that said, simply, "Wait").
- Notice which writing experiences bring the small successes underlying self-esteem (a powerful ingredient of resilience); and, too, notice when you waste efforts on pessimism or on solving the wrong problems (such as working for short-term relief of emotional distress).

Exercise 4. Extend Mindfulness to Other Domains of Living.
In the longer run, the most resilient writers notice that writing does not occur in isolation from the rest of their lives. The hardier they become, the more actively they look for ways to build more constancy, moderation, and resilience in other things they do. Consider just two of the related things they commonly do to enhance their strength: Sleep and physical conditioning.

Sleep.   Mindful writers notice that chronic insomnia and tiredness sap resilience in writing and so they combat sleep problems with mindfulness practices they already know as writers: They hold back (wait, actively), near bedtime, from exertions that arouse them in sustained ways (e.g., arguments); they begin early, several hours before bedtime, to relax and calm themselves; they limit the time they spend in bed by getting up at a preset time in the morning, no matter what (and so ensure they will be ready to sleep at a reasonable hour later that day).

Physical Conditioning.   Resilient writers, having noticed how regular practice of mindful ways makes them stronger writers, suppose that physical exercise will add even more resilience in the face of stresses. Writers in my studies who exercised with constancy and moderation (e.g., weight lifting, Yoga, aerobics, running) rated higher on scales of self-esteem and self-efficacy (i.e., they more often stated that they would succeed; they more commonly took a process stance in simplifying a writing problem). This idea, like all the others in this book, is not new:

> *The better your physical condition the easier it is to write. . . . Whatever discipline you expend on your body will affect your artistic output. . . . You need to eat properly and get enough sleep. . . . If you aren't prepared to put your writing first, you really aren't a writer.—RITA MAE BROWN*

In my own programs for writers, these sorts of advice elicit an understandable objection. The point is often made like this: "Aren't you asking us to change our *whole* lives? I just want to be a better, happier writer." Sometimes the reservation is said this way: "Isn't there an escape from rules and hard work anywhere in all this? Isn't there room for magic here somewhere?" My answer to all these questions begins with a calm "yes" and moves to explanations like these:

- Mindful ways of writing generalize, rather spontaneously, to other aspects of working and living. Mindfulness, once habitual, simplifies lives in general ways.
- Writers who achieve this resilience and its self-esteem display more openness to learning from all manner of sources, even popular writers. One program participant even put special value on a mindful insight from a writer he had formerly scorned:

> *Too often, the way taken is the wrong way, with too much emphasis on what we want to have, rather than what we wish to become.*
> *—LOUIS L'AMOUR*

Section II Summary and Extension of the Mindful Ways of Writing

Here, at the end of Section II, I pause for contemplation, just as I did with the new faculty members in my more formal programs carried out in person. Those periods were, most of all, an opportunity to appreciate how far we had come, what we had learned, and where we would like to go next. I hope that you, as a reader, can join in the spirit of these collegial meetings, at least in appreciating how we reviewed now familiar ideas about working and generated new ones.

The first thing that stood out for me in these sessions—at the end of participants' second academic years in the program—was the change in attitudes since beginning. Worries about survival now seemed distant; good starts had been made at both teaching and writing. Participants rarely lamented about falling behind schedule; they no longer did or expected to. The change that participants listed as most telling, though, concerned principles of constancy and moderation: Their writing had grown so dependable and comfortable that they had begun to turn away from concerns about doing enough to doing better quality work. Said one participant to her group: "I'll meet the minimums but I'd like to do more, on my terms. I want to think clearly about issues and their essences. I know now that I can become a very good writer." Everyone else in the group, it seemed, had similar intentions. "That's the most important change in how I feel now," said someone else who had been listening and nodding.

Then, we looked for other changes, including a simpler image of how to work at writing. In one instance, this topic led to a respecification of timely stopping and its lessons (e.g., knowing, beforehand, how much will be enough for the day). That sort of reflective reduction was expressed in ways like this:

- The astonishingly broad importance of moderation (as opposed to rushing)
- The wide role of constancy in supporting moderation (and vice versa), especially in terms of comfort enough to pause and stop
- The far-reaching value of working in a process mode, say, by focusing on doing the important things first, and getting them underway in the present moment

- The expansive power of recursiveness in writing to keep bouts of generation and reading brief, interactive, and more creative/productive/economical
- And, most fascinating, the joy in discovering that so simple an act as timely stopping helps move the writing to a higher plane (e.g., using pausing and stopping to induce a rhythm of working that clarifies the image for writing and then the writing)

Mindfulness, for all its emphasis on calm, brings a surprising enjoyment and optimism to writing.

Mindfulness and Metacognitions

As we generated and revised broader ways of seeing mindfulness, we called them metacognitions, despite the grandiosity of the word. These cognitions *about* cognitions helped us to resee processes in a wider perspective (e.g., to see what mindfulness does as it moves outward from its traditional roles in not doing and not thinking, all the way to forming images that compel writing). Said another way, our metacognitions relied on mindful nonattachment from experience to get a broader picture, a clearer seeing, of what matters and what doesn't.

One prized metacognition in these reflective groups helped clarify what had still seemed a difficult concept: The generation of prewriting, intermixed with revision/rewriting, into prose. Writers at this point could explain the two essential and interactive components but they remained unsure about their own abilities to put them into practice. What helped was a reseeing of generation and revision, by way of reliving our attempts to practice them. The essential move went from reseeing to relabeling.

Internalizing

One part (generation) we now called *internalizing* or *inning* (i.e., holding back to calm and clarify internal experience as ideas/themes for writing). Those words better described one basic process of generation and they more readily instated that process. When writers now practiced holding back to keep the process internal, and did so in front of the group, they began to talk about how this simple act helped generate ideas for writing: Waiting, directed inward, revealed a sufficiency of ideas and images already in mind, especially if allowed to appear without rushing. With further patience (and a bit of preliminary, implicit revision) those bits of prewriting would grow clearer, especially as writers began to ready them for outward expression in linear and verbal form.

What helped most specifically in conjuring this metacognition among several participants? Prior, many writers hadn't quite visualized themselves generating ideas and themes, apparently because they supposed the process more complicated than it is. Now they saw and did it more realistically.

Externalizing

When the same writers reconceptualized the other part of the duo as *externalizing* or *outing,* that designation seemed too obvious for any of the self-congratulation they had been feeling. So we slowed to think and talk a bit about how this outer-directed mode of mindful working reflects its opposite: Inning seems mostly visual and nonlinear, outing mostly verbal and linear. Inning is more wholistic and affect-laden, outing more step-wise and disciplined. Indeed, it seemed to us, that each process is optimally located within or without.

That, in turn, cued an examination of benefits of working at writing from those two vantages. Each mode, in its own way, helped clarify and expand the other—inwardly on the form of more compelling images and outwardly as increasingly directed and direct writing. And with that came a linking insight, one that may have occurred to you: Inning and outing are not so discrete and separate as they first seem:

- Visual images might remain foggy until we hold back, early, to freewrite and conceptually outline what we could say.
- Visual images, even before we start to put them outward, soon suggest enough verbal substance in faint auditory approximations to allow us slow and reshape.
- As we move those increasingly verbal images outward for even clearer verbalization and revision, we may be most motivated to write; a special relief comes with saving those images out onto paper or screen. That same anticipation of relief, kept patient and moderate, also helps generate the images in the first place.
- A related sort of image stays with the writing even longer in its outward movement, often to project completion: It portrays how the manuscript should look and sound.

That interaction of inning and outing, we noticed, made the writing easier to generate and ever more open to change. How, exactly? The answers came more slowly, after the meetings:

- First, because the two processes of inning and outing could sometimes be kept in mind at the same time.
- Second, because these juxtapositions at two levels, imaginal and verbal, encouraged more shortcuts between ideas or themes.
- Third, because the growing interactiveness between generation and revision simplified and clarified images until they compelled outing of more finished, confident, and satisfying writing.

What if you feel short-changed by not experiencing these insights directly? Wait. Work in brief, daily sessions and in other mindful ways. Consider starting a writing group on your own campus. And generalize your mindful ways back to teaching (e.g., by way of an acquired preference for recursions between generating and revising before going to class and once in it).

Look, too, at how these participants in my formal programs summarized the chapters of Section II as a closure to the discussions I abstracted above. This sample perspective, from just one group, emphasizes the natural movement of mindfulness outward.

Veteran Participants' Reviews

Outing is just as odd a word as its more technical counterparts, *exteriorization* and *externalizing*. All those words refer to the mindful act of putting images/ideas for writing outside our minds, the sooner the better (so long as we consistently return to inning as we are outing). Externalizing is so valuable because its expansiveness helps us let go to trust vague, imperfect images as the basis for writing. Externalizing works because it gets us to model after fluent (and least blocked) writers.

Once we understand outing, we better comprehend why internal images need externalizing into talk. Personal speech is cryptic and unstable, sometimes not fully verbal. The longer it is left untended and unexternalized, the more likely it will grow distracted, mean spirited, and blind. The more quickly and often we transpose it into publicly understandable messages, the more readily we write productively and painlessly. Prose writing in our heads is possible but doing it on paper or screen is far more practical.

Outing first came up in the program as the essence of holding back to begin early. Writing Rules 1 and 2 admonish writers to move beyond merely avoiding or worrying about a project to actually putting ideas and plans outward as hard copy in the following ways:

- By waiting, actively, to generate ideas and imagination (instead of rushing into writing or running away from it, impulsively)
- By talking aloud notions and/or images for writing to oneself and to others
- By freewriting and conceptual outlining before fully knowing what is going to be said, even before images begin to appear

These initial kinds of outing have two proven benefits: First, they induce lasting momentum via growing approximations to prose. Second, they help us clarify our thoughts in the linear, logical fashion necessary for most writing (cf. Gertrude Stein's famous automatic writing).

Outing practiced in the *intermediately numbered Writing Rules* revolved around constancy and moderation, particularly working in brief, daily sessions and publicly charting our progress against plans. Outing was also a part of noticing maladaptive thought patterns by talking them aloud, by disputing and replacing them aloud (i.e., externally). Outing was an essential aspect of getting in touch with the emotions that accompany our work at writing; by noticing and noting their outward presence and effects, we moderated them and gained more control over our writing and ourselves. All these forms of outing are about gaining control (as Zen teachers might say) by first giving up familiar controls and their short-term objectives/impulsive actions.

Outing in the *later Writing Rules* helped as a more social act. It included sharing early materials with critics and letting others do some of the work (Writing Rule 9) as a means of making writing more socially acceptable and more efficient, even of moderating the attachments to writing that cause overreaction to public criticism (Writing Rule 8). Outing turns intentions into action, and its mindful economy strengthens resilience (Writing Rule 10).

Said another way, *inning and outing are really nothing but patience and tolerance,* the two essences of the *nihil nimus* approach. These two processes could be the most essential outcomes of education in general, certainly for writers learning to write (even those who might suppose themselves already well educated). We need patience to hold back and tolerance to deal with the often surprising results, including creativity and criticism.

After all this, participants and I felt optimistic about having sorted out two essential, simple, and manageable actions of mindful writing. That, in turn, inspired me to add a brief review with more emphasis on the broadly functional theme of Section II: Mindfulness. I began by wondering if the concept of mindfulness would still prove useful. It did.

Reseeing Inning and Outing in Terms of Mindfulness

In the Introduction to this second Section of the program, I showed how traditional information about mindfulness approximates exemplary ways for writing among new faculty. Here, at the end, I've relied on group reflections to draw a similar parallel about how traditional experts on mindfulness hint at these notions of inning and outing. See if the following progression helps you, as it did us, to better understand the specific ways in which writers can practice mindfulness. Ideally it will ready you for the last stage of this *nihil nimus* approach, a compassionate path to collegiality, mentoring, and service (Section III).

Sources of Expertise, Most Revisited and One New

Pema Chodrin (1997).   For Chodrin, mindfulness is largely a matter of replacing struggling with relaxing, mainly by stopping one's self-talk and coming back to the freshness of the moment. Even though there is some "doing" in her formula (in stopping the ongoing discourse), the action is largely internal and different from, say, trying to solve a working problem like writing. Mindfulness practice for her is largely a commitment to staying awake, with a gentleness and a letting go of narrow, selfish reality. When she does specify ways of externalizing mindfulness, she imparts the feeling of modesty, of not trying to do too much. Her approximation of outing begins by "noticing"—with the precision and gentleness of a becalmed mind at the ready—what needs doing and then doing it, unimpulsively and patiently, as though it were the only thing that matters (i.e., with strong involvement).

Sylvia Boorstein (1996). Boorstein, much like Pema Chodrin, characterizes mindfulness as seeing clearly, as awakening to the happiness of the uncomplicated moment. But Boorstein is a bit more revealing about ways of extending practices based on "sitting" and "nondoing" to other activities. She emphasizes her discovery that the periods of formal sitting make possible the mindful practice of everyday activity. That is, once in possession of the continuous, calm, and focused attention of mindfulness meditation, we can carry it over into activities such as walking from one place to the next, so that "the journey itself becomes the practice." How, specifically, does this happen? Mindfulness helps us uncomplicate and enjoy activities by not letting them elaborate into more complex, emotional experiences than they need to be.

Philip Kapleau (1969). In his classic interpretation of Zen Buddhist practices of mindfulness for Westerners, he highlights meditation (zazen) as a means of keeping the mind free of discriminating and judgmental thoughts, of giving full attention to the moment. He eagerly relates the benefits of daily "sitting" to daily tasks: Involvement in work becomes easier because practice at zazen lessens tendencies to squander energies in purposeless actions and compulsive drives. The sitting also helps us face daily struggles because it teaches better alternatives than the mindless impulsivity of escaping or mitigating pain:

> *No longer are we dominated by intellect at the expense of feeling, nor driven by emotions.... Eventually zazen leads to a transformation of personality and character. Dryness, rigidity, and self-centeredness are transmuted into self-mastery and courage.*

A clue to the importance of working mindfully in the Zen culture that Kapleau studied is that novice monks spent most of their time at simple tasks, not sitting.

Jon Kabat-Zinn (1994). This contemporary popularizer of mindfulness techniques begins with exercises for contemplative sitting: paying attention, on purpose, in the present moment—nonjudgmentally. But he, too, hints at how mindfulness can be put to use in external matters, notably in replacing actions driven by blind thoughts with those undertaken in awareness. One mechanism sounds like a writing rule of this book:

> *I like to practice voluntary simplicity to counter such impulses [to blind action]. . . . It involves intentionally doing only one thing at a time and making sure I am here for it.*

Mark Epstein (1995).   Epstein, like Kabat-Zinn, is a psychotherapist working from a Buddhist perspective and he, too, begins with a caution about assuming that mindfulness is limited to internal acts:

> *Despite Buddhism's reputation as passive, stoical, and anti-ego, classic ego functions of taming, mastering, self-control, and adaptation are clearly valued in the Buddhist cosmology.*

Epstein also explains why initial practices of mindfulness might discourage us from pursuing outer-oriented practices: Both modes, inning and outing, inevitably produce humiliating experiences that we don't want, but the latter ("outed" practices) are more publicly visible and so more readily avoided. What we need, then, is the momentum from inning. Once we're doing the hard, regular work of *holding* our thoughts, images, feelings, and actions in suspension in order to see them clearly, we then write them more confidently and tolerantly. That effort of externalizing by putting experiences and insights out into spoken and examined narratives, helps us "break identification" with inadequacies such as impatience. And it is invariably therapeutic. That mindfulness also, in Epstein's view, accomplishes something else akin to what we, as writers, have practiced in the exercises of our own book: It puts the buzzing, confusing mass of our thoughts about writing out into linear prose by switching from a spatially based sense of self to a linear experience that operates in the moment and with more awareness of our bodies and feelings.

Ellen Langer (1989).   Langer found fame in her demonstrations of how mindlessness in the elderly—particularly as evidenced in their unthinking acceptance of stereotypes for their age group—unnecessarily restricts their activity and undermines their health. She also devised ways of teaching the elderly mindfulness, and thereby helped them reassume more productive, healthy lives. Although she neither advocates practices of meditation nor speaks directly about externalizing mindfulness, Langer does provide its functional equivalent: She outlines ways of coaching elderly people to take more active control in a problem-solving task, by helping them make explicit more of the decisions about how to proceed, and, in turn, to act more independently and confidently, with less helplessness and depression. Her influence on the rules of the present book can be seen in admonitions to work in process modes, with clear seeing and calm but always with a readiness for externalized "doing."

Joanna Field (1936).   Field's may be the best modern examination of mindfulness as outing. She came to understand the sources of her unhappiness, tension, and inefficiency by putting her usual thoughts outward into spoken and written forms as an ongoing diary of what was happening in the moment. She was surprised at how often her thoughts were blind and anxiously distracted by the prospect of something more important just ahead. This constant looking ahead for a better experience, she noticed, kept her from living in the present; it also left her unaware of how her mind usually worked and where it was taking her. Moreover, the implicit self-talk that occurred in the meanwhile, without her full awareness, tended to be mean-spirited, unhappy, and unable to set clear goals.

Part of what helped Field's progress beyond that insight was putting her thoughts and emotions outside herself for careful examination—into calm speech and writing. She discovered this complimentary step when practicing mindfulness elsewhere, while listening to music by putting her consciousness outside herself. The result was the complete and joyful immersion she wanted in what she was doing in the moment, one free of the distractions of chattering thoughts. She then extended the same principle to working and playing, realizing, for example, that ping-pong performed with one's consciousness in the arm and hand is far easier and more effective than giving in to usual temptations to let the head do the hand's work. This, my writing groups and I agreed, is an unusual way of seeing the difference between inning and outing: Letting the mind do some of the hand's work versus letting the hand do some of the mind's work.

Field's discoveries may at last be coming to recognition (e.g., Oatley, 1992)—so are even far older, more obscure insights that deal directly with externalized and mindful ways of writing. I'll finish, despite my love for history and my desire to include many more case studies, with just one.

Samuel Johnson (circa 1700s).   You may already know something about Dr. Johnson, perhaps his pithy sayings as related by his biographer, Boswell. You might be aware of his *Dictionary,* the first of its sort in English and an accomplishment not surpassed for over a century. You might even have read his classic introductions to great poets. But you may not know that he practiced mindful ways of writing and living (Bate, 1977; Boswell, 1934).

His progression to mindfulness was largely self-taught and his goal, consistent from the start of his work as a writer, was to learn to live and work in the present. The move apparently began with his discovery that work itself (such as learning to bind books as a way of supporting himself) was therapeutic. This was not, in itself, an unusual insight; his further conclusions were and still are.

Johnson discovered that full, undistracted immersion in one's work (including writing) keeps blind thinking at bay, focuses attention on what needs doing, regulates imagination and its tendency to extremes of emotion, allows seeing things both realistically and in ways that readers will appreciate. Not least of all, he liked to point out, this mindful step to outing rewards the worker with the see-ing of progress in the moment—an important incentive for writers.

From these insights and practices, Johnson developed more specifically mindful ways of working at writing—probably more than any writer before or since:

- An "essentialism" (i.e., simplicity and directness) of expression found by way of working with the focus of clear seeing and a planful readiness to get to the point
- A broadened seeing, while patiently holding back for reflection, whose inter-connections suggest insights and aphorisms for writing
- A "promptitude" (including an element of deliberate risk taking) to compress experience into generalities, followed by care at pinning them to concrete examples
- More readiness and health for writing because of regular practice of general disciplines (e.g., arising at eight o'clock each morning, thus curing his insom-nia; or managing procrastinated tasks in brief, regular sessions, and so dimin-ishing the guilt he felt about neglecting, say, his Bible reading by managing it at a constant, moderate rate of 21 pages per Sunday)
- More ease and happiness in writing by using a present-orientation to see the "stability of truth" (what Freud later would later term the *reality principle*), and consequently to appreciate the benefits of living in the present—all while conquering that fearful combination of anxiety, self-punishment, and exces-sive self-demand that would otherwise afflict him.

A few excerpts from the writing of Samuel Johnson illustrate his notions of mindfulness. This one exemplifies his belief that we need mindfulness to manage our imaginations:

> *No mind is much employed on the present: recollection and anticipation fill up almost all our moments. . . . So few of the hours of life are filled up with objects adequate to the mind . . . that we are therefore forced to have recourse every moment to the past and future for supplemental satisfac-tions.*

This is one of his suggestions for a solution:

> *If it [imagination] is an indispensable ingredient for human happiness, when it is kept sufficiently open and regulated by reality, it is [otherwise] also the source of most human misery.*

Here, he writes, with essentialism, about the difference between living mindfully and mindlessly:

The flights of human mind are not from pleasure to pleasure but from hope to hope.

And here, he writes about the real discipline behind the difference—not just the fortitude to meet great occasions or exceptional disasters, but the resiliency to live and work in the moment, in the midst of mundane or serious problems:

The real test is what we do in our daily life, and happiness—such happiness as exists—lies primarily in what we do within the daily texture of our lives. Life is very short and very uncertain: let us live is as well as we can.

So Samuel Johnson was clear about the need of "interiority" (as it would have been called then) for writers. It was the core of his methods for moderating the imagination and it centered around holding back and living and working in the present moment. But he was also prescient about ways of externalizing mindfulness; some are like those of this book and some are far more advanced:

- His self-disciplines to enhance his strength for staying in the present and facing reality head on
- His resort to manual labor, including writing, to "get himself outside himself "
- His preplanned moves, once outside, to see even more broadly, while taking the whole context into account
- His mindful simplifying of thoughts into writing, by way of the essentialism we saw earlier
- His compression of broadly seen ideas (i.e., metacognitions) into memorable generalities
- His concrete, simple, direct, and reassuring thinking by way of first saying what he might write in the social conversations for which he is so famous

Why else might we want to emulate his methods? Because Samuel Johnson may have been the greatest writer ever. He helped pioneer direct styles of expression, including short phrases; he stands second only to Shakespeare, as the most quoted author ever. More important, I believe, Johnson's ways of writing provided him with courage, generosity, a childlike playfulness, and a juxtaposition of wisdom and action that still inspires unusual trust, even joy, in readers.

That realization of what mindfulness did for Samuel Johnson, notably the happiness and acceptance it brought him as a sociable writer—the program participants and I decided—primed us for the third stage of working in the *nihil nimus* approach: The extension of an involvement in the professoriate that had seemed largely a matter of teaching and writing well enough, to a more sociable, caring, and generous style of professing. Not only do all experts on mindfulness conclude that its practice brings more compassion (perhaps the ultimate kind of outing) and social responsibility. Its results, they note modestly, make practitioners far easier to get along with, to like, to learn from—and far more committed to the happiness of others. Consider what it did for Samuel Johnson—by universal consensus one of the homeliest, most awkward, but beloved people who ever lived and worked.

Section III

<hr />

Socialize and Serve with Compassion

Why Compassion Is Ultimately Important

I've put socialization and service last in this book because they are primed by the practices of moderation and mindfulness of Sections I and II. When we first slow down and notice our own needs, we are more likely to see others' needs. When we first care about ourselves, we more readily care about others.

While compassion naturally moves outward in the *nihil nimus* way of teaching and writing, it's up to you to make optimal use of it, even to allow its meaningful expression *at all* during your tough first years on campus. If you downplay socialization and service, you greatly increase the risk of a poor start.

There is another reason to give more than cursory attention to the social side of your initiation rites. Decisions against retention/tenure/promotion (R/P/T) are just as often made subjectively, on the basis of sociability (e.g., "Can we get along with this person; will he treat students humanely?") and citizenship (e.g., "Is she likely to carry her share of departmental duties?") as on productivity numbers or teaching ratings. There is a real but often overlooked principle behind this custom: To fail because of teaching and writing, you have to prove yourself incompetent beyond doubt. To fail because of social problems, you need only the appearance of aloofness and uncooperativeness. After all, a decision to award you permanent appointment (or its equivalent) may mean having to work and socialize with you for 50 years. Think of it!

My guess about why academe keeps its criteria for socialization and service vague is this: Unstated and uncalibrated rules leave the most control for gatekeepers because they can adjust their implicit criteria to fit their biases. Given the customary ambiguity about socialization and service, who among new faculty can model the right stuff while retaining their individuality?

Exemplary New Faculty

In my studies, even some of these quick starters sense the peril of unwritten rules somewhat belatedly. But they, far more quickly than struggling peers, make four key moves to help correct that oversight:

1. They inquire discreetly and briefly about the *faux pas* that commonly sink unwary new faculty, often by questioning peers who have recently undergone a R/P/T decision for better or worse. And they quiz a trusted advisor. Just as often, they query friends on the faculty at another campus.
2. They quickly look for ways to extend already familiar methods of mindfulness to socialization and service, particularly once they see that their challenges may be more difficult than for writing and teaching.
3. They expect that a studied mastery of socialization rules will save more time than it takes (just as with mindful ways of working at writing and teaching).
4. They soon lessen their involvement in "worry groups" of new faculty who obsess, helplessly, on rumors about injustices in the R/P/T process. Exemplars quickly learn that not all kinds of socializing in academe are adaptive.

[handwritten margin note: take yourself away from neg. ("moderate emotions")]

Thriving new faculty also reflect on the social side of new faculty experience to consider how success at, say, writing depends on social skills (e.g., getting to know leaders and learning from them). They notice how academe rewards writers in return for service (e.g., volunteering to review manuscripts and grant applications in their field educates them as writers/planners and acquaints them with gatekeepers who accept or reject manuscripts and proposals). And they recall that prowess at teaching depends on using positive, social motivators with students (Section I); presumably, the same compassionate process applies to socialization with colleagues.

What seems to matter most in this progression of reflections is the recognition that the simplest rules for teaching and writing—including balance—apply here.

How the Social/Service Side of New Faculty Life Brings Balance

To help make sense of where we're going, I'll step back for a moment and review the book to this point—very briefly. (You know the importance I put on setting and resetting contexts.) Section I of *Advice for New Faculty* was about *economies* of working at teaching as per Adam Smith and his insight into the value of constancy and moderation. There, we concentrated on first doing what matters most, *and* on doing it with constancy and moderation. In Section II, we extended the *nihil nimus* approach to mindfulness in writing, with Samuel Johnson as our primary guide. There, I emphasized working in *process* modes. That is, we not only aimed to work in the present moment, by way of constancy and moderation, but to do it in ways that mindfully enhance creativity and productivity. In that second stage, we moved beyond simple economies to learning about *inning* and *outing,* all the while keeping the complex act of writing surprisingly simple.

Here, in this last Section, we move to an even more exteriorized and sociable mode of action. Dr. Johnson is among those who suggest that mindful simplicity is best gained by way of social orientation. Recall his practice of clarifying what he would write by first saying it to friends to notice their comprehension and appreciation. New faculty who thrive help illustrate this outward trend:

- They are more outgoing than other new faculty (but in moderate and constant ways), and more likely to model after colleagues already faring well.
- They, far more constantly than struggling peers, communicate with colleagues, on and off campus (but not to an excess that interferes with necessary work).
- They more often impress colleagues as consistently cheerful, optimistic, and socially sensitive, particularly as interested in what other faculty do.
- They less often complain publicly of being too busy to chat with colleagues and students, or of spending their probationary years in social isolation.
- They talk about gaining a wider perspective on all their efforts at moderation and mindfulness. Said one exemplar: "I need to see other people using these principles." In response to my request for a specific example, this person answered, "Well, I was fascinated by how [the star of the department] showed an interest in my teaching. I was flattered, naturally, and I was struck by how his own social style allowed me to relax and listen, and observe. He listened carefully and, how can I say it, patiently, without pressuring me. I learned a lot from that; he showed me that the basics are simple . . . well, maybe not simple, but understandable and doable."

There is a balance in all this, too. While exemplars take a genuine interest in what colleagues do, they maintain a modicum of assertiveness with them. So, they more often disagree with colleagues, but in civil ways. And they more commonly resist pressures to work fully within traditional boundaries. Similarly, exemplars set clear limits on how much departmental and campus service they agree to perform during their 'probationary' years: "I've been nice but firm about it. During these make-or-break years, I serve on one committee in and out of the department and only in a beginner's role . . . no way do I agree to head-up projects or whatever. Not for now. I do, though, promise to do more, somewhat more, if and when I survive the tenure process. Saying that always seems to break the ice."

Another, Older, Exemplary Approach

An idea I haven't yet mentioned helps set the social theme for this final Section. It is Francis Bacon's (circa early 1600s) explanation of how to simplify and improve work by "outing it" to a more sociable level. You'll soon see what I mean, I trust.

Bacon is an oft-misunderstood pioneer of scientific method (Mathews, 1996) who taught himself and others economical ways of working. In particular, he looked to see how expert scientists made discoveries. The key, he decided, lay in taking new methods out into society to see if they served people well, and then revising and simplifying the methods until they proved widely practical. That notion is so fundamental and unpretentious that it has largely escaped the notice of us moderns.

Bacon provides such a clear-seeing and practical perspective because he lived during the beginnings of Western science and was able to appreciate the need for scientific discovery based on broad but fundamental principles. He hoped his teachings about simplicity and broadness would influence the training of scientists, and that his admonitions would deflect the growth of science away from the complex and "particularistic" approaches already entering the scene. Without his socially based method, he feared, scientists would become more and more likely to opt for very specific phenomena and laws. The problem then would be a science developing a sense of a world so seemingly complicated and overloaded with facts that fewer and fewer of us would search for, or believe in, first-order principles. Scientists and other scholars of his own day already seemed in peril of learning a great deal about a few things, little about others of broader import. The longer-term result, he warned, would be a mass of insufficiently broad knowledge and a disinclination to apply it to far-reaching problems such as efficient ways of working (Crowther, 1960). Bacon would not, I imagine, be surprised to discover that researchers on higher education have nowadays amassed thousands of articles and books on specific aspects of teaching (e.g., curriculum design), but few proofs of having helped broad samples of college teachers teach better in significant, lasting ways. Said another way, Bacon favored a generalist approach and most other scientists prefer specifism.

Bacon's forgotten method of simplifying science by keeping its development focused on general and socially tested solutions explicates patient, mindful ways of attending to the process of discovery itself. It also suggests patterns of discovery that both encourage and reward more sociability in work. Bacon's socialized ways of working are effective because:

1. They must first demonstrably help diverse others.
2. To carefully determine the extent of that help, the investigator has to ascertain the most basic and general principles involved.
3. The scientist, now aware of those fundamentals, applies them, where appropriate, to himself or herself.

How would these socially based, Baconian ways pertain to new faculty members? Easily. They are, in essence, the basis of the same old *nihil nimus* rules we already know for working with constancy and mindfulness. But here, they grow even simpler and more effective because they are made more social. That is Bacon's point—of a science kept more basic and practical by way of compassionate application to others and then oneself (and vice versa, much as in the recursive fashion we've been learning to write).

The chapters in this section will seem familiar for their emphasis on beginning early to acquire social awareness/knowledge of the culture you are joining, with their reliance on socializing in patterns of constancy and moderation. Even so, they may surprise you with their implicit assumption that you'll fare even better in teaching and writing by devoting about as much time to sociability as you do to them. Francis Bacon could have told you that; he believed that science and compassion should operate hand in hand.

Evidence for the Efficacy of Socialized Work

First, this Baconian method of putting work into serviceable forms is reliably and distinctively modeled by the same exemplars I've touted throughout this book (e.g., they spontaneously make social contracts for regular writing sessions). Second, when I devised programs for initially-less-advantaged peers that had them mimic this exemplary strategy of working with broad sociability, the results (compared to nonparticipating peers) included:

- A larger increase in knowledge about socialization criteria, such as the publishing expectations of R/P/T committees or their equivalent
- More consistent and larger increases in ratings of their progress toward surviving the R/T/P process from more senior colleagues and chairpeople
- Higher self-ratings of efficiency and enjoyment in managing professorial work
- Clearer reports and demonstrations of how compassion, in particular, can be built on constancy and moderation (e.g., "I'm pleased that I noticed something as basic and good for myself as that the principle of brief, daily writing works with socializing. When I learned to work at it [socializing] regularly, it helped me to explain my plans . . . to myself and to the people around me. I felt more patient about explaining myself to them. Now I appreciate why they otherwise might have seen me as withdrawn—I'm shyer than some people realize")
- Higher levels of self-rated happiness, largely over having simplified and clarified social life, especially in moderating the usual concern about whether colleagues are approving or not (e.g., "Once I became more consistently outgoing and friendly with them, once they could see that I'm making good progress, because I showed them my ongoing work and asked for their advice and appraisal, I simply didn't feel the old anxieties about what their occasional moodiness or absent-mindedness meant—or mine")

Where can you get information about the program behind these outcomes? In the chapters ahead about socially patterned ways of working (as Bacon would have called them).

What Are Socially Patterned Ways of Working?

Socially patterned ways of working extend the *nihil nimus* themes of constancy and moderation to their natural conclusion, outward but always in balance with inner processes. Specifically:

1. As increased *social awareness,* beginning with learning the cultures of one's new department and campus and their usually unwritten rules of socialization
2. As self-rewarding *social involvement,* based around mentoring and other socially based experiences
3. As intrinsically motivating ways of providing *social services* to needful others, by further clarifying what works for oneself via helping other newcomers learn the same efficient, joyful actions

Those three aspects of sociability and service are the topics of the three chapters remaining in this book. As you consider them at more length, I hope you will experience their mindful essence of compassion, toward yourself, then toward others, then back again. I end this Introduction to Section III by previewing those three chapters.

A Preview of Section III

Foremost, Chapter 19 coaches exemplary ways of learning what matters in academic cultures, before you actively join them. It even helps after you've come to your new campus because the secrets of this learned priesthood (now reluctantly accepting women and others once thought to be lacking souls) often take years, decades, lifetimes, to learn. At either time, early or a bit late, it is the compassionate thing to do for yourself and those you work with.

Its basic rule resembles earlier advice in this book for waiting patiently while beginning to begin, early: Learn about academic culture early, patiently. The result is enlightening and enjoyable, according to my early readers.

Ours is a culture that fascinates and amuses. In many respects, its socialization rituals resemble those of medieval monasteries with a scholastic bent. Only recently have most of us shed our full-dress robes and hoods in everyday work on campus; now, we might like to don them more often but we are limited to grave ceremonies such as convocations and graduations. More important, we continue to treat the professoriate as an elite priesthood, with mysterious and sacred rites of initiation that generally go unexplained to outsiders, especially to initiates. There is more to this analogy: We separate ourselves from the lay world and its mundane tastes. We still expect initiates to leave old ties behind and wed themselves to their work. We too often accept the most inhumane practices toward them as apprentices (e.g., the ways in which we treat dissertation students struggling to finish their writing, worse yet during their oral exams where candidates are reduced to contritions and tears). And we continue to reward a fondness for currently favored doctrines and "correct" belief systems; our culture directs surprisingly strong disapproval, even shunning, to infidels and heretics. What impels us to do these irrational things? Perhaps a tradition of excessive reverence for saintly leaders and their cults. Or maybe an understandable desire for salvation.

You see, I hope, why this seemingly arcane information merits reading. Tradition continues to matter, like it or not. The overview of the literature about professors in this chapter—even the intentionally humorous examples—warns about fatal mistakes to be avoided, about eccentricities to expect of colleagues, and about unwritten rules you will be expected to follow.

No, you won't join a group that, as in my day, pressured its newcomers to drive Volvos or Peugeots, smoke a pipe, wear tweed jackets with elbow patches, rave about all foreign films, and affect a private school accent. Or will you? As I reflect on the experiences of new faculty I know now, it seems to me that you'll still fare better at faculty gatherings by choosing wine or brandy over beer, by publicly admiring a string quartet instead of the Rolling Stones. Alas, I'm getting ahead of myself.

Chapter 20 accentuates an exemplar-based strategy that we already know in a way: Letting go of complete independence and permitting others to do some of our work. To place this advice in a realistic context, I include data and lessons learned from a uniquely direct study of mentors paired with new faculty. From that study I draw principles about why mentoring is usually uncommon for new faculty, about why some mentoring pairs fail while others succeed, and about how to select, even educate, a mentor. Mentoring done well proves beneficial far in excess of the modest amounts of time and energy it requires.

An openness to letting others do some of the work, I suggest in Chapter 20, inclines new faculty to other socialized ways of working, including cooperative learning and classroom research—both popular approaches to teaching improvement.

The final chapter addresses ways of improving your own work patterns by providing services for others. Here, I become most Baconian. I advocate the seemingly odd idea of developing your service orientation close to home—with other, newer new faculty who could benefit from your informal mentoring about first-order principles of working. Such an approach helps you learn more about the *nihil nimus* methods by teaching them and noticing their general patterns of effects on diverse others. And it inevitably brings more compassion for colleagues, more understanding of how their frustrations and irrationalities resemble your own, and more patience with yourself.

I put that idea into a real-world context by summarizing my own study of new faculty experiences of women and minorities. The disappointments and hurdles they face, many of them exaggerations of the rituals faced by all new faculty, offer broad lessons about how academe could help itself and its carefully recruited new hires with even a modicum of compassion. In the longer run, I note in the last chapter, this service orientation provides an early, lasting sense of belonging and worth in academe unavailable elsewhere in professorial careers.

— how you dress
— how you address people
— etc.

19

Learn about Academic Culture Early, Patiently

How best can you learn about so secretive a culture as academe? I suggest beginning with books written by professors about academic life. These writers entertain; they are, after all, like us. Better yet, they inform novice academics of what to expect in unusually candid fashion.

Consider how Professor Jane Smiley (1995), in her best-selling book *Moo*, pictures a typical provost savoring his large midwestern institution (provosts actually run campuses; presidents are more for display and fund raising):

> *While a state university, unlike an Ivy League institution, did not promise membership in the ruling class (Wasn't that the only real reason, Ivar thought, that four years at Harvard could cost $100,000?), Ivar's university, over the years, had made serious noises to all sorts of constituencies: Students could find jobs, the state would see a return on its educational investment, business could harvest enthusiastic and well-trained workers by the hundreds.... At the very least, students could expect to slip the parental traces, get drunk, get high, have sex, seek passion, taste freedom and irresponsibility surrounded by the best facilities money could buy.*

What, besides Smiley's delightful cynicism, is worth noticing here? For one thing, that higher administrators take a far more optimistic view of how well trained most students are than do their faculty. Second, that we can too easily forget what matters more to undergraduates than the things we hope to teach them.

Michael Moffat's (1989) direct-observational account of dorm life at Rutgers University is even more informative. Here, for example, he summarizes what freshmen most need to learn as students and where they typically get it:

> *The crunch often came after the first midterms. C's and D's??!! So, sitting around in the lounge with a book open was not really studying. Reading something through quickly did not make it stick. Listening to lectures without taking good notes was not enough. Most freshmen made adjustments. Sometimes friends helped, but more often the novices figured out new study routines for themselves.*

Moffat's inside information can help you understand your own students, even to fathom your own struggles as a freshman in the professoriate. At the least, it is good reading.

Then, for the ultimate in succinctly useful books, look at Burton R. Clark's classic, *The Academic Life* (1987). In this excerpt, he uses his extensive studies to point out the four pivotal determinants of most professorial careers:

> *First, and most important, is the obvious divide between research and teaching, redefined as specialist and generalist careers. The second is the distinction between full- and part-time appointments. . . . The third divide lies between tenured [or tenurable] personnel, an important matter for the stability of academic employment and the fundamental beliefs of the profession. Last is the pure-applied distinction.*

Put simply, Clark says that your probability of career satisfaction, as measured traditionally, depends on situating yourself in the first position for each of those dualities. Why, for instance, is it true that teaching counts less than research? On campuses where teaching is the true emphasis of faculty work, the institution is client driven. That means less administrative valuing of faculty as individuals, less individual freedom, less time and support for individual scholarship, more likelihood of faculty becoming professionally obsolete and immovable. No, I don't always like this reality either, but I believe we do better to face it than ignore it.

In Burton Clark's surveys of which professors were most valued by colleagues at a variety of campuses, a consistent pattern emerged: Those of us who matter most in the professoriate teach and research well, but with clear emphasis on the latter in ways that are elegant, individualistic, and entrepreneurial. Moreover, professors with esteem as researchers report the most career excitement and happiness; in contrast, those of us at "teaching campuses" are most likely to report feeling mismatched and intellectually understimulated. My own studies of new faculty replicate Clark's findings.

Another key revelation in his book on academic culture shows how nonobvious some unwritten rules are. Those of us in "upward-tilting" disciplines, such as the hard sciences (with tilt defined in terms of proportionately how many departmental courses are offered at upperclassmen versus underclassmen levels), reap the highest status and pay. Those of us in "downward-tilting" disciplines, such as English Composition, where the bulk of teaching occurs at freshman level, have the lowest salaries, security, and caste. Why point this out, given that you've probably already committed yourself to one tilt or the other? Because it helps prepare you for realities that often upset new faculty in the humanities and some social sciences—too often, in my experience, to the point of distraction and demoralization.

If we are wise, let us prepare for the worst.—GEORGE WASHINGTON

He is a man of sense who does not grieve for what he has not, but rejoices in what he has.—EPICTETUS

If, as I hope, I've stimulated your interest in a brief but systematic enquiry into academic culture, how, exactly, should you proceed? The following strategy proved most palatable and useful for the new faculty in my programs:

- Begin by finding informative excerpts and general principles about academic cultures; this sets a useful backdrop for appreciating the generalities and learning the specifics of the culture you are joining.
- Learn about colleagues at your new campus before you meet them (e.g., scan their publications; talk to mutual acquaintances). Sometimes this step comes as early as preparing to apply for professorial positions.
- Anticipate some of the eccentricities of your new colleagues, or take a closer look at your graduate campus and imagine its faculty as your colleagues.
- Begin early to practice ways of working with particular relevance to the jobs you hope to be offered (e.g., fluent ways of writing grant proposals or course plans).

That is, do these things instead of rushing ahead without noticing how your new culture differs from (and resembles) what you've known. Specifically, prepare early for unpleasant realities that may confront you, by (1) discovering, well before you feel the inclination or need to, the predictable disappointments connected to your discipline, your campus, your background, and your racial/ethnic/social class status; (2) understanding potential "fault lines" in your career, such as a dysfunctional relationship with your departmental chairperson (no one else, in all likelihood, will prove more crucial to your initial survival and success than this person); and (3) uncovering the reasons why faculty at a certain campus like their setting enough to stay. In addition, do the exercises that follow.

Rule 1: Wait.

Rule 2: Begin Early.

Exercises for Rules 1 and 2

In the case of writing (Chapters 9 and 10), these rules meant holding back from impetuous starts to figure what needed saying and doing. Here, it amounts to early discovery of effective ways to make reasonable first impressions and good starts as a colleague. And here, the waiting and beginning early may be easier: They start with the simple act of reading the summaries ahead about the nature of academic culture.

But before you set off on these exercises, beware of the length of text that accompanies them. Here, as just above, I abstract and explain suggested readings while assuming your ability to skim or scour them as you wish. (But here, alas, I cannot threaten you with the prospect of tests down the road, as I might if I were a mean-spirited teacher. Or can I?)

Exercise 1. Peruse the Literature on Academic Culture, the Earlier the Better.

We've already seen examples of the sorts of readings that can be helpful—information about the real interests of provosts and undergraduates, about some of the predictors of high status and disabling disappointment in academic careers, even a clue about why freshmen often struggle. Here, I present some related excerpts from readings, arranged this time in more systematic fashion. I begin with ways of anticipating the eccentricities of your colleagues and knowing the unwritten rules of conduct before you need them. Some of the best information lies in 'fictional' accounts of professorial life.

a. Humorous Fiction about Professors.   Following are excerpts from David Lodge's classic comedy—*Changing Places* (1975)—about professorial life in Britain and the United States. It takes the perspective of exchange professors who've crossed the Atlantic to experience new settings in their work; the realities are much the same in the old country and the new, then and now. This first excerpt depicts an all-too-typical senior faculty member, someone whom many new faculty don't quite expect as a colleague (or expect they could eventually resemble):

> *There was one respect in which Philip was recognized as a man of distinction, though only within the confines of his own Department. He was a superlative examiner of undergraduates.... In the Department meetings that discussed draft question papers he was much feared by his colleagues because of his keen eye for the ambiguous rubric, the repetition of questions from previous year's papers, the careless oversight that would allow candidates to duplicate material in two answers.... A col-*

league had once declared that Philip ought to publish his examination papers. The suggestion had been intended as a sneer, but Philip had been rather taken with the idea—seeing in it, for a few dizzy hours, a heaven-sent solution to his professional barrenness.

Next, Lodge provides a devastatingly realistic indication of how we, once in the professoriate, might overrespond to a book reviewer's comments about our published writing:

I skimmed through the columns to see whether there was any comment on my contribution, and sure enough there it is: "Turning to Professor Zapp's essay . . . " and I can see at a glance that my piece is honored with extensive discussion. [But then, on closer reading] Imagine receiving a poison-pen letter, or an obscene telephone call, or discovering that a hired assassin has been following you about the streets all day with a gun aimed at the middle of your back. . . . This guy really wanted to hurt. I mean, he wasn't content merely to pour scorn on my arguments and my evidence and accuracy and my style, to make my article [i.e., a chapter in an edited book] seem to be some kind of monument to imbecility and perversity in scholarship, no, he wanted my blood and my balls too, he wanted to beat my ego to pulp.

These excerpts come from David Lodge's *Small World* (1984/1995), an insightful and irreverent account of faculty behaviors at conferences:

The MLA (Modern Language Association of America) is the Big Daddy of conferences. A megaconference. A three-ring circus of the literary intelligentsia. . . . Imagine ten thousand highly-educated, articulate, ambitious, competitive men and women converging on mid-Manhattan on the 27th of December to meet and to lecture and to question and to discuss and to gossip and to philander and to party and to hire or be hired. For the MLA is a market as well as circus, it is a place where young scholars fresh from graduate school look hopefully for their first jobs, and more seasoned academics sniff the air for better ones. The bedrooms of the Hilton and the Americana are the scene not only of rest and dalliance but of hard bargaining and rigorous interviewing.

The next selection portrays the sort of position many successful professors actually aspire to, one with a magnificent and unparalleled salary, with a support staff always at the ready, and—most important among status considerations—with no teaching requirements. Here, too, Lodge captures the usual and politicized result for serious aspirants (in this case, Professor Zapp, waiting expectantly at a conference meeting for his name to be announced as the winner of just such a position):

"As most of you know," Jacques Textel was saying, "UNESCO intends to found a new chair of literary criticism tenable anywhere in the world, and I think it's no secret that we've been seeking the advice of the doyen of the subject, Arthur Kingfisher, as to how to fill this post. Well, ladies and gentlemen, I have news for you." Textel paused, teasingly... "Arthur has just told me," said Jacques Textel, "that he is prepared to come out of retirement and allow his own name to go forward for the chair." ... "Of course," said Textel, "I can't speak for the appointing committee, of which I merely am the chairman. But I should be surprised if there is any serious rival candidate to Arthur."

I'd like to go on with quotes from David Lodge, Jane Smiley, and other writers on academic culture, but I hope you'll read them yourself. There is also a plenitude of murder mysteries set in academe (including, as you might expect, clues about fatally interpersonal tensions therein), but little of worth, tellingly, in science-fiction/fantasy or in romance novels.

b. Systematic Studies of Academic Culture.   There are surprisingly few of these studies, and, woe on you, many are mine. I'll present just two:

Obligatory dinners for new faculty.   This first study is small and concerns ways in which exemplars managed the seemingly trivial ritual of dinner invitations during their first year on campus. The invitations always came from a few senior colleagues and attendance seemed obligatory. All such dinners occurred at the homes of seniors and all were a bit stiff and boring, at least in my studies. Most important, all were, or could have been, occasions for faux pas early in professorial careers.

Exemplars avoided memorable mistakes because they (1) ingested and imbibed moderately, no matter what others did; (2) listened more than talked, even attended, in moderation, to spouses/companions; and, (3) wrote thank-you notes to their hosts afterward, no matter how old-fashioned and unnecessary it seemed. In sum, exemplars exercised social moderation, especially in not underestimating the power of offending their hosts—at least one of whom would be reencountered for a long time. If all this sounds like common sense, I assure you it is not in actual practice.

Another of my studies carries an even more somber message, one I almost hesitate to present here, among our earliest looks at the obstacles facing new faculty. But with the words of George Washington still ringing in my ears, I press on.

A systematic inquiry into middle-aged, disillusioned colleagues.   This second study is far lengthier to read and far more informative.

Rationale. Once they are hired and settled into campus routine, few things, in my experience, astonish new faculty more than the burned-out and angry departmental colleagues they encounter. Usually, newcomers find only one or two in their departments, sometimes more. But always these middle-aged, disillusioned colleagues (MADCs) have an impact far beyond their numbers. These most unsociable sorts usually go unmentioned and unseen during the hiring process and interviews. And, because academe still tries to ignore these discomforting members, they have been little studied. When I noticed how these peculiar professors often distract and demoralize new faculty, I decided to learn more about them. Once I saw that they had much to teach about the long-term effects of poor starts in professorial careers, I studied them more systematically (e.g., Boice, 1986, 1993).

First look at MADCs. I began my study with a goal you might have anticipated; I needed to convince most academics, including higher administrators, that MADCs were common and problematic. Those who already believed were the department chairpeople who most often had to deal with MADCs, usually as quietly as possible. I interviewed 88 individuals to discover if they, too, had noticed MADCs. Table 19.1 depicts the most common kinds of chairs' descriptors of least-valued faculty, in the modal order they were mentioned to me.

A methodological aside: I took pains *not* to lead chairs into saying what I expected. First, I simply asked them to list and briefly describe their faculty in two groups with regard to experience levels—those within their early years and those at midcareer and beyond. Then I asked them to detail those colleagues whom they saw as most or least valued and valuable. The most valued faculty almost always resembled the exemplary pattern depicted throughout this book. Their opposites, faculty listed as least valued, elicited far more description.

TABLE 19.1   Estimates by Chairs of Their Faculty Who Qualified as Salient on These Dimensions

	Seniority Levels of Faculty Rated	
Dimension	*< 12 years as faculty member*	*>12 years as faculty member*
1. Socially isolated from colleagues	16%	34%
2. Regularly unfriendly to chair	5%	24%
3. Disrupts departmental meetings	11%	32%
4. Inactive as scholars/researchers	42%	71%
5. Frequent source of student complaints	16%	22%
6. Shirks student advising	32%	49%
7. Explosive with students and colleagues	11%	22%
8. Commonly suspicious/paranoid	5%	12%
9. Qualifies (in 5 of 8 prior categories) as disillusioned	16%	24%

Three things surprised me while collecting and analyzing these ratings and descriptions:

1. Departmental chairs were eager to talk about their problematic faculty, especially about the individuals they rated so difficult that they met what became a broad criterion for MADCs (see the ninth dimension in Table 19.1). Chairpeople were so expansive, they told me, because they had virtually no one else with whom to commiserate about these puzzling colleagues. Two chairs, as soon as they mentioned an especially difficult colleague, pulled an impressively large container from under their desks (one an enormously fat leather valise, the other a large squarish case) to show the extent of materials they had collected about just one MADC; these were displayed with the kind of reverence usually reserved for battle wounds. Virtually every chairperson I queried in this study showed me or told me about an especially thick file on a difficult colleague.

Chairpeople talked most about MADCs who made emotional phone calls to their homes late in the evening (often after apparently having obsessed until impelled to call in a maddened frenzy), who sent barrages of memos and letters (many were copies of letters of complaints about chairs sent to the authorities), and whose threats were litigious or worse. Most such files shown me (in strict confidence) included an accumulation of student complaints and notes from proceedings of campus hearings. The great majority of these chairs told me that their MADCs constituted the most stressful part of chairing—and their prime temptation to quit the position.

2. Ratings by chairs of faculty misbehaviors were generally far more common and problematic than I or almost anyone else I had consulted beforehand imagined. All but 25 of the 88 chairs I interviewed (and followed up within a month or two later to see if they had changed their first impressions) specified at least one highly problematic colleague. All but 2 of the rest designated someone closely approaching that level. The chairs and I (in retrospect and with the data summarized) were also shocked to see how many truly serious problems, such as paranoia and explosiveness, were commonly cited. For example, 3 MADCs had been formally cited for pushing or striking students in classrooms, 2 others for intimidating and shouting students out of their offices. Most such cases, chairs supposed, went unreported to campus administrations.

Many chairs recognized a likely reason why they had overlooked the wider reality of MADCs; prior, they had supposed MADCs were more common in their own department than in others; and they had worried that bringing attention to MADCs under their aegis might reflect poorly on their skills as chairpeople.

Chairs expressed especial alarm and disappointment about the numbers of relatively junior faculty depicted in Table 19.1 (see column for less than 12 years on campus). Too many of them already displayed patterns as unsociable, unhappy, unproductive, and oppositional. Indeed, like most other well-meaning administrators I interviewed over my decades of studies in academe, these chairs had seemed blissfully unaware that their newer faculty struggled with much more than slow starts at writing and teaching. "I guess the psychological side needs more of my attention," said one of the most compassionate chairs among those 88.

3. I now more clearly saw that the roots of dramatic displays of MADCs might be discernible well before midcareer. To explicate that point, I abstract a study of MADCs designated to me as extreme cases.

Follow-up study. I looked for signs in the early careers of extreme MADCs ($N = 22$) that distinguished them, in retrospect, from a sample of peers now nominated as most valued/exemplary at midcareer ($N = 22$). Each of the 44 interviewees was told that he or she was part of my program of interviewing colleagues about the academic experience to collect ideas on how better to treat new faculty. None of these 44 were told they had been nominated as abnormal and none seemed to suspect it.

I first asked each of the 44 to remember their starts on that same campus, particularly what helped or hindered during their first few years. Because MADCs specified few helpful influences during their career starts, I focus here on factors these midcareer faculty recalled as most handicapping. A summary of those data appears in Table 19.2. Even a quick glance at these data suggests that MADCs put heavier blame on early experiences for any disillusionment they now felt. Given that they began at the same campus as did their matched controls, can we dismiss the MADCs as whiners from whom we have little to learn?

TABLE 19.2　Midcareer Faculty Who Agreed Strongly That an Early Experience Handicapped Their Careers

Early Scenario Strongly Endorsed at Midcareer	MACF	Valued
1. Not knowing R/P/T expectations for publishing, etc.	86%	41%
2. No useful information/help from colleagues/campus about publishing enough	55%	45%
3. No useful resources/help from colleagues/campus about teaching well enough	91%	18%
4. No useful direction/information about sufficient or appropriate service	95%	14%
5. Supposing R/P/T information as especially withheld from them	100%	5%
6. Experiencing R/P/T process as politically biased	100%	5%
7. Seeing themselves helpless regarding early survival	91%	0%
8. Experiencing self as only marginally accepted in R/P/T process	100%	0%
9. Being too busy, too overscheduled to do the expected	100%	18%

Not, I trust, after reading the first two sections of this book. Recall that new faculty I observed as unlikely to meet R/P/T expectations complained of nearly identical problems (e.g., busyness) most vigorously and angrily. Those slow starters were apparently on their ways to either leaving academe or staying on amidst disillusionment and oppositionalism. MADCs, then, provide a valuable second sight about the nature of early career fault lines.

Put simply, MADCs (and those on their way to becoming so) exhibit a contradictory mix of high ideals/intentions with helplessness and pessimism about meeting them under conditions common to the professoriate. They usually:

- Direct blame outward, with a small sense of self-responsibility.
- Perceive suggestions for change as criticisms of their person (and as coming from someone unqualified to give them advice).
- Express volatility toward others who might question or evaluate them, including students, peers, and supervisors.
- Display growing social isolation.
- Obsess about wrongdoings, real and imaginary.

What, in contrast, are the typical ways that newcomers on their way to success perceive their experience? Table 19.3 draws the comparison.

The information suggests adaptive and maladaptive ways of experiencing career starts. The next exercise admonishes you to take a more active and involved step.

Exercise 2. Learn What New Faculty (after 4 to 7 years) Would Do Differently if Starting Over.

This is something I urge you to do on your own or with another new hire on campus, largely by way of interviewing junior faculty who will reflect on their own starts. I illustrate what can be learned by summarizing inquiries I've carried out.

TABLE 19.3   Predictive, Dominant Early Experiences of New Faculty

New Faculty en Route to Disillusionment	New Faculty Making Good Starts
1. Experiencing collegial isolation/ neglect	1. Finding useful social supports/networks
2. Perceiving general collegial disapproval	2. Finding ways to admire and enjoy colleagues
3. Self-doubts about own competence	3. Acceptance from students
4. Feeling victimized beyond long-term repair	4. Getting outside requests for reviewing/ consulting/travel

The following are the most common regrets (restated in general ways by me) volunteered by "slow starters" nearing the final decision about reappointment (and already resigned to rejection). They represent diverse study campuses:

"If I could start over again, I would ... "

1. Finish essential tasks in more timely fashion at my graduate campus, before leaving, especially the dissertation and sending it off for publication.
2. Start sooner, immediately after arriving on campus, to work at things like writing regularly, instead of waiting until in the mood.
3. Make more effort to find out about unwritten expectations for new faculty like me, early. I would start, even before leaving my graduate campus (or, later, by calling back), to learn what to expect at my new campus by talking with the younger faculty where I was, and with people I knew who were just starting professorial careers.
4. Read more about early experiences of new faculty (added one to me, humorously, "Maybe even your books").
5. Keep my early interactions/questions with colleagues light-hearted and non-anxious, nonobsessive.
6. Make more effort to know and get help from my chairperson. I'd want to learn what sorts of mistakes or oversights distinguish newcomers who are not reappointed.

Are you surprised that slow starters knew so much, albeit so late? Don't be. New faculty are smart, very smart. Too many just don't learn early how to work and socialize with constancy and moderation. The usually tacit knowledge about how to *work* in academe is intelligence of a different sort, a kind of problem-solving uncommonly taught in schools. When you're in touch with how this oversight penalizes people with great potential, you may be more compassionate toward yourself, your colleagues, and your students.

While you're interviewing a small sample of experienced junior faculty, try to include some quick starters. They, in my experience, do start early at the things just listed. Once they near the tenure decision, though, quick starters in my inquiries usually say that if they could begin anew, they would work with even more moderation, less hurriedly at writing and teaching, more regularly at seeing what matters broadly.

One thing you may not find readily on your own is a sense of how best to conduct these inquiries/interviews. My observations of new faculty carrying out this assignment suggest the following methods and cautions:

1. Engage in small talk and show genuine interest in the other person's expertise and interests. That is, prime the conversation, then wait and listen patiently and compassionately. Expect some of your colleagues to be surprised if you ask process questions—about how to work. Expect, too, that they may be vague at first;

academics are more accustomed to discussing products than processes, more comfortable asking than answering questions.

2. Calmly point out your understandable interest in wanting to do well, for yourself and for your new department/campus. But make it seem that your concerns amount to more than generalized anxiety.

3. Know what questions to ask and what challenges to expect in return (e.g., when you ask what vision your interviewers have in mind for you in your professorial role, they will likely ask you for your own vision of what you hope to accomplish in the next three to six years). When you've replied, ask for opinions about how realistic and on track your plans are. Odds are you will hope to do more than any mortal can.

4. Hold back and don't insult the person you're questioning with many trivialities (e.g., "Is Santa Barbara a nice place to live?"). Avoid obvious ingratiation—a cardinal sin in academe—and, similarly, hold back from bragging or arrogance.

5. Don't actively solicit or reinforce criticism and despair in discussions about your department and campus (but do make note of what your prospective/new colleague seems dissatisfied with and look for patterns across interviews while considering the success and happiness levels of your informers). Why should you seem neutral and only mildly interested in hearing complaints? Because otherwise, interviewers will tend to see you as negative, even if they do most of the complaining while you listen eagerly.

6. Let go of your questioning in timely fashion, earlier than you might like. Stop as soon as the other person persists in stonewalling or awkward rambling, before he or she seems fully annoyed or distracted. Walk away without annoyance. Realize, for example, that your chosen informer may never before have thought of such matters in systematic fashion—and, too, that many professors expect you to ask the questions they, as new faculty, once asked others.

7. Finally, be careful about what kind of curiosity you display:

> *There are two sorts of curiosity: one is from interest, which makes us desire to know what may be useful to us; another which is from pride, and arises from a desire of knowing what others are ignorant of.*
> *—LA ROCHEFOUCAULD*

Next, I overview my own findings about a particularly crucial new faculty experience and I put them in terms of exemplary correctives.

Exercise 3. Consider Reasons for Holding Back from Assuming Collegial Rejection.

Once you're interacting with new colleagues on campus (or even beginning to correspond with prospective colleagues at campuses where you plan to apply), anticipate one of the hardest realities of academic life. People you might suppose will encourage you may seem oddly distant and indifferent.

Pause to reflect mindfully on the probable reasons why: First, most academics are as shy as you are and they do not excel at making small talk with strangers. (If they talked to you with ease at the departmental party after your job talk, you now know why such alcohol-aided events are necessary in academe.) Second, many professors are caught up in busyness, so much so that they unwittingly seem impatient and abrupt with your inquiries. And third, professors are potentially sociable but often prefer isolation and near invisibility, except, perhaps, with their graduate students. If you were to ask them why, they would tell you it is the only way they get any work done. Remember, finally, that introverts find social contacts distracting and wearing—and that they need others to take the initiative in collegiality.

This shock of social isolation is a key source of stress and disillusionment for brand new faculty; seismic overreactions to colleagues who seem uncaring and indifferent create major fault lines in the careers of newcomers. If you find yourself nearing this experience, amid broken promises and shattered spirits, review the common reasons why new faculty often feel abandoned *and* why the stimuli are usually not personal to the new faculty who experience isolation. Consider, too, the following, exemplary ways of responding:

- During prehiring rituals, such as lunches or individual meetings with interviewers, professors are often uncharacteristically friendly; in the euphoric spirit of recruiting, some of them give misleading appearances that they will be close friends and collaborators.
  —Quick starters, in particular, noted that they had made useful adjustments to this scenario by stopping, soon after arrival, to reflect on the likely reasons for feeling abandoned. Said one, "These people probably feel pressured to help recruit candidates, and during interviews they probably get carried away with appearances and promises. Sort of like being rushed by a fraternity."
- Candidates given obvious priority by the department often experience interviews and departmental parties at levels of intensity usually reserved for courtship rituals—including the bobbing and so nodding well known amongst prospective mates in the bird world. The problem is that once such a candidate is hired and on campus, most of those former courtiers return to customary ways of working, largely in an isolating nest all their own.
  —Prospective hirers do this, some new faculty decided, because tradition in academe leads them to expect that you will, once hired, be self-starting, much as they had to be: "Yes, they are cordial but they also keep their distance. I think they're waiting to see if I can manage by myself."
- Many new hires first come to campus in temporary or adjunctive positions. Tradition excludes these newcomers from even the most cursory of amenities—private offices, clear welcomes to faculty meetings, and class assignments at times regular faculty are present.
  —The most successful of academics subjected to this ordeal do four things

that set them apart: First, they take advantage of their freedom from committee work and other departmental responsibilities to get the sort of work done that will enhance their attractiveness on the job market; indeed, new adjuncts are often more productive as writers and teachers than new faculty. Second, they find someone on the full-time faculty with whom to collaborate, someone who can become a champion for them in the department. Third, they make sure they do not remain invisible or aloof. And fourth, they face their ordeal of uncertain status/continuation with the same serene but productive mindfulness that all the other quick starters do.

Problems of acceptance once on campus are clearest where they are most extreme, often among new hires of color. Campuses I studied made special efforts to find such individuals, often before they applied. Select committees with famous members swept them away with warmth and flattery during calls and interviews. The kinds of things not usually arranged for new faculty were provided, even housing arrangements and jobs for spouses. But rarely did these search and capture groups persist beyond the recruitment. After that, it was business as usual: Departments were generally dilatory about providing needed information beforehand or at hand (e.g., where resources and services were located, sometimes at so simple a level as the location of the mailroom). And new colleagues, while friendly, seemed rushed and distracted. Moreover, promised facilities such as an office with a window or a usable lab space were generally not ready, often not even likely. While special new hires might have noticed that other, more traditional new hires were treated with similarly benign neglect, they had a much harder adjustment to make, given the contrast between pre- and posthiring experiences. Moreover, they themselves came to campus with academic histories of expecting but resenting marginalization. So it was that they often accepted indifference and isolation with a sense of resignation. No wonder, I thought, that several such new hires soon opted for corporate careers with established programs of support with labels such as *fast-tracking* for all newcomers.

Traditional new hires felt almost as astonished and discouraged over their campus welcomes and made these usual comments to me during their first few months on campus:

"I realize now, more than ever, what made my start in graduate school so hard. No one paid me much attention when I arrived and I had to figure out almost everything for myself. It's the same deal here. But at _____ , at least, there were other students eager to do things with me. We worked in the same lab and on the same projects. Here, there isn't even that. Why?"

"I've never felt so alone in my life. In graduate school I had friends but I don't know if I will here. Sometimes I get very depressed."

"I wonder if I've chosen the wrong career."

I urge you to notice a commonly overlooked problem in these reactions: The change from student to professor is far larger than most new faculty anticipate. Indeed, it may surpass the transition from living with your family and near life-long friends to independent life at college. In either situation, the adjustment is unlikely to be painless or easy. But in both, the same simple predictor of success applies (e.g., Pascarella & Terenzini, 1991): Constant but moderate involvement in campus activities (e.g., attending cultural and sporting events; participating in campus organizations), in productive interactions with teachers or senior colleagues, and in identification with the institution (i.e., pride of membership). Said another way, effective ways of socializing prove as important at first as do hard work and sacrifice. Socialized work is, after all, the theme of this final section of the book.

The difficulty of that transition, incidentally, is not limited to young new faculty. Consider the scenario where experienced and accomplished people (e.g., conductors/composers, writers/editors, former congress people, civil-rights leaders) were hired as new faculty, usually as full professors, ostensibly to meet specific departmental needs for expertise and collaboration. Imagine how magnificently they were courted and how amazed they were once on campus and left alone (sometimes even targets for resentment from insecure colleagues).

Does this general phenomenon of cold starts mean that they and you should avoid professorial careers? Not at all, I say. It simply shows the benefit of understanding academic culture and how to moderate its perils. Disruptive feelings of isolation can be avoided, most directly by involvement, but also by remembrance of an old maxim:

Pride goeth before destruction, and a haughty spirit before a fall.
—PROVERBS XVI, 18

Exercise 4. Take the Initiative in Collegial Matters.

You've just seen ways of doing this vis-à-vis inquiries and initial contacts with colleagues. But those strategies may seem insufficient in a setting where almost everyone seems remote, indifferent, or worse. The immediate problem of coping with isolation often overwhelms and demobilizes new faculty, so much so that I'll be redundant in restating the common ways that exemplars manage:

1. They soon realize that almost all professors, even though introverted, will gladly offer help if asked. And they know that tradition discourages more experienced colleagues from seeming intrusive or manipulative; concerns about academic freedom often come first. They hope, too, that their compatriots have chosen professorial careers because they enjoy helping others; while professors may readily initiate help with students, they feel more reluctant with peers. The point: You'll need to reach out and ask for help (the brief bouts of inquiries in Exercise 2 may be a good beginning), even if you've felt slighted.

2. They begin early, well before feeling ready, to establish supportive relationships with some colleagues. Preferably they start to communicate and bond before applying for the job, as early as getting their dissertations underway. You'll have little to lose by getting to know outside people in your interest area, perhaps at first as informal readers of your dissertation proposal.

I could list other kinds of specific kinds of advice almost indefinitely, but I want to economize with just two more to keep the scope simple and general.

Exercise 5. Set Inquiry/Work Routines Early, within an Increasingly Sociable Context.

Remember, from the first two sections of this book, why failing new faculty in my studies hadn't put this action first, as they wished they had later: They felt they needed to settle in and wait until large, undisrupted blocks of time appeared before they could work properly at writing. Almost as often, they didn't want regimentation or rules. Recollect, too, some of the other mindless processes that put off their important work unnecessarily:

- Habits of rushing and bingeing that made delayable work seem better put off until there was nothing else that needed doing immediately
- Notions that creative work, like writing and teaching, needs suffering for excellence
- Inquiries not made about how new faculty manage to thrive, including facts to the effect that writers who work with constancy and moderation produce the most and best product over the long run, with the most health
- Entrenched habits of trying to live and work in either the future or the past, not in the present moment

How—early on—can you help prevent this wasteful procrastination? In particular, by consulting Section II and its *nihil nimus* methods for finding time and motivation for writing. But also by making yourself a scholar of sorts about advice for scholarly writers. By at least perusing books besides mine, you broaden your base of advice. That small but important act of socialization is also a kind of service to yourself and your institution; if you help yourself thrive as a newcomer to the professoriate, you ease the lives of colleagues; if you learn enough to help yourself, you can impart that knowledge to other new faculty.

Some new faculty I've known wanted to supplement my *nihil nimus* approach with books that focus more on mechanics and specifics; most other books of advice do.

The first step in Exercise 5 is this: Find at least one other useful guidebook about writing for publication and/or for grants. There are many, many books of advice for scholarly writers, from how to write dissertations to writing for publication in academic outlets, even some about writing while you sleep or dream; I have a large bookcase full of them. But few readings, according to my tracking studies, have proven so useful as the two I overview here and abstract in more detail in the Appendix at the end of this book. I hope to induce you to read them for yourself but I've tried to depict enough of their essential themes to make the appended abstracts useful.

The first is the most useful and confidence-building book I know for imparting detailed information about how to write for publication and fare well in the editorial process (its assigned number helps locate its abstract in the Appendix at the end of the book):

> #1. Sternberg, R. (1993). *The psychologist's companion: A guide to scientific writing for students and researchers.* New York: Cambridge University Press.

Ignore the apparent specificity of the Sternberg book to psychology. It works nicely for new faculty in all disciplines where writing and publishing are de rigueur. Moreover, it is written by a professor with unquestioned success as an academic writer and esteem as a teacher and editor. His highly scientific style of writing may make his book a welcome change from mine. Another reason to read Robert Sternberg is to broaden your perspective on how successful professors work at the most elite level. The best reason, in the view of new faculty in my projects, is that no one excels him at succinct directives on avoiding fatal errors in manuscripts and on what editors want to see from submitting authors.

But know too that Robert Sternberg is stern and seemingly snobbish; he represents high-stakes players with the highest success at the most aristocratic universities. He broadens our scope with anecdotal information about what may distinguish the elite of scientific writers, and he conveys the sense that few new faculty will ever meet his standards. Still, he provides just the kinds of high ideals that many new faculty have told me they value (e.g., "Why not try to be the best?" said one).

Robert Lucas, author of the second guidebook for writers mentioned here and reviewed in the Appendix is more relaxed and democratic in his approach. He, too, models his own pattern of success, one very different from Sternberg's. Lucas made a disappointing start in the professoriate but recovered to learn exemplary ways of working and socializing. Now he travels widely, from his home in remote San Luis Obispo (CA), to coach faculty who want ease and confidence as writers, particularly in the domain of preparing effective grant proposals.

> # 2. Lucas, R. (1992). *The grants world inside out.* Urbana: University of Illinois Press.

No one, according to new faculty I've queried, puts novice grant writers more at ease and in possession of smart first moves in the grants world than Bob Lucas.

No one in this chilly context even approaches his sense of humanity and humor. And no one, in my own studies of new faculty, has proven as helpful to new faculty applying for external funding.

The second step in Exercise 5 is: Find another useful guidebook for preparation as a new faculty member. This suggestion of a reading represents a striking alternative to my own manual: Richard Reis coaches students, as early as undergraduates, about ways to prepare and apply for professorial careers.

> #3. Reis, R. (1997). *Tomorrow's professor.* New York: Institute of Electric and Electronic Engineers.

Reis's text is a far more detailed and specific guidebook than mine; it conveys essential concepts by way of lengthy vignettes—case studies based on recalled or ongoing experiences of individuals. Its material about thriving in graduate school and about wise ways of applying for academic positions should prove especially informative (and not just those of you in engineering).

The third step in Exercise 5 is: Find other guidebooks more exclusively concerned about teaching than mine. I end this introductory representation of readings abstracted in the Appendix of this book with three suggested readings more specific to teaching well. These were most clearly rated by new faculty as most useful. The first, oddly, gives no direct advice for new teachers, nor is its research based on college teachers.

> #4. Bullough, R. V., Knowles, J. G., & Crow, N. (1991). *Emerging as a teacher.* New York: Routledge.

Still, it provides unusually practical insights into what factors typically make beginnings as teachers difficult. In their close and empirically based study of how novice teachers experience starts, Bullough and his colleagues detail usual surprises for school teachers that generalize completely to the college teaching level (e.g., struggling between the moderate stance of making a safe haven for students and the extreme position of becoming their rescuer).

I follow the clear-seeing book of Bullough and colleagues with another reading about the problem of balance in teaching. It, like many other useful writings on balance, prescribes a recursive process of nearly equal time for generating and evaluating.

> #5. Elbow, P. (1983). Embracing contraries in the teaching process. *College Teaching, 45,* 327–339.

Peter Elbow is primarily revered for his books on writing; he wrote the contemporary classic on how to freewrite. He has also written one of the best ever articles on teaching—this one. His premise is intriguing: An essential struggle in teaching well comes from conflicting loyalties, on the one hand to maintaining standards and on the other to nurturing students.

I'll tempt you to glance at just one more abstract in the Appendix to this book by mentioning it here. (I'll add a few more abstracts in the remaining two chapters with direct pertinence to challenges of belonging to special groups—e.g., cooperative teachers, adjunctive faculty, and women and minorities in academe.) This last reading not only teems with broad wisdom and practical specifics but it addresses that most fearsome of teaching assignments for new faculty.

#6. Erickson, B. L., & Stommer, D. W. (1991). *Teaching college freshmen.* San Francisco: Jossey-Bass.

Erickson and Stommer's pioneering and oft-praised guidebook is absolutely essential for new faculty teaching large introductory classes. It also proves invaluable for anyone teaching large numbers of students. (I know whereof I speak; as a first-year assistant professor, I was suddenly assigned to teach well over a thousand freshmen in a generally required survey course that met in two successive sessions per day, in a huge and poorly lighted auditorium.)

Even if you find these six sources worth a closer look, you might continue to wonder why I consider this sort of reading-for-action a useful step in socialization. One reason, again, is that it takes you beyond the exercises of this book, into experiences of gathering more advice and insight from others. Second, it acquaints you with the real voices of experts giving advice—a useful comparison for advice you collect on your own from colleagues. And third, the varied perspective I model in suggesting those readings (e.g., one from psychology, English, science and engineering, higher education, and administration) can only broaden your own. The exemplary way to implement these advantages, finally, is in the Baconian sense: Learn which specifics from readings are helpful to you by putting them outward for public testing, in the public view of others, including peers and students. Better yet, begin to synthesize those specifics across experts and with the *nihil nimus* approaches of this book in order to draw more general but simple principles for working.

Exercise 6. Begin to Find Colleagues for Ongoing Advice and Support.

Because I have already specified the entry skills for getting to know colleagues, I'll be brief about what comes next. None of it, I suspect, would surprise you. This, for instance, is the compilation of what one program participant noted from her initial chats with a colleague who agreed to spend more and regular sessions listening to concerns and offering advice. This more senior colleague was, herself, a near exemplar—a nice qualification if you can manage it in your advisor. So, here is a sample of what one participant valued most from her notes of advice sessions:

- Get to your essential work *immediately* now, not at some later point when you must because you're running out of time. If you don't, you'll find yourself a whole lot less productive over this period than you had imagined. And you *will* be at risk of a rejection for permanent appointment, believe me, and you'll fail in an astonishingly miserable way. I've seen it happen.
- Soon, very soon, establish your plans of where you want your work to take you and then share it with someone who has been there, like me. You need to be certain that what you want to do will fit in here, at least in some general ways.
- Don't isolate yourself and don't suppose that meeting with me alone is enough.
- Get ready to share your written plans, while they're tentative, to a few others here who know the ropes. I can suggest some and I could even arrange a meeting where we give you a friendly evaluation.

None of that was new to the novice listening to her mentor but all of it was reinforcing and indicative of what you, too, can elicit from an a regular advisor.

Next is a brief sampling of this newcomer's notes from just such a first meeting with her informal steering committee of three more senior colleagues:

[her] Q: How much is enough here?

[their] A: Usually at least four publications in the next four to six years in refereed journals, depending on their quality.

Q: How will I know about quality?

A: You let us see what you're doing as you do it and submit it. In a way, we [will] steer [direct] you on that by looking over your plans for research and publishing now.

Q: Am I likely to have to or want to change my plans?

A: Some junior faculty do, but they probably don't do it wisely unless they work it out with good advice from the department or a good representation of colleagues

Q: When are you likely to advise a change?

A: If we see you're overloaded. If you're working hard with too few satisfying results. But we are most concerned about your changing in a fickle and impulsive way. It happens and the result usually isn't good.

And this, finally, depicts advice from a subsequent meeting with just her mentor:

- Get visitors to your office to leave in timely fashion (i.e., within a reasonable period, especially when there are others waiting to see you) by mentioning that you worry about keeping the next person waiting or that you have a phone call to make. If necessary, walk your present visitor to the door, and wish him or her a pleasant farewell. Then, ask the person waiting to give you a minute to rest before entering.
- Don't socialize too much with old friends from former lives at first. Don't invite them for weekends or longer, not during this probationary period. Just explain your temporary situation and they'll understand if they are friends. Whatever, don't get into such things out of a need for escape. A brief rest? Fine. A long escape? Not good.
- Resist temptations to visit, call, or mail your old schools. You need to be here, at least for now.

Exercise 7. Accompany and Observe Your Advisor(s).

This is a natural step, but one you might suppose an imposition on one of the colleagues you've picked as advisors. If you're brave enough to take it, you will almost surely find that he or she will regard your "shadowing" a compliment, so long as it is kept occasional and moderate.

This exercise produces too much valued information to list in a book that I've tried to keep brief enough to entrap busy readers. Here, too, I've chosen examples from notes taken by shadowers—new faculty following and observing their advisors. None of their records seemed more important than having seen how the most experienced and successful professors avoid unnecessary affronts to colleagues:

- They wait and listen in faculty meetings, at least until something needs saying. They suggest that emotional interchanges be put off for calmer times.
- They notice norms of dress codes and stay within broad boundaries of acceptability (as opposed to constantly dressing up from colleagues in a casually attired department).
- They never criticize colleagues in classes/offices, even in retribution; they know that the same people who encourage them to gossip are most likely to repeat (and probably distort) their offhand comments.
- They don't shrink away from an administrator who has broken a promise (e.g., about teaching load). Instead, they react calmly but firmly by negotiating for some sort of useful compensation (e.g., an extra research assistant for the semester). They show compassion for administrators who must make such thankless decisions.
- They keep up with colleagues' accomplishments/interests, even enough to comment in brief but meaningful ways on their new publications and media appearances (but without being ingratiating).

- They talk aloud the costs of intimacy/harassment with students, colleagues, and staff. They constantly but moderately remind students and others of their attachment to a significant other—often by displaying photos of that person in their office or by mentioning her or him in their anecdotes during classes and discussions.
- They remain aware of faculty power groups and how they operate. In a traditional department, that group may operate as a poker-playing, cigar-smoking, private club of sorts [it is still so at my final campus] and as the setting for secretive decisions about departmental matters.
- And, not least, these advisors had found good mentors in their own career beginnings.

Your early advisor(s) may be ideal as a mentor; remember to do the following things before you make a binding decision: Ask your advisor for her or his opinion of where you should turn for mentoring (and don't assume that your advisor wants to take on that larger role). Look around you to see which more experienced colleagues, in or out of the department, might best meet your needs. For example, some offer possible advantages of taking you along in projects of grant writing, researching, publishing, and service. Some excel at promoting you behind the scenes. And some are excellent teachers of simple survival skills.

Most important, first read about the proven benefits of mentoring, and about the specific acts of effective mentoring. Where? In the next chapter.

20

Let Others Do Some of the Work

Compassion for yourself is more than slowing and calming, nice as those are. It is also more than simplifying your work by way of mindfulness moved outward and into action. The hardest part of practicing self-compassion is letting others do some of your work.

We already know why this "letting go" is difficult, because we struggled with it during earlier exercises as teachers and then as writers. The same rule is no less important in socialization to the professoriate. And it is no less challenging. The usual obstacles apply, including excessive pride, personal reluctance about sharing the credit for work with others, and beliefs that collaborators more often hinder than help. That much you already know; you may suspect the rest.

These inhibitions also owe to customs unique to academe. What better model for working alone and with little direction than the way most of us do our dissertations? What more effective discouragement of sociable sharing than the expectation that dissertations must not be submitted until finished? And what better basis for dread of public scrutiny than the customary uncovering of a shameful ignorance during oral exams?

When I repeatedly queried struggling new faculty about their reluctance to reach out for social support, one explanation emerged most saliently: These novice faculty supposed that *dissertation rules* still applied (e.g., work on your own and share it only when perfect). And they believed that displays of weakness in the presence of more senior faculty could be fatal. But some novice faculty let go of these hardened views when I reminded them of my research findings:

- The sooner new faculty abandoned vicious cycles of isolationism and perfectionism, the more readily they thrived during their probationary periods.

- Struggling new faculty who conserved these unnecessary and counterproductive attitudes more often left campus or stayed on under a cloud.
- These conservatives were less involved in programs for junior faculty, such as the one outlined in this book (however, they did listen, more than other new faculty, to stories about the unfairness of reward systems at their campus).
- They remained unusually private as teachers and as writers; that is, they put off appointments with classroom observers and submissions to editors.
- They more often procrastinated writing while waiting for ideal work conditions and for impressively clever ideas; they typically reworked lecture materials beyond the point of diminishing returns.
- They unintentionally seemed aloof and distant to colleagues, and they themselves saw colleagues in much the same way.
- Conservatives made no sustained attempts to find mentors; moreover, they resisted approaches by prospective mentors (especially when women were offered direction/support by successful men).

Those reluctances remind me of the questions that puzzled me most when I began my programs for new faculty: What makes struggling new faculty so resistant to accepting help from colleagues? Why do individuals who need help most seem least willing to accept it? I didn't quite figure an answer until I repeatedly saw struggling newcomers reject the advances of experienced colleagues who could offer substantial help. I was at last reminded of an insight from Samuel Johnson in his own attempts to assist the needy. They, he noticed, were most skeptical and suspicious, most determined to display their cunning by working alone. Why? Because they, already on the defensive, found it hardest to trust others and to admit even obvious failings. Worse yet, he noted, they were caught up in a pride that made them regard offers of help as little more than condescension.

No wonder, then, that many new faculty need to understand why a sound mentoring relationship is worth letting go of excessive pride and suspiciousness. That understanding, you may have noticed, is the point of this chapter. Toward that end, I will ask you to scan traditional notions of mentoring, to reflect on a pioneering study of mentoring, and to extend the kind of collaboration/trust learned in mentoring to acts such as cooperative learning and classroom research.

As usual, I'll mention proven correctives for poor starts among new faculty: Exemplar-based ways of working and socializing. And I'll try to be compassionately brief in setting a context about where we are and where we are going. A key to getting underway here with ease lies in the clear seeing of what compassion means—as in this simple definition:

[*compaſſion,* French from *con* and *patior,* Lat.] Pity; commiseration; sorrow for the suffering of others; painful sympathy.

Ye had compassion for me in my bonds. (Heb. 10:34)—JOHNSON'S DICTIONARY

What Helps New Faculty Find Self-Compassion through Socialization?

Compassion, excluding Dr. Johnson's definition of pity, comes most reliably and directly from the kinds of mindfulness we practiced explicitly in Section II of this book. When we live and work largely in the moment, we more clearly see how we usually bring ourselves to misery (e.g., trying to do two things at once). And as we give up neurotic conflicts of approach/avoidance, we not only simplify our own experience but we also more readily admit to our own inefficiencies and needs for expert coaching. In my programs, at least, that inner awareness is most readily moved outward to accept help when the action is least threatening—as with the inquiries about academic culture modeled in the prior chapter. That first move can prime you for an understanding of how mentoring helps.

What, specifically, happens when you begin to socialize your perceptions of academic work by reading and applying some of the advice of varied experts? (Here I ask you to resume the mindset of Francis Bacon, our official guide in Section III.) Expert advice, assembled and refined in a perspective of public action, provides socially tested knowledge that shortcuts the trial-and-error learning we would otherwise have to undergo. Equally important, that socialized learning allows us to proceed with especial confidence about using our time and energy wisely.

If this Baconian notion seems confusing, reconsider this: Early in this book we learned much the same thing about looking outward for public demonstrations of which strategies work well and which do not. One instance with special promise of savings was about reliably distinctive qualities of new teachers whose classes were uncomplicated and unimpaired by incivilities. And in the preceding chapter, again, we enacted the same pattern of moving outward by accepting social support and direction: First with regular advisors, then with advisory groups, along with broad expertise from writers worth reading because of the seeming social generality of their advice. The next exemplary step is reaching out for information on mentoring, initially by considering potential values of mentoring and the simple actions that ensure them.

Mentoring

In preliminary studies where I observed but did not intervene, I could see that mentoring proved a powerful predictor of "good starts" (as I've defined them throughout this book) for new faculty. Yet, like many other exemplary factors, effective mentoring was generally neglected amongst new faculty left to their own wiles.

Most newly arrived faculty told me they probably would not want or need a mentor. These were their most common reservations (condensed here for the sake of clarity):

- I'm too busy.
- Mentoring is remedial help.
- Dissertation directors are ostensibly mentors but mine was of little help.
- I'm tired of other people telling me what to do; I'm overdue to work on my own.
- I'll ask for advice if I need it; I don't want to be pinned down with regular meetings or annoyed by constant criticisms.
- Mentoring is a fad. It is almost always superficial and done for appearances.
- A mentor would pressure me to be like him or her, maybe even to be a lackey in his or her work.
- I'm not sure what a mentor does.
- Someone who would want to mentor me would probably expect a sexual relationship.

Where might these newcomers to professorial careers have acquired that sort of pessimism? Probably in realities like these: Previous experiences with advisors who were too negative or uninvolved to help; supervisors who allowed too little freedom of expression; and superiors who pressured for inappropriate favors (e.g., collaborations where the novice did most of the work but got second authorship). Add to those experiences customary assumptions that the best work in academe is done alone, and you may feel compassion for such skepticism and reticence. If that compassion needs to be directed to yourself, resume practice of something you know from exercises at teaching and writing: Letting go of excessive attachments, especially to bad experiences. Start by joking about this defensive stance:

> *A pessimist is one who feels bad when he feels good for fear he'll feel worse when he feels better.—GEORGE BERNARD SHAW*

> *An optimist sees an opportunity in every calamity; a pessimist sees a calamity in every opportunity.—AUTHOR UNKNOWN*

But how do you actually get past the nagging realization that pessimists are right? Thriving new faculty generally say they do so by way of mindfulness like this: They see that all these bad things can happen to people who dare venture outward with work done more socially. They remind themselves why that risk is worthwhile (e.g., "Life is a risk, anything worth doing entails some risk"). And they notice that pessimistic new faculty demonstrate the penalties of conservatism: Because they do not learn how to avoid or manage embarrassments and injustices, they risk feelings of helplessness/hopelessness and their likely sequelae of poor self-esteem and low self-efficacy. Moreover, pessimists isolate themselves from too many of academic life's best experiences.

An especially effective way of moderating pessimism, according to my studies, is entering a compassionate mentoring relationship. To illustrate this, I ask you to abide yet another account of my field researches, this time about the surprising ease and effectiveness of mentoring done in exemplary fashion. Therein lie some insights about what makes mentoring useful.

A Systematic Study of Mentoring among New Faculty

I developed an interest in mentoring much as I did for other experiences of new faculty emphasized in this book: Its presence or absence seemed to matter in my day-to-day observations of newcomers. Here, too (as in my examinations of, say, binge writing), there were fewer useful precedents than I hoped for.

A Brief Look at the Literature

Mentions of mentoring can be found in very early writings; it is as old as its kin, including apprenticeship, coaching, and teaching (maybe even parenting). Except for ways in which some apprentices were coached in crafts, such as gunsmithing, we know little about the particulars. I, for one, still associate apprenticeships with the oppression of Oliver Twist, sleeping on a shelf amid the coffins he helped build—but I suspect we can learn more from other cases.

The clearest descriptions of mentoring nowadays come from the corporate world where ensuring good starts is obviously economical. While some business writers extol mentoring for its nurturing properties, almost all their evidence is conjectural or anecdotal. Its critics dismiss any value of mentoring in business because it forces participation and conformity, more so because mentoring done well presumably requires more time than can be managed in the real world. Not surprisingly, pessimists who could be mentors or mentees in academe recite the same objection, one that comes down to busyness.

Even so, recent publications about mentoring in professorial careers merit our attention (e.g., Bova, 1995; Gaff & Simpson, 1994; Johnsrud & Atwater, 1993): Intense mentoring relationships generally predict political saavy, more advanced professional skills, higher levels of research productivity, and greater career advancement. The problem amid these optimistic findings is one we've seen earlier in this book, notably in the attitude romantics bring to scholarly writing: Most campus leaders in a position to help new faculty believe that the best mentoring occurs spontaneously, without unnatural arrangements. Said one dean to me with great certainty: "That only works as a hands-off proposition. Mentors have to do the picking, and they have to do it their own way, without outside interference."

That last assumption—about spontaneity being preferable to informed interventions—was the focus of my earliest studies about mentoring. I began, with my partner Jimmie L. Turner, by observing how often and to whom mentoring occurred "naturally," and how effective it proved to be.

Pilot Study: Does Naturally Occurring Mentoring Suffice for Diverse New Faculty?

Our year-long field observations showed the following:

- Spontaneous mentoring occurred for only about one-third of the new faculty; nontraditional hires and newcomers who struggled most were even more likely to go unmentored.
- The great majority of those natural pairings died an early, natural death, almost always because mentors and mentees claimed that their own busyness necessitated putting off meetings.
- Because they generally had no clear sense of which actions and interactions would be most helpful, almost all natural mentors tended to disappointingly narrow styles (i.e., meetings only in the mentor's office, usually with the mentor doing most of the talking from behind his or her desk, much of it anecdote telling, bragging, and complaining).
- Most natural mentors were reluctant interventionists and champions for their mentees; they gave some concrete advice but they rarely modeled ways of working (e.g., how to prepare a lecture) or introduced mentees to useful resources and influential colleagues. Instead, they mentored much as they taught, by lecturing to passive listeners.
- Exemplary new faculty, in contrast, took the unnatural initiative of selecting their mentors after careful consideration (e.g., advice from their department chairpeople) and patient early contacts with several possible mentors. All had near-exemplary or exemplary mentors, and most had more than one (usually one primary and the other secondary and more specialized). Exemplary new faculty and their mentors typically met in brief, regular meetings that persisted quietly over several years, and their interactions included direct coaching, even collaboration, in domains of writing, teaching, and socialization.
- Thriving new faculty helped arrange meetings and interactions that took place outside the mentor's office. Curiously, these people were unlikely to publicize their mentoring experiences, apparently because they were more interested in getting work done than in proselytizing about how they did it. They knew that tradition in academe carries a strong prohibition against "outperfomace" (outperforming others) made public (Exline & Lobel, in press).

So the answer to the question I posed at the head of this list—Does naturally occurring mentoring suffice for diverse new faculty?—is no. Natural mentoring is uncommon and usually ineffective. Moreover, exceptional instances of mentoring that works remain generally unknown.

Formal, Funded Mentoring Study

Project Designs (see Boice, 1990; Boyle & Boice, 1998 for additional information).   The first study site was a large comprehensive university. During this two-year formal project, 116 new faculty were hired on the tenure track, 48 of whom were novices in the professoriate. At the second site, a public research university, 95 new faculty were hired, 45 as novices, during the four-year period of study.

Mentees.   Pilot research (above) indicated the importance of tracking each mentoring pair on a weekly basis, with attention both to individual pair members and to mentoring duos. We used friendly and individual encounters to recruit a total of 19 new faculty at both campuses who, by their own admission, would otherwise have remained uninvolved. We included no mentees performing at the level of exemplary new faculty.

We selected novice faculty distributed across the sciences, social sciences, and humanities (although at Campus 2, some departments—under the influence of a new provost with an initial prejudice against faculty development programs—permanently prohibited participation by their new faculty). One recruit quit the program after a luncheon with her prospective mentor and she was replaced by a peer with similar demographics; the other 41 mentees at Campuses 1 and 2 persisted in the program for at least an academic year. All participation was voluntary and, so far as possible, confidential.

During the total six years of study, we got the consent of 36 novice faculty who proceeded without apparent mentoring to serve as control subjects who would provide us with occasional data about how well they were faring. An additional 6, none of them exemplary new faculty, found "natural mentors" on their own and agreed to the same ongoing scrutiny as directed at project pairs.

Mentors.   Public appeals on both campuses for mentors brought an oversupply of volunteers. At Campus 1, interest might have been augmented because our federal grant could supply mentors with a summer stipend after completion of a project year; nonetheless, volunteers seemed as plentiful and enthusiastic at Campus 2 without funding. At both campuses we picked mentors largely on the basis of their productivity and optimism as teachers, writers, and socializers; all seemed genuinely interested in learning about mentoring and helping their appointed mentees in substantial ways. At Campus 2, because I was better prepared to find near-exemplars among experienced faculty, I sought only mentors who qualified as successful teachers, writers, and socializers who had already mentored in a demonstrably effective manner.

At Campus 2, I found exemplars and their close kin among the experienced faculty by looking at:

- The records in departmental files about which faculty were consistently published in archival journals and highly rated by students (cf. strict reliance on public teaching awards or on campus reputation as well liked, hard working, and self-promoting)
- Their classroom immediacies and involvement (see Chapter 8), by way of direct observation in classrooms.
- Their patience during individual interviews
- Their recounting of benefits from mentors of their own
- Their description of a recent experience as mentor, confirmed by mentees as beneficial
- How clearly and willingly they could imagine themselves mentoring in active ways such as coaching at writing or co-presenting in classrooms

One thing struck me as surprising about the accomplished group selected as mentors at Campus 2. They were usually not highly prominent or political on campus (cf. members of special advisory groups to the president; vocal leaders of the faculty senate).

Schedules, assessments, and obligations.   While at Campus 1, we knew of no systematic mentoring programs in academe that had succeeded in keeping its pairs assessed and meeting regularly for more than a few months. So we assumed that our usual emphasis on brief, daily sessions (BDSs) for writers might bring more constancy and persistence to mentoring than customary methods (e.g., pairing and inspiring mentors/mentees in a weekend retreat before letting them work on their own). Our pair members promised to meet in brief, weekly sessions of about 10 to 20 minutes each over the whole of the academic year just underway.

Each pair agreed to share experiences and methods with other pairs in monthly group meetings of about an hour each. They also tolerated several kinds of constant scrutiny: (1) our presence during about half of their scheduled mentoring meetings; (2) our weekly phone calls or direct visits to each pair member along with requests for descriptions and ratings; (3) our weekly looks at their updated logs of ongoing experiences in the project; (4) our frequent demands for completion of self-inventories such as personality tests; and (5) our noting of what they did and said in monthly meetings with other mentoring pairs.

I extended the same essential methods to Campus 2. (This period of my career stands out for the exhilaration I felt in cycling from one observation or interview site to another on campus about every 20 minutes for as long as four to six hours a day. Never before had I felt so connected with the new faculty experience.)

Participants also knew they would be rated as individuals and as pairs in terms of a Mentoring Index with 10 basic dimensions (e.g., "Pair meets regularly, persistently, in substantial fashion" [i.e., more than small-talk and for more than five minutes]). Each of these items was rated weekly on a 1- to 10-point scale, with 10 = maximum at both campuses. In all measures, I made my own ratings independently of of those of the participants.

Project Results

Involvement.   Of the 25 mentoring pairs at Campus 1, 22 met regularly and persistently over an academic year. That is, they missed no more than three weekly meetings and no more than two group meetings overall. All 16 of the pairs at Campus 2 met this criterion of constant but moderate involvement. Why was participation so high? Pairs eventually explained it in three ways: (1) The worth and pleasure of the meetings, (2) the brevity of meetings that did not interfere with other obligations, and, most important, (3) the awareness that they would be visited at meeting times or else asked soon after to describe the meeting. Even though we were invariably gentle in these reminders to meet regularly, participants told us that when tempted to skip a meeting, they decided it would be less painful to meet their partners on schedule than to explain their "sloth" to us. Over time, mentees reported a related factor behind their constant but moderate involvement: The efficacy and self-esteem that accompanied this version of BDS. (For a similar point about writing in BDS, see Chapter 11.) Mentoring pairs at Campus 2 evidenced even higher levels of involvement but they placed less importance on feeling forced to meet.

Mentoring styles: Campus 1.   These 25 pairs interacted in a wide variety of styles. Six pairs began by focusing on just one activity, usually writing but often teaching or early preparation of materials for reappointment. By the second semesters, though, those 6 pairs had broadened their scope to three or four topics. By the same juncture, the 12 pairs that had begun by discussing just about everything that came to mind had narrowed topics to three or four specifics. The other 7 pairs established patterns we had not anticipated, patterns that proved instructive to us. Of those, 4 were stymied when, after a few weeks, they had run out of small-talk and could see no need to continue. After a bit of coaching from us (i.e., to continue meeting until worthwhile topics emerged; to spend time reflecting on what kinds of needs most new faculty might have), these pairs functioned at levels we rated as moderately effective. That is, these somewhat reticent pairs remained that way, somewhat reticent.

The remaining three pairs were unique as the only duos who had been close friends beforehand. Each of the prefriendly pairs eventually rated as "failed," apparently because once the relationship was formalized, their mentors generally assumed more authoritarian styles and unrealistic expectations/demands than did other mentors. Another explanation may lie in research by social scientists: People who rely most on "weak connections" (i.e., acquaintances but not close friends) fare best in making wide and useful social contacts (Gladwell, 1999).

Mentors were otherwise initially reserved about acting as experts or advisors (e.g., "I don't really feel comfortable calling myself a mentor because I m not even sure I know what one is"). What helped break this impasse was the ready insistence of all mentees, in monthly group meetings, that they considered their partners as qualified mentors with things worth teaching and taking pride in. Said one to her mentor: "Listen: It not only isn't presumptuous to call yourself my mentor, it also comforts *me*."

Mentoring styles: Campus 2.   I selected only mentors I had designated, beforehand, as exemplary or nearly so. I gave none of these 16 mentors explicit directions for mentoring, except a research-based document about the usual experiences of new faculty on campus (e.g., their surprisingly lonely starts and their disconcertingly busy and uncivil beginnings as writers and teachers). In a group meeting of mentors alone, held before they met their mentees, mentors settled quickly and congenially on a format of what they called *active mentoring*. They would all begin, they decided, with actions to (1) break the initial feelings of isolation among new faculty (e.g., by taking mentees around to meet people who could help and/or be friends; by showing them how to use the campus computer center); (2) observe mentees' classes from the first to check for incivilities (e.g., lecturing at too fast and uninvolving a pace); and (3) involve mentees quickly in regular sessions of scholarly writing. One result was a far higher level of confidence about being able to help as mentors than I had seen at Campus 1.

The mentoring index: Campus 1.   We used pilot research to preset criteria for rating that would result, ideally, with every pair scoring a mean of at least 70 overall; such a score required little more than consistent, balanced, and substantial ways of mentoring. Our mean rating for these 25 pairs was 70.8; only about half of the mentoring pairs met our expectations for moderate involvement and success; fewer pairs met their own. Still, even the most poorly rated pairs in the project scored generally better than the naturally occurring pairs we monitored; the best two pairs outside our program scored at $\bar{x} = 51$ and 57 (and both were prearranged by mentors before mentees got to campus) but the others rated no higher than $\bar{x} = 30$ during the two months or less they persisted. The three failed pairs who began as strong friends scored $\bar{x} = 29$, 56, and 62. One other pair, weakly and cordially connected, self-described as too busy to meet regularly, ended with $\bar{x} = 29$. I speak to the reasons for this generally poor performance as we proceed.

If this small sample is worth sorting for effects of other variables, these suggestions emerge: Mentoring pairs arranged across departments scored higher ($\bar{x} = 73.9$) than did those with both members in the same department ($\bar{x} = 67.8$), a difference that only approached statistical reliability. Pairs with more senior mentors (15+ years) rated only slightly higher than mentors five years or less past tenure.

Four mentors who paired again with new mentees in the second project year dropped in ratings ($\bar{x} = 77.1$ vs. 81.5), apparently for two reasons. They reported burnout in starting with new and demanding mentees so soon, and they felt conflicted about not giving their original program mentees as much time as before. Indeed, the latter reaction seems understandable in considering that all but one mentor rated above $\bar{x} = 70$ continued to meet with their mentees in brief, weekly sessions for at least a year beyond the formal project, usually two years. (Only two of the less successful mentors persisted in similar fashion.) All pairs that continued with regular meetings into a second year judged it as more valued and productive than the first, and the third year best of all.

The mentoring index: Campus 2.   Compared to those on Campus 1 these mentors took a more definite and active role, and their scores based on the same Mentoring Index produced predictably higher ratings overall, $\bar{x} = 90.5$. No pair at Campus 2 rated lower than 79 (and that score came from a within-department pair who decided to put off sustained attention to teaching until the second or third year of meetings; their department had a clearly stated rule that initially poor teaching ratings would not count in R/P/T decisions).

Pair's self-ratings: Campus 1.   Pair-members made weekly entries in their logs on a variety of dimensions. Just 3 of the 25 pairs at Campus 1 showed consistently high ratings in both directions (mentor-to-mentee and vice versa); retrospectively, mentees in the other pairs blamed themselves for most of the slowness with which trust and rapport had developed.

Figure 20.1 depicts the average pair ratings for the dimension participants valued most after the project at both campuses: Consistency of meeting. (These data, not surprisingly, closely resemble my own counts of actual meetings.) The first four quarters represent the formal year of participation; the fifth quarter depicts the carryover of consistency into the first quarter of the second year. Natural pairs (Campuses 1 and 2) fell off most markedly and reached nader within the first year. Experimental pairs (Campus 1) were highly consistent until the fifth quarter of recordings; there, the divergence between groups with overall above- and below-criterion scores lowered the mean level of consistency. Finally, pairs with near exemplary mentors or better met most consistently.

Those same groups also divided in similar ways along lines of reported congeniality. This suggests that experimental pairs, most of whom could not find compatibility, fared only marginally better than natural twosomes on this crucial dimension. Said another way, our failure to select more exemplary mentors at Campus 1—and, perhaps, to provide them with a clearer sense of what needed doing first—produced pairings less likely to cooperate than at Campus 2.

Pairs ongoing ratings: Campus 2.   Again, pairs with near-exemplary mentors showed the most consistency in meeting (see Figure 20.1). They also reported the most congeniality by far (Figure 20.2). My own observations indicate that exem-

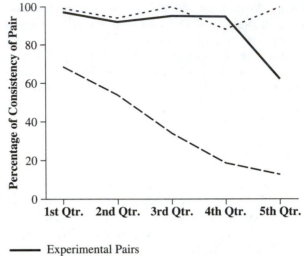

——— Experimental Pairs
– – – Natural Pairs
· · · · · Exemplary Mentors

FIGURE 20.1   Consistency of Pair Meetings

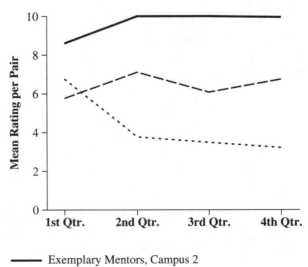

——— Exemplary Mentors, Campus 2
– – – Experimental Pairs, Campus 1
· · · · · Natural Pairs, Both Campuses

FIGURE 20.2   Pairs Reporting Congeniality

plary mentors came to pairings with more confidence and congeniality at hand; said in terms of this book, they more readily displayed the immediacies and positive motivators we saw for the exemplary teachers of Chapter 8. This, in turn, seemed to enhance the readiness with which mentees could respond to suggestions for on-target actions. That same readiness also seemed to amplify their sense of congeniality. Mentees of exemplary mentors rated their "coaches" with uniformly high scores, at least by the third week of regular meetings. Mentors did so almost immediately.

Put simply, the pairings at Campus 2 (all formed between strangers—as strong weak connections—and half across departments) worked surprisingly well for both mentors and mentees, many of whom had initially described the other as disappointingly different with regard to personality, appearance, or apparent interests. Mentors said that these pairings had gone far better than their own, earlier, natural mentoring experiences, probably because they now had so clear a sense of what new faculty experienced and needed in general. As a result, mentors reported, they could move quickly to specifics and early actions for mentees. One mentor put it this way: "It was as though I could read his mind." And they put high value on the confidence they felt in so helpful a path with their mentees (e.g., "I was at ease, immediately"). I anticipated the final explanation of why their pairings worked from what mentors had said, retrospectively, at Campus 1: The more they got into coaching, the more they benefitted in seeing their directives put into action by mentees (sometimes in other mentors' mentees, in monthly group meetings). This meant that mentors clarified their advice about, say, teaching by way of pointing out classroom immediacies. But that pleasant experience was only the half of it. One exemplary mentor's explanation seems so memorable that I present it with emphasis:

> *Let's see, maybe it will make sense this way: At first I had to admit that I had never been totally clear about what I did as a teacher until I tried to put it [advice for teaching] into discreet assignments or whatever. That took some thinking and some observation to see how she [my mentee] did it to our mutual satisfaction. Then, of course, I put those somewhat clearer techniques to work in my own teaching. Now that was an unexpected benefit of mentoring. I may be getting more out of this than she is.*

Francis Bacon would have, I believe, beamed at this outcome. I surely did.

Conclusions about the Mentoring Study.   Overall, my 6½-year inquiry about mentoring for new faculty took me a long way beyond my anticipations. (I could have used a mentor, an expert about mentoring.) At the outset, I had no good understanding of how rich and rewarding mentoring relationships in academe can be. And I had begun without imagining what deprivation new faculty suffer without effective mentors. At the two study campuses I've just depicted, and at several others I have monitored, truly effective mentoring occurs for far fewer newcomers than Jim Turner and I had originally estimated in our pilot studies. The irony is that effective mentoring is neither too difficult nor too time consuming to effect in useful fashion. In my observations, effective mentoring took no more than one hour per week, on average, for mentors (including time spent in meetings, in preparing for meetings, and in related contacts with faculty/administrators who could help their mentees). When mentees found a secondary mentor (40 percent of mentees in pairs rated highly did so; none in poorly rated pairs), time expenditures for primary mentors decreased somewhat. For mentees of exemplary mentors, time reported spent on meetings and exercises averaged 2.5 hours per week. Mentees at Campus 1, in the better half of mentoring pair ratings overall, reported $\bar{x} = 1.8$ hours per week; those in the lower half reported $\bar{x} = 0.7$ hours per week.

At the beginning of my mentoring studies, I would not have guessed that my own mentoring/coaching of mentors would become a prime stimulus for completing this book of advice. In practice, *Advice for New Faculty Members: Nihil Nimus* seems as useful for mentors as for mentees.

I'll end my overview of the mentoring studies with some data that may have mattered most in terms of survival. Mentees from highly rated pairings at Campus 1 and from all pairings at Campus 2 evidenced greater long-term benefits than did poorly mentored or nonmentored new faculty. These are representative specifics for new faculty with effective mentoring:

- Always came close to departmental expectations for scholarly productivity (mode = three or four manuscripts accepted in refereed outlets before formal tenure consideration)
- Always exceeded departmental expectations for adequate teaching by year 2 on campus (criterion = teaching ratings in the top half for the department)
- Always were rated, beforehand, by reappointment committees as adequately collegial and cooperative

Amongst new faculty *not* exposed to excellent mentoring, one-third were on track in regard to these criteria early—within the first two years—and one-half within the first three years. Most new faculty who were just below par at reappointment but who showed promise and congeniality were reappointed for a second three or four years and with painful feedback. Roughly 15 percent of new faculty without excellent mentoring left campus early or were terminated while probationary; *none* with effective mentoring did or were. Of course, mentors with success had help from their partners. Mentees in excellent pairings were also distinctive in supporting mentors, even in asking for specific help they wanted.

What might you do to be as proactive? How can you be informed enough to select a mentor likely to help you in substantial ways?

Rule 3: Let Another Person Do Some of Your Work, as a Mentor.

Exercise for Rule 3

Exercise 1. Consider Optimal Ways of Arranging Mentoring.

1. Know enough about mentoring to appreciate how useful, essential, and fun it can be. In particular, appreciate that joy and comfort are nearly universal for mentees in mentoring relationships carried out with constancy, moderation, directedness, meaningful assessments, and compassion. Also, anticipate that you can also derive other benefits, such as good beginnings and easy passage through R/P/T rituals.

2. Understand why most natural mentoring isn't more common and useful. The usual process is no more effective than waiting at home for new romantic prospects to show up. You must be proactive in finding a qualified partner; you might even have to cultivate your mentor as much as he or she educates you.

3. Appreciate one good reason for carrying out this difficult assignment of letting others do some of your work: Most campuses set expectations higher than can be attained without it.

4. Understand that exemplary mentors and their close kin may not be the most luminous and obvious faculty on campus. They are usually not so competitive and busy as politicians.

5. Be patient and mindful in selecting/accepting a mentor; wait while you sample the advice and modeling styles of prospects before coestablishing a formal relationship. Try to arrange at least one mentor from a department other than your own in order to ensure that some of your foibles are observed by a colleague not on your R/P/T committee.

6. Remind yourself of the actions of excellent *mentors* (e.g., willingness to mentor in active ways, including coteaching) and, just as thoroughly, of the exemplary qualities of *mentees* (e.g., ready trust, openness, and involvement—once confidentiality is assured)

7. Let go of perfectionism if necessary; you'll do better to find a young partner than no mentor or an uninvolved senior mentor. Settle, if necessary, for two or three mentors (not more; be moderate), each with different kinds of expertise. If your campus has no mentoring program, prepare yourself and your mentor with a guidebook such as this. And agitate for a mentoring program on campus.

8. Enquire about outstanding mentors of new faculty. Put your departmental chairperson in a separate and limited category, as someone you should regularly ask for advice but who shouldn't know all your shortcomings.

9. Expect that mentoring experiences, if done well, will persist, with constancy and moderation, at least three years. Expect, too, that mentoring, if done amid overattachment, will lead to occasional strife, including a difficult period of "leaving" your mentor.

10. At the least, coach yourself mindfully in proven ways of overcoming the usual early fault lines described in this book.

You might even want to consider two related things that can help strengthen your willingness to share work with others—involvement in cooperative learning and classroom teaching. Here, the mentoring amounts to letting nationally organized groups of experienced teachers help direct you to work on your own and with others on campus.

Other Kinds of Socialized Work

We already know some of what happens with socialized work, such as joining a mentoring relationship. Two more possibilities you may not yet know are cooperative learning and classroom research.

Cooperative Teaching/Learning

Few strategies for teaching improvement have amassed so strong a set of affirmations as this one (Smith & Walker, 1997). And, arguably, few have made so strong a contribution to teaching improvement at the college level. Formally, the movement for cooperative learning is a response to calls from researchers and national commissions to more actively involve students in the learning process (Cuseo, 1996). Traditional lecture methods, in contrast, carry the assumption that students learn best by simply listening to knowledgeable people talk about their knowledge (Chickering, 1974).

While the push for active and cooperative learning is as aged as attempts to coach teachers, the movement for cooperative teaching/learning has become widely popular only in the past decade (e.g., Gaff, 1994; Johnson, Johnson, & Smith, 1991). The leader of this surge is Jim Cooper, editor of the *Cooperative Learning and College Teaching Newsletter* (New Forums Press, Stillwater, OK) and author, with team members, of a book with the same essential name (1990). Cooper and colleagues have studied the effects of cooperative learning in thousands of college students.

What makes this approach "cooperative" is its focus on learner-centered teaching. In practice, it begins with letting go of strict reliance on the lecture method in favor of having students do some of the work in classrooms. And, far more radical, it means involving all students as active learners, not just the usual minority of dominant class members. It has students teach other students (what we might term letting others do some of the work) and its related specifics are these:

- Teachers place students in teams and assign clear roles to individuals (e.g., team captain, recorder, spokesperson), assignments (e.g., a different subsection of learning projects), and rewards (points for meeting individual and team goals).
- Teachers use peer group influence to enhance performance and learning. Peers may be better than teachers at explaining concepts at a level more congenial to students. And peer teachers, much like the mentors depicted earlier in this chapter, learn more than do recipients because they must clarify what they teach and observe how it gets put into practice by a student or mentee.
- Cooperative learning may be best arranged in small groups where students not only teach each other but also work for collective grades. Telling measures of learning come from student reports about the processes of team practice and from dialogues about their own performance. Students prefer group efforts where their individual efforts are reflected in their course grades. In the end, though, they may value the social bonding of team learning as much or more than the grade.
- Done optimally, cooperative learning balances group problem-solving sessions in teams with activities for the whole class, including some lecturing and discussion. Even within teamwork formats, emphases include constant attention to learning goals, reasonable levels of student involvement, and the teacher's feedback. Cooperative learning does not mean lessened responsibility or work for teachers.

Here is an opportunity for the instructor to assume the role of coach. As teams progress through their assigned activities, the teacher can observe, encourage, and intervene to provide requested clarification, offer encouragement, ask questions to stimulate deeper thought, or redirect efforts as needed. In most cooperative learning activities, students must perceive their peers as the major resource, and the instructor must avoid the temptation to provide immediate answers.—JIM COOPER

One thing might still puzzle you: How do teachers facilitate cooperation within student teams? Some team-building activities are as simple as modeling small-talk and self-disclosure to students as they get to know each other (e.g., having team members interview each other and summarize the information to the team). Other kinds of bonding come by way of immersion teams in tasks as easy as making sense of what the teacher has just said in his or her brief lecture.

Measurable results for students learning in teams are consistently superior to those in traditionally individualistic and competitive formats. One key to this outcome apparently lies in students' access to diverse teachers—and not just the professor. So here, too, as in the *nihil nimus* approach, there is balance between group and independent learning. A second key is freedom from sole reliance on lectures and readings for learning. That shift alone seems to help students develop more autonomy, self-expression, and sociability with peers and teachers. Third, cooperative learning may foster more critical thinking in students and teachers (e.g., Kurfiss, 1988). When students are allowed to be less dependent on and attached to professors, their independence fosters a "standing back" from what is being done and said in order to reflect, mindfully and metacognitively, on alternative processes and economies of solving problems. We saw a related approach in Section II, of teaching ourselves less dependence on traditional methods of writing in mindless/passive ways and more on recursions between broad images and clarification into linear writing—so that the whole process of writing or learning is made simpler but broader-minded.

Indeed, cooperative learning does facilitate writing by encouraging its sociable practice in small groups. Writing, as we have seen, is initially eased and clarified by talking it aloud; social conversation about what students plan and write helps break narrow conceptions and self-conscious blocks. In a cooperative learning approach, even the shyest and least self-confident students can be coaxed into active and effective participation.

Worth doing? Yes! As easily done as it first appears? No. Few, very few, *new* faculty in my studies fared best in a full shift from lecturing to cooperative learning during their first two years of teaching practice. They did better to wait and move into cooperative learning formats slowly but surely. Even exemplary novice teachers (and those who modeled after them with success) focused on first things first; they began with attention to classroom incivilities and classroom comfort. So, for example, they mostly lectured but they took pains to slow the pace, make fewer main points, and encourage questions, even discussions. They often primed chosen students before class to ask certain questions to help make discussions more predictable at first. Did their cautious approach work? Theirs were classes where student involvement and comprehension were as high as in any teaching format I've assessed. Later, usually by the third year of teaching, these new faculty felt confident enough about gaining student cooperation (especially in large introductory classes) to do what Jim Cooper and his team would call cooperative (or Cooper-ative) teaching/learning, during about half of total class time.

But when new faculty tried to move abruptly to general reliance on discussions and small groups, the results were usually anarchy and embarrassment. Students didn't really know what to do, largely because of their own unfamiliarity with cooperative learning, and they complained loudly about being taken away from the familiarity of lecturing and listening. New teachers panicked when groups floundered, particularly when some students resisted involvement. Student comprehension after such class meetings was dismal and teacher satisfaction was no better. Were there exceptions to this pattern? Yes, but they were exceptional.

So a larger question looms: Why, in my own studies, if exemplars and their mentees were succeeding as teachers who lectured, did many of them move to a cooperative learning mode? These were active lecturers who commanded high levels of student involvement and learning; the gradual and democratic involvement of their students as active participants led to cooperative learning almost spontaneously. The optimal pattern amongst new teachers I studied had students doing the following:

1. Individually writing abstracts outside class about readings, for circulation among peers
2. Writing abstracts for brief discussion in class, with the authors fielding questions from the class
3. Writing abstracts outside class and in small groups who then presented/ defended them, collectively in class (or, as part of large introductory classes—in lab or discussion groups headed by teaching assistants)
4. Working in small groups in class, still with mentoring from the professor, each preparing parts of classroom instruction and then presenting them with economy to the class
5. Having small groups conduct early, informal evaluations of what the class valued and learned in lectures and in teamwork
6. Doing more and more things prescribed by leaders in the cooperative learning movement

The fifth of those cooperative tasks consists of course evaluations/analyses carried out by students (one we saw much earlier in Section I), and it sets the stage for considering a similarly shared action of teachers and students.

Classroom Research

This popular approach to teaching improvement is also cooperative and sociable. But classroom researchers do more of what their group label suggests: research. The literature of the classroom research movement encourages (1) mastery of the literature on teaching improvement as a meaningful form of scholarship in an academic career; (2) extension of that scholarship to empirical research in classrooms; (3) results that can be written up for an audience of other teachers (sometimes even students); and (4) involvement of students as fellow data collectors and analyzers of class experiences. All this can turn out to be little more difficult than managing cooperative learning. Classroom research can also be a legitimate source of scholarship and publication for new faculty, especially at campuses whose R/P/T guidelines credit nonrefereed manuscripts.

Classroom researchers began to bond together for support and ideas in the 1980s, largely under the leadership of Thomas Angelo (e.g., 1990). The movement continues to grow in size and importance; whole sessions at national conferences are devoted to cooperative sharing of what members have learned in classroom research at various campuses. If you'd like to socialize your work at teaching and produce worthwhile manuscripts, you probably won't do better than this.

Even if you don't intend to join this crusade, I encourage you to know something about its advice for collecting data about how (and how well) your students learn. To give you a sense of what classroom teachers teach (and learn), I mention a reading here that I abstract in the Appendix at the end of this book:

> #7. Angelo, T. (Ed.). (1998). *Classroom assessment and research: An update on uses, approaches, and research findings.* San Francisco: Jossey-Bass.

The book is edited by Tom Angelo and it includes chapters by many of the leading research-practitioners in this sociable approach to improving teaching.

I could go on with similarly socialized ways of letting others do some of the work but instead I'll begin to stop by reminding you where we've just been and where we will go next. In our journey through Chapter 20, we've looked mostly at ways of bringing more social support and socialized knowledge to new faculty experience. We prepared for this move in the previous chapter, with simple and painless ways of learning about the culture being joined—by way of reading and sifting expert advice, by interviewing saintly colleagues about proprieties and efficiencies for novitiates. We even, in that first chapter of this section on socializing with compassion, looked at beneficial ways of finding an especially useful advisor and, better yet, candid advisory groups. In this chapter, we moved outward a bold step further, to finding and optimizing mentoring. Here, we saw evidence of the worth of mentoring for new faculty and about what effective mentors do that helps ensure easy beginnings and timely tenurings. Most important, I used the research on mentoring to advise you about ways of arranging effective mentoring for yourself. A key point was this: Mentors, like other teachers, need educating by mentees.

That same point extends to cooperative and researched ways of learning how to teach. When we make students collaborators (or when we act as active learners with our mentors), we see beyond our own needs to the needs of our students. And, as per Francis Bacon's notions, this move informs us about how others learn what we teach in ways that make us better learners, too.

One more step remains in this progression outward to more sociable beginnings for new faculty (always balanced with time and energy for thinking and working alone): Exemplary new faculty usually take the compassion they've learned as mentees and teachers to yet another level. I advise you to perform that same service as part of making your own career and that of others easier and more rewarding. In the next and final chapter of this book, I show how service, defined here as an extension of help for yourself to other new faculty, can reward and educate more than serving time on committees.

21

Combine Self-Service with Service for Others

Consider why public service too often seems superfluous among expectations for new faculty. Administrators exhort newcomers to do it but they rarely evaluate or reward it the way they do archival publishing, external funding, and outstanding teaching. And most new faculty, in my experience, know or suspect this duplicity. Nonetheless, well-chosen kinds of service have been observed as useful in replacing the usual helplessness and anomie of new faculty with a sense of self-worth and belonging (Jarvis, 1991; Mandel, 1977).

So, I've framed this last set of activities as both self-serving and social-serving; I've deemphasized customary admonitions to do service only because you *should*. What may surprise even more about this exemplar-based approach is that it starts close to home, as cooperation and collaboration with other new faculty. It is inherently more interesting and valuable than most traditional kinds of service in the professoriate. The mechanism behind its immediate value turns out to be familiar and Baconian: New faculty who coach/teach peers in *nihil nimus* strategies for quick starts learn and benefit at least as much as do partners. The satisfaction of helping other newcomers is a bonus.

How large a step is this? You already know how to enlist peers for regular sessions of writing where each of you work on your own manuscript, where both of you act as occasional supporters and listeners. You're accustomed, I hope, to noticing classroom incivilities and correcting them with immediacies toward your students. You can easily do the same in the classroom of your partner and, in turn, enlist him or her to do the same for you. And, I suspect, you can coach someone as shy as you to act more collegially in, say, going to departmental gatekeepers for a preliminary sense about the appropriateness of their plans as scholars, researchers, writers, grant proposers, and teachers.

Most of the substance in this chapter, then, is not about these same simple methods. Instead, I've invested it in information about the diversity of new faculty who could use your interest and understanding. I also encourage you to consider the possibility, sooner or later, of extending your direct service to peers who face the most daunting challenges as new faculty: Nontraditional new hires. Why do I suggest this extra step despite my skepticism about the worth of traditional service during our first six years on campus? In part because it surpasses customary limitations. In part because the move comes naturally, as part of the growing sociability and compassion we've been developing. And in part because it is fully characteristic of those same exemplary new faculty who find success and serenity most readily.

Noticing the plight of new faculty with the toughest beginnings—nontraditional new hires—sharpens your understanding of what you experience as a newcomer. Nontraditional peers offer alternative ways of coping you may not have considered; they have as much to teach you as you might teach them.

Even if you do little more than appreciate the new faculty experience of women and minorities, you perform a quiet but important gesture toward them. Few things dismay nontraditional new hires more than the realization that colleagues misunderstand and misjudge them. Few things are more unrealistic in an academic culture that discourages obvious self-promotion than placing the responsibility wholly on women and minorities to make colleagues understand their special challenges and needs. Your small effort in taking some of that initiative and interest can make a large difference in an academic culture overdue for change.

Am I, as usual, setting up this brief look at nontraditional new hires to tempt you to extend your self-serving cooperation and collaboration to a more altruistic level? Of course. But before I do so, I'll take a formal look at service.

Usual Definitions and Shortcomings of Service

Service, first of all, is usually (and implicitly) distinguished from more obviously necessary activities like teaching; service usually means simple helping or participating. In its traditional sense, service is less work than, say, teaching because its demands are occasional and its duty generally passive. It apparently needs no training or evaluation. We *perform* service but we *work* at writing and teaching. In that perspective, service cannot count much.

Most of what I've seen new faculty do that counted as service on R/P/T forms consisted of sitting through committee meetings. Only in about a fifth of those experiences did newcomers judge the service as worth the time compared to that spent on other academic activities. Nowhere during my 20 years of systematic tracking studies did I witness an instance where service actually mattered in R/P/T decisions. Never did I know a junior faculty member who, having gotten promotion and tenure, listed service as crucial to the attainment—*except* for exemplars (and *nihil nimus* program members modeling after them) who had concentrated their service on peer mentoring/learning. With new faculty who quit academe early, who failed to get reappointed, or who got by with litigation, views of service were clearly negative. One Black woman denied tenure put it this way:

> *What hurt me most was the time I spent on committees that just had to have a Black and a woman [among its members]. What killed me was the time and energy that so many, many needy Black students needed from me. You know, I heard my dean joke in a meeting that the campus should limit the number of publications to one per year for junior faculty who write too much and too superficially. He couldn't have been more pleased with himself. If he had really been in touch with what someone like me needed, he would take steps to make sure that we have relief from some of the extra demands placed on us. Writing too much was the least of my problems. Ha! He doesn't have a clue.*

The Most Serious Problem in Service: Excess

We already know the results of excessiveness in other activities of new faculty, including writing and teaching. Here, too, struggling new faculty tend to perform either no service or else too much. When they overdo, they fret because they know it will help them less toward reappointment than working at teaching, writing, and socializing. Why do they do it anyway? Service offers more immediate rewards (e.g., friendly interactions in a nonthreatening atmosphere) and less hard work. And why is it that some strugglers do no service at all (and, so, project an image as selfish and uncaring)? Because they feel too busy, too far behind to attend meetings and because they resent requests from higher-ups for service.

As usual, moderation characterizes thriving new faculty. Exemplars perform some traditional service from outsets of careers but not much at first. Specifically (as a reminder of something I implied earlier in this section), exemplars ask to be appointed to no more than one committee at a time and once on it excuse themselves from consuming roles such as secretary or recorder. (They might say, "I'd like to start out as a good listener; I have a lot to learn.")

Strugglers, in contrast, often volunteer for extra committee work. They customarily spend more time on committees than on scholarship and writing, and by far the most time counseling/befriending undergraduates. Many strugglers not only welcome extra advisees but they also leave their office doors constantly open, thereby encouraging unnecessarily long visits (commonly twice as much time per week than hours spent presenting classes). Combine that excess with usual overpreparations for classes, and you'll find a busyness that leaves too little time for constructive socializing. Perhaps the greatest irony of this pattern is that it rarely accompanies excellence in teaching; instead, it predicts busyness and rushing at teaching.

Values Exemplary New Faculty Bring to Service

1. *Moderation:* Exemplars limit service to about one hour a week during their first four years in the professoriate. They do more later.
2. *Balance:* Exemplars generally keep time for service in line with another worthwhile but occasional activity such as attendance at cultural events.
3. *Letting go:* Exemplars consciously, deliberately give up the immediate satisfaction of saying yes to the nice people who ask for their service and the opportunity to win their constant approval/affection.
4. *Early knowledge:* Exemplars realize that it isn't enough to join a committee or sponsor a student group for the sake of making new acquaintances; as new faculty members, they've already met enough colleagues whose acquaintance deserves more development. So, they ask about histories of committees on campus in general (e.g., "When do they really make a difference in the long run? Can you give me a specific example?"). They inquire about the records of specific committees they might join (e.g., "If you do recommend new programs on campus, do your considered findings usually get implemented or are they generally overruled by higher administrators with agenda of their own?" or "Does this committee's ratings of graduate students as teaching assistants demonstrably lead to improvement in their teaching?"). Such questions are, of course, best asked with gentleness and genuine curiosity.
5. *Benefit for self and recipient:* Some committees, like some mentors, are well worth joining, but you'll do well to look out for yourself before committing to them. I'm not suggesting you avoid service altogether—just that you moderate your service until you are secure and productive in your start. And, again, I urge you to perform most early service in selfish but social-serving ways.
6. *Close to home:* In practice, this tactic isn't as selfish as it sounds. Most commonly, exemplars choose service roles closely related to their own most essential activities—a domain where they can most readily help themselves and others. This usually means helping peers as an interested and compassionate observer—better yet, as a friend, mentor, and collaborator.

Imagine a scenario where you strengthen your habit of writing in brief, daily sessions by enlisting a peer to meet with you for mutually independent writing on a similar schedule. You would, at the least, ensure more constancy for your own writing. But what if you suppose such an act too self-serving and easily done to qualify as service? Or as too private to impress those on campus who value service? Realize, first, that other new faculty will probably not get useful help in surviving from these campus leaders. Realize, second, that when descriptions of your efforts reach them, evaluators will be remiss not to count them a high form of service (even when they cannot identify the new faculty whom you're helping). I challenge you to name many services you could perform with more value and within the time constraints you face, or to specify more worthwhile recipients in academe than novice college teachers.

Collegial services displayed by thriving new faculty follow the model of mentoring we saw in the preceding chapter: First, hold brief, regular meetings with peers/partners to share plans and progress in writing, to assess each other's classes, to exercise together. Second, establish a clear sense of what needs doing most, for both of you, based on mindful listening, noticing, and communicating. And third, understand why these sociable acts take little more time than doing them alone. In fact, this form of cooperative learning is rated as most instructive and rewarding of anything participants do in my studies.

How Exemplars (and Those Who Model after Them) Begin Their Nontraditional Service

Once they let go of less useful acts of service, exemplars start slowly but constantly by learning about new faculty experiences in general. Some even read this book. What surprises them most is the susceptibility of new faculty in general to unforeseen disasters. What interests them most are the even stronger perils faced by nontraditional new hires.

To provide you with a quick sense of the sorts of things exemplars value in gaining information, I mention three classics I've abstracted in the Appendix at the end of the book, one on feminist efforts to improve college teaching, the second about adjunct faculty's efforts to manage more than marginal membership in academe, and the third on how to deal with racism in your own classes.

I recommend the first reading for its feminist (and so nontraditional) approach. I particularly like its authors' reliance on conclusions drawn from direct observations of classrooms:

#8. Maher, F., & Tetreault, M. K. (1994). *The feminist classroom.* New York: Basic Books.

Maher and Tetreault found that feminist-oriented teachers made a difference by shifting classroom climates away from assertive, competitive, and hierarchical customs instituted by men. Conclusion: Political, historical, cultural influences on universities and their teaching need more of our attention.

What, specifically, do I hope you will take from this abstract? For one thing, a reminder of the oppression experienced by women in the professoriate. For another, a realization that, along with their differences from male-dominated tra-

ditions, women bring useful values and workable alternatives to customary teaching. And, finally, a sense of an effective way of teaching that is slowly but surely
gaining ground because it works.

Many of us may be less aware of another kind of inhumane and unproductive
exclusionism in our midst toward part-time faculty; few newcomers to academic
careers face more overt discrimination and discouragement than they. I've
abstracted this book because it alerts us to what may now be our worst inhumanity, one that we might want to confront as part of our outreach to do service. Just
as important, it addresses a condition of professorial life that many of you might
be considering or already enduring.

#9. Gappa, J. M., & Leslie, D. W. (1993). *The invisible faculty: Improving the
status of part-timers in higher education.* San Francisco: Jossey-Bass.

Part-timers, who now approach 40 percent of all faculty in the United States
are usually young, overqualified, and underbenefitted; they are constant victims
of a general lack of appreciation for their work and a lack of power to change their
classes. What, in actual practice, limits the likelihood of help and equality for part-
timers? The general indifference of most campuses about their plight and the
implicit support of full-time faculty of having others teach large survey courses.

So what should you do—besides being lucky enough to join an enlightened
campus—if you will or must begin your career as a part-timer? Acquire a realistic
picture of part-timers' usual experience. And consider yourself a legitimate new
faculty member in the sense of visiting and seeking help of the sorts discussed in
the preceding two chapters. Few such brave souls, in my studies, were refused this
or other kinds of help once they made themselves visible and cordial. Finally,
explore ways to help yourself in much the same ways that other new faculty do.
Part-timers are usually included in the orientations for full-timers if they ask to
join. And part-timers are just as privy to information of the sort presented throughout this book on *Advice for New Faculty Members* (although I'll admit that their
campuses are less likely to buy a copy for them). Who better to share the exercises
with than another new hire, of full- or part-time status?

When I've gotten funding to extend my own *nihil nimus* programs to part-
time newcomers, the results have often been more impressive than for most full-
timers. Why? Because part-timers coached to find ready contentment and productivity moved quickly to finish dissertations and to publish things about work done
after that. Optimists among them believed that because they were freed from obligations to advise students and serve on committees, they had more time for writing. Virtually all newcomers in part-time roles were motivated to perform well in
their quest for full-time positions. "I'll do anything to get out of my present job,"
said one part-timer to me.

Still, I usually advise against beginning faculty careers part time. In my own
observations, part-time positions too often become dead-ends for faculty who

merited and wanted more; some never get beyond transiency, moving from one campus to the next, sometimes from day to day. In large metropolitan areas, such part-timers are known as *freeway fliers*. Treatments of part-timers too often leave the self-esteem and scholarliness of new faculty irreversibly crushed and they exacerbate the usual problem that part-timers bring with them, of unfinished dissertations that are delayed indefinitely. Several survey studies show that students who leave campus early, ABD (all but dissertation), greatly increase the likelihood of slowed completions of dissertations, of dissertations never finished, and of subsequent careers in low-paying and frustrating positions. Yes, part-time teaching often seems preferable to assistantships or loans, but they are generally deleterious to professorial careers and general satisfaction. Better to be poor for a while than frustrated for the rest of your life.

If there is a value in part-time teaching, beyond its neglected potential to bring retired professors back to the classroom, it lies partly in reminding us how readily and mindlessly academe can subject its new hires to poor conditions, to deprivation of necessary supports, and to invisibility.

What remains conspicuously absent in our brief look at the professoriate's inhumanity and counterproductivity with its novices? Experiences of racial minorities as new faculty. In what follows, I first mention an abstract in the Appendix of an action-oriented article about how we can begin to deal mindfully, thoroughly with usually unconscious issues of race and racism, as part of teaching in our own classes.

> #10. Tatum, B. D. (1992). Talking about race, learning about racism: The application of racial identity development theory in the classroom. *Harvard Educational Review, 62,* 1–24.

Tatum is direct and deals in process issues. She has found that the best way of inducing awareness and change with regard to racism lies in casting the learning experience in terms of predictable stages of progress toward antiracism: preencounter, encounter, immersion/emersion, internalization, and, finally, internalization/commitment. She models ways to incorporate their awareness as part of teaching and learning to move ourselves and our students past the unnecessary constraints of racism.

Second, I provide information from my own studies of new faculty to put Beverly Tatum's information into the broader context of understanding the special challenges faced by women and Blacks. Here, too, the eventual goal is commitment to change; the service we provide needs foundations in objective information about problems and in Tatum's enlightened ways of understanding their root causes.

I have a secondary motive in presenting the following inquiries, modeling a way you can provide service that matters, via understanding nontraditional colleagues, better yet as a way you make your service part of your research. What follows may be far more ambitious than a project you might want to carry out but useful in depicting general processes that worked for me.

New Faculty Experience of Women and Minorities

In this study (Boice, 1993), as the title implies, I tracked nontraditional newcomers to the professoriate. I came to this inquiry much as I did with other aspects of new faculty experiences; I had noticed a problem not being addressed in meaningful ways. People of color and women, at least in my own studies, were more proportionately likely to display poor starts in academic careers than were White males. Specifically, these nontraditional newcomers were more likely to leave campus before R/P/T decisions were made, they more often took years off during their probationary periods to rest and catch up on writing, and they struggled or failed proportionately more often in campus decisions about R/P/T. Women and minority new faculty more frequently suffered from unmistakable instances of illnesses such as influenza, from psychological complications such as depression and/or anxiety attacks, and from sustained periods of fatigue. Academe, it seemed to me, needed far more than its usual admonitions and anecdotes to change this inhumane and wasteful situation. It also, I soon discovered, needed more openness about acknowledging this problem.

As I began my inquiries, I encountered higher administrators who heatedly denied the problem was real (e.g., "We've spent large amounts of time and money on affirmative action") and who supposed my study would do little more than embarrass the campus (e.g., "Whatever problems we do have you could find anywhere else; you need to ask yourself why you want to make us look bad"). More surprising, some powerful feminists complained that my efforts to point how women and minorities fail could only prolong negative stereotypes. I erred, they warned, in "blaming the victims instead of the institution and culture." The problem could, they insisted, lie only outside the people being oppressed. "You," one critic told me, "are a tall and dominant White man who could never understand our experience in a million years." I hoped it would take somewhat less time than that.

I listened carefully to those objections and I relied on my best practices as a Buddhist to detach myself from the seemingly personal nature of the criticisms. It seemed to me that my critics were still stuck in the "immersion" stage of development (as per Tatum's article abstracted earlier in this chapter). More important, they were not doing things in direct ways that could help the nontraditional new faculty I was tracking survive and thrive. I decided against waiting for someone more acceptable or qualified to do the study.

A Brief Overview of the Literature

Writings about nontraditional new hires are most useful in helping readers move through what Beverly Tatum would call the "confrontational" stage. That is, they can raise our consciousness about the wrongs academe inflicts on the faculty it once openly resisted hiring. Both women and minorities in professorial roles characterize their experiences in terms like hardship and victimization (e.g., Exum, 1983). Both groups suffer deprivations of social supports, including mentors, models, and sponsors (Banks, 1984). And too many of these nontraditional new hires feel marginalized, unwanted, invisible, and, at times, crazy (Winckler, 1988). In view of these injustices and others, the usual outcome is not surprising: At the least, these new faculty feel overworked, incompetent, and, worst of all, unqualified (e.g., Cohen & Gutek, 1991; Fox, 1985). Add to these handicaps the stigma of gay orientation and the data about higher failure rates become undeniable (Rothblum, 1988).

One problem with these reports is that they provide little factual basis for concluding that women and minorities meet more and different kinds of problems than do traditional new hires. Another is that they rarely prescribe specific and proven interventions to address the special needs of nontraditional novices. A third problem is that they too rarely seem to base advice on women and minorities who make quick starts and excel across domains, including socialization and research, while maintaining their individuality and special missions.

Still, this literature merits a close look for its anecdotal accounts of new faculty experiences of women and minorities like these: Women come to academe valuing their personal warmth and gentleness more than the competitive, aggressive climate still enforced by many males (Bem, 1974). Mentoring for women more likely addresses personal than professional problems (Landino & Owen, 1988). Women and minorities almost always end up in lower-status and lower-paying positions than male counterparts (Clark, 1987); moreover, these customary roles may make them feel less confident about doing things most valued in academe (notably research) and more inclined to work hardest at things valued least (in particular, teaching) (Schoen & Winokur, 1988). Also, nontraditional new hires start out amidst the surprising realization that their more senior colleagues, virtually all of whom consider themselves as deliberate and fair supporters of affirmative action programs, are especially unlikely to see their own racism and sexism (Exum, 1983).

How many truly effective programs have these reformist accounts generated to moderate those obstacles in professorial careers? Virtually none. But what about, say, the study about feminist teaching that I abstracted earlier in this chapter (Maher & Tetreault, 1994 *[The Feminist Classroom]*)? It, at least, looks to possible exemplars to draw general suggestions about ways they teach in accord with feminist ideals. Alas, it says nothing about how effectively these teaching philosophies and methods improve the teaching/learning of other teachers. What difference has it made in terms of improved teaching or enhanced survival of teachers? Hard to tell.

Something else about "standards" such as Maher and Tetreault's book worries me—their exclusive attention to teaching. Consider other problems, according to my direct observations, that usually go overlooked in reformist writings:

- Nontraditional new faculty more often miss or avoid general socialization experiences, and so proportionately more often impress senior faculty as distant and uncaring about wider missions of the university.
- Newcomers who bring nontraditional alternatives to academic customs lose opportunities to model some of what they themselves might do better to more traditional colleagues because the communication is not direct, congenial, and convincing.
- Nontraditionals more often devalue publishing for reasons of "immersion" (again, as per the developmental scheme in Tatum's article) and spend far more time with student as counselees and close friends than involving themselves and kindred students in writing.
- Nontraditionals launch professorial careers with even less awareness than other new faculty about the usual perils/pitfalls that await.

A Rationale for the Study

It is the last problem in the preceding list that I decided to study first. I not only wanted to learn more about the fault lines that occur quickly for new faculty in general but also to determine whether these perils were more telling for women and minorities. In fact, they were. And, consistent with the exemplar-based approach of this book, I hoped to show how some new faculty avoided these career fault lines and thus modeled ways for others to emulate. The most informative of these new faculty were thriving nontraditionals.

Methods

I drew subjects for individual tracking from six cohorts of new faculty, two from a comprehensive and four from a research university. I selected 30 women (5 of them Blacks) as newcomers and a matched sample of 30 males, 5 of them Blacks. I enlisted each participant in this study during his or her second or third semesters on campus; all were deemed strugglers in terms of pace towards R/P/T standards.

I observed and assessed the early experiences of these struggling new faculty in five ways:

1. I used open-ended questions as I followed them around campus (e.g., "What has your day been like?").
2. I conducted structured interviews where they rated experiences and described plans.
3. I tracked participants through office hours and classes and rated their interactions according to the dimensions regarding civilities and other immediacies I mentioned earlier in this book (including interviews with students about what they took away of substance and value from their classes—see Chapter 8).

4. I used more formal and retrospective ratings from the New Faculty Faring Index (NFFI—see Boice, 1993). Briefly, the NFFI is a format for rating new faculty in comparison to exemplarly peers in regard to (a) immersion (e.g., involvement in collaborations with students as collaborators; participation in campus events); (b) regimen and productivity (e.g., works at writing on schedule and produces verifiable manuscript pages; conducts early, informal evaluations of classes in timely fashion); (c) self-management (e.g., optimism; energy/resilience, timely work); and (d) social management (e.g., finds effective mentoring, interacts in a conflict-free way in the department).

5. I specified crucial turning points in career beginnings. For this final and most interesting assessment, I relied on established theories and methods of documenting and mapping those critical events. The first (Blackburn & Havighurst, 1979) is a simple method of eliciting faculty responses about pivotal career events. The second (Baldwin & Blackburn, 1981) identifies a broader format for the content-analysis of faculty careers as developmental processes. I duplicated these essential procedures with two exceptions: I modified the interview schedule to elicit information about new faculty experiences (e.g., "What were the first signs of how well you would do here?"). And I repeated these recollective, hour-long sessions at least two more times, until each individual felt comfortable with the technique of thinking aloud and, as nearly as possible, reliving the moment of a turning point (Perkins, 1981). I followed Perkins's rules for such inquiries by coaching each participant, individually: To speak as continuously as possible; to not explain, interpret, or justify; and to report only what happened from the vantage of an internal observer by reliving the experience directly and in that moment. My role was nondirective except for encouraging participants to think of the most telling experiences that either made them, as newcomers, feel welcome or unwelcome. Repeated sessions helped participants move beyond interpretive reporting to simpler and more direct accounts—and to sort significant from insignificant events. As a rule, first sessions evoked halting but emotional recollections with no useful focus. Second sessions brought more calm and clarity of recall and more certainty about significance. In third sessions, subjects generally pared initial lists of 8 to 12 turning points to the 4 or 5 most significant and then reconsidered them in the broader context of their new faculty experiences.

A year later, without forewarning, I rechecked these memories as an informal test of reliability; recollections were always virtually identical, perhaps because (as participants suggested) they had been made so clear by talking them aloud in initial trials with me. What had been largely nonverbal and emotionally-laden images were clarified by externalizing them in talk; what at first seemed vague in talking aloud was cleared up by referring that talk back to the mental images. (Recall that this process resembles the mindful ways of writing we discussed toward the end of Section II.)

Results

As you might remember, I made my observations at four different levels of complexity; I begin with the simplest.

Informal Interviews. To simplify these findings, I juxtapose the modal responses for struggling White men, White women, and Blacks in Table 21.1.

This qualitative outcome suggests that struggling Black new faculty were more closed/private in their reactions to challenges than were members of the other two groups of new faculty. Their interactions with their students in class, with colleagues in departmental commons, and with me remained cordial but reserved on campus. When I pressed them for explanations, their responses were generally, "I have to do this on my own. I have to be better and stronger."

Whites also gave responses of a markedly different sort from those we've seen as typical of exemplary new faculty throughout this book. White men still struggling during their third semesters on campus most often reacted to my queries about how well they were doing with angry reassurances that they would succeed on their own terms but at a slower pace than the campus (or I) might prefer. "If they want my best work, the kind that most of my colleagues are not capable of," said one to me with annoyance, "they'll damn well have to trust to the potential they saw when they hired me. I don't intend to be average." Struggling White

TABLE 21.1   Modal Comments Made Spontaneously, Arranged in Most Common Categories

White Men Struggling	White Women Struggling	Blacks Struggling
I'll manage acceptance in classes by lowering my standards.	I won't coddle students or try to entertain them.	I'll try to be formal and impressive in class.
I'm angry about being lied to about resources during hiring.	I'm disappointed about the social caring of my colleagues.	I'll be all right once I get settled in here and show what I can do.
I'm feeling overworked, tired.	I feel panicked.	I need to keep my problems to myself.
I'm too busy to write.	I'm too busy to write or have a social life.	It's hard to know what to do.
I belong here; they'll accept me once they see my best work.	I act outrageously and I feel crazy at times. I want to fit in but I don't.	I don't belong here, except to help students like me.
I don't need a mentor; I already know what to do.	I'm anxious about mentoring that goes beyond friendly conversations.	Unless I can find a mentor like me; I'm not interested.

women, in contrast, revealed less self-confidence and more conflict about the discrepancy between their need for social supports and their anxiety about accepting it in ways that the culture offered it (e.g., mentoring focused around problem solving, not just support). They, compared to the other two groups, were most apt to blame themselves for their slow starts.

Structured, Sit-Down Interviews. Information from this second format proved harder to interpret and simpify. These are essential outcomes:

- Struggling women—White and Black—rated lowest in terms of how well and often they were welcomed to campus by colleagues; they scored even lower in terms of subsequent outreaches for (or acceptance of help from) mentors with problem-solving approaches than did their White male counterparts.
- Struggling Black men rated lowest in terms of finding collegial support on campus, especially in regard to writing.
- Struggling women usually claimed five or more close friends on campus; struggling men usually had none. Exemplars, by comparison, generally had one or two.
- White men were the only strugglers who had met several times with departmental chairpeople.
- Struggling women rated highest for sharing scholarship and research in small groups and in conference papers, lowest for progress in writing up those presentations for publication. At the same time, these women reported feeling the most pressure to publish, usually at levels accompanied with chronic anxiety.
- Finally, my ratings of stress, illness, and depression were by far highest for all struggling White women, second-most for Black women. Struggling men, Black or White, fared better on this index of adjustment, perhaps because they often explained difficulties as new faculty as similar to "making" an athletic team by dint of hard work and few complaints.

Some more general patterns emerged from these data.

Struggling White women suffered most for their lack of self-esteem and self-efficacy—most for their unwillingness to face even moderately competitive/evaluative challenges (e.g., "I worry most about students comparing me to their other teachers; I hate to imagine where I fall short"). Yet, without exception, they came to campus with higher expectations about balancing research with teaching and social life. And they, better than other struggling groups I studied, were far more receptive of my advice, more likely to attend workshops, and more likely to express intentions of adopting more successful strategies. But, during these first three semesters on campus, they were most likely to hesitate and block when trying to put these intentions into practice. Typical examples:

I think those ideas might work for other people but I'm pretty sure they wouldn't for me. I'm just different, I guess.

When it comes down to it, I can't do it because I don't know the exact steps I have to take.

What I'm lacking, in some way I don't understand, is trust. I don't trust what your exemplars do because they must be more belligerent and confident than I am. What may be good for them isn't necessarily so for me.

I was left wondering, as you might be now, whether these women were right to completely reject male-oriented approaches. But I was brought back to center by recalling what thriving White women did in contrast. They avoided or moderated the problems I've just listed while seeming to make an autonomous and loosely defined system work well for them by congenially communicating how and why they deviated. Said one of these optimists, "It isn't the obstacles I worry about, it's how well I handle them."

Struggling Black new faculty were self-handicapped most often by social isolation. While the culture of academe traditionally distances these new faculty, the victims reinforce it, however unintentionally. I justify this hard judgment with my observations of Black new faculty who thrived. They were more at ease, less in anger. They far more often reported seeing resemblances between their own initial experiences (e.g., feelings of isolation and abandonment) and those of other new faculty in general. And, most basic, they were more optimistic—without giving up their individualism.

Struggling White men showed patterns that seemed simplest and toughest to change. The more these newcomers expressed resistance to help by claiming it would demean them, the lower were their general position in the rankings based on success regarding student evaluations of teaching, manuscripts completed and submitted, and useful social contacts made among colleagues. These new faculty were easily the most contentious, immodest, and unlikeable of new faculty. A surprisingly strong predictor of this syndrome was a doctorate from an elite graduate school and a disdain for the new campus.

Ratings According to the NFFI (New Faculty Faring Index).   Here, an independent observer and I rated participants on dimensions already proven critical to good starts among undergraduate students new to campus (e.g., Pascarella & Terenzini, 1991). Presumably, schemes that explain student faring/retention can illuminate how new faculty struggle or thrive during their own freshman years.

Immersion.   This reflects measurable levels of new faculty involvement with colleagues, with students, and with peers overall. It also measures participation in campus services (e.g., workshops for new faculty) and activities (e.g., cultural events). In regard to teaching, for example, this index depicted struggling newcomers in a paradox we already know about: They worked longest and hardest at teaching preparation but were associated with lowest levels of student involvement and comprehension. They rated lowest on (1) involving themselves in clear learning goals before class and (2) then directing themselves and their students toward meeting those same goals.

Constancy and moderation.   Just two of the 25 struggling White women in this sample met the simple criterion of one page per week of writing during their first three semesters on campus; none of the struggling Blacks or slow-starting White men did.

Self-management.   Overall, struggling White women scored lower than peers in terms of externally rated optimism and self-esteem—so too for behavioral signs of energy and resilience as they left class meetings, writing sessions, and problem-solving sessions with collegial advisors. Slow-starting White women also scored lower than all other participants on objective measures of procrastination, including delaying completion of grade sheets until overdue at departmental offices and missing deadlines for funding proposals.

Social management.   This broad measurement of skill in winning supporters and finding needed help also distributed most clearly by gender: Struggling women, Black and White, were far better than men at finding close and compassionate friends. White men, but not Black men, fared better at finding useful advice about problem solving in ways that approached mentee-mentor relationships. And White men scored best at knowing what problems most needed solving (e.g., moderating content and pace for teaching; working at writing before they felt ready to).

In even so brief an account of the patterns in the first three levels of assessment of faculty faring, you might begin to perceive some early turning points. The final kind of assessment in this study, career mapping, may be most useful because it is most concrete.

Career Event Maps.   Recall the talking-aloud procedures I mentioned earlier as the essential component in this mapping of early experiences. Four things stood out in my analysis of these data: First, most major turning points occurred early, usually during the first 3 semesters. These early events had the potential to make or break careers. Second, the maps of new faculty faring poorly were not only marked by more such incidents but they also displayed a different pattern compared to peers faring well. Third, the numbers of crucial incidents and their variety were greater for struggling White women than for struggling men, and still higher for Black new faculty. Fourth, the patterns in these maps had apparently been preset, more or less, before these new faculty arrived on campus; strugglers most often came to campus with the least optimism, constancy/moderation in ways of working, and social acceptance of diverse others. Virtually every fault line judged significant by their victims involved those deficits.

To make my comparisons more substantial, I extended my sample to include 15 thriving White women during their initial three semesters. Compared to their equivalents, the strugglers we already know, pivotal events of good starters differed in striking ways. Table 21.2 shows those patterns plainly, as rank-orderings of commonality in final recollections of crucial experiences. The most striking difference in Table 21.2 appears across domains of social acceptance of diverse others, optimism about potentials amid the challenges of initiation rituals, and permission for self-esteem about professional worth.

I could not manage so complete an extension of early career maps for Black new faculty on pace versus those not meeting R/P/T standards. Table 21.3, then, offers even more tentative patterns.

Again, nontraditional new hires fared better when they accepted useful supports, readily interacted with and accepted diverse others, and made social adjustments while maintaining their individual missions for social change. On the other hand, nontraditionals fared worst as they experienced subtle but hurtful racism, sexism, and deprivation to the point of distraction and derailing.

Did struggling individuals (represented in the right-side columns of Tables 21.2 and 21.3) meet more challenges that necessarily undermined their beginnings in professorial careers? In my extensive tracking of thriving and struggling

TABLE 21.2   Most Common Turning Points Recollected and Judged Crucial among White Women

Best Faring White Women ($N = 15$)	Worst Faring White Women ($N = 15$)
Finding a ready social network, including problem-solving help	Skeptical/disappointing treatment during interview for job
Appreciating students as enthusiastic and as wanting personal contact	Finding lack of respect from colleagues and students once in job
Realizing that most obstacles are impersonal and potentially self-educational	Students demanding to be pandered to and entertained
Finding classroom comfort and involving students as contributors	Finding that the high level of stress makes the job seem unworthwhile
Deciding to let go and feel/express confidence	Feeling more disorganized and incoherent in class
Beginning to help struggling students and peers	Despair that busyness interferes with social life

TABLE 21.3 Most Common Turning Points Recollected and Judges Crucial among Black New Faculty

Acceptable Starts (N = 4)	Unacceptable Starts (N = 10)
Came to campus with social network and mentor in place	Faced with unmangable demand for advising and counseling students of color
Compassionate acceptance of students and then by students, in and out of class	No surprises and no pivotal events reported
Finding ways to fit socially meaningful study into solid and publishable research	Social rebuffs, usually as rushed or missed interactions, from colleagues and administrators
Diverse interactions, mostly with optimistic and fun colleagues	Told that research plans/progress were unacceptable and responded with quiet resentment

new faculty around campuses, I saw no obvious difference in signs of sexism and racism presented to them—nor did they, in their recollections to me. Much like the exemplary teachers we saw in Chapter 8, thriving women and Blacks seemed to anticipate and notice these challenges while compassionately dismissing them as understandable and generally not worth anger or rebuttal. I agree that this question demands more precise research by more diverse investigators.

Whatever the reason, women and Blacks proportionately more often struggle as new faculty in my studies. Whatever the excuse, I say that *we* could provide them with far more ease and support as they learn to cope with the mysteries and irrationalities of White male culture. Following is a modest example of my own attempt at such a service.

A Brief Intervention Study with Black New Faculty
This was the most intimidating but rewarding challenge I've experienced in my work with new faculty. I tracked five of the struggling Black newcomers mentioned earlier, three women and two men, into their fourth and fifth semesters. We worked together in ways most obviously related to teaching; we shared more spontaneous values of managing student approval, involvement, and comprehension. As you might expect, I coached them in the immediacies and prosocial motivators that can halt classroom incivilities and moderate most aversions to teaching/learning. They, in Baconian fashion, taught me how real, diverse people put those strategies into practice.

In that first semester of this study (their fourth on campus), I involved all five participants in mindfulness exercises, particularly in slowing, calming, and reflecting on how they came across to students. I supplemented these reflections with information from my own observations/recordings of their students' reactions during and after class. None of the five participants resisted this evaluation; none judged it as contrary to their own value systems. Once classroom incivilities were clearly seen and their effects appreciated, we treated them as problems easily corrected; even the most imperfect first attempts to do so were immensely rewarding and involving. I could discern no differences in how African American new faculty understood and implemented this approach from how earlier groups of White new faculty did. Major struggles at teaching ended for both groups and early fault lines were erased with equanimity.

Before that first semester of participation had ended, I helped coach these five new faculty to broaden these insights/solutions to collegial interactions (e.g., making sure they didn't self-present as seemingly formal and distant). In the first two "trials" of this extension, I accompanied each participant and took the lead in drawing our hosts, usually shy and experienced colleagues, into sociable and useful conversations with the two of us as visitors. In the second two trials, I took less of the lead while subtly reminding participants what to do during these social interactions. Five more such visits sufficed to help participants reassure senior colleagues of participants' interest/enthusiasm about faring well in their careers, and of their openness regarding listening to and learning from them. In the view of these five participants, none of this felt like submission or adopting White values. None of it detracted, they said, from their own individualism or social missions. But all of it, they agreed, helped make them feel more welcome and appreciated, more likely to succeed on their own terms but in ways that would contribute to the campus in general ways.

I liked those claims of relief from oppressive and disappointing beginnings but I relied more on long-term outcomes before supposing that this sort of approach might be worthwhile. All five participants were rated by R/P/T committees as having made major turn-arounds on their own during their third years on campus in regard to teaching and collegiality. All five arranged social contracts for writing in brief, daily sessions and in meeting usual writing/publishing criteria on campus; three persisted. In the end, I realized that this process and outcome were no different from my other projects for involving/immersing new faculty in *nihil nimus* programs. The only variation, it seemed to me at first, lay in the stronger efforts I employed to recruit these struggling and reluctant newcomers. On reflection, though, I suspected something else: I had been unintentionally distant and uncivil in communicating with new faculty of color during my earlier and largely unsuccessful attempts to make program participants of them. I had felt intimidated, mostly because I wasn't sure I would like what colleagues with histories of mistreatment from people like me would say to me. So *I* remained somewhat formal and reserved unless I sensed immediate openness and acceptance from new faculty of color. That insight and the changes it led to came as a great relief to me.

Rule 4: Get Struggling Peers to Accept Some of Your Help.

Exercise for Rule 4

Where does this long look at the new faculty experiences of women and minorities leave us? More inclined, I hope, to understand their problems in coping with our dominantly White and priestly culture. More compassionate toward yourself for your own early missteps. And more motivated to interrupt those patterns of poor starts, your own and theirs.

The exercise consists of focusing your service on actions that help new faculty work in mindful, economical, and enjoyable ways. How? By following Beverly Tatum's prescriptions for developing mindful ways of accepting diverse, different colleagues to the point of committing yourself to helping change the culture that limits all of you. By practicing other suggestions in this last chapter for scholarship about new faculty experiences, even collegial research, as a self-reinforcing manner of performing service. Or at least by taking this information to heart as you grow into senior roles such as gatekeeping.

There are, I believe, enough benefits in this close-to-home approach to make it memorable: More understanding of turning points in early careers—a clarity enhanced by seeing those perils in their extremes, among nontraditionals. More opportunities to use simple and effective *nihil nimus* strategies as correctives, for yourself and others. More collaborative learning where you teach and you are taught survival strategies. And, not least, service made more stimulating and useful by testing it socially for broad but simplified efficacy.

How might our guide through Section II, Francis Bacon, have summarized this approach to service? By noting that it begins in seeing that the seeming complexities of new faculty life are really just variations on a few basic themes (and not an infinite collection of particulars). Then by explaining how this path to service leads us toward the substance revealed in a simple *pattern* among particulars, by way of strikingly typical instances. Finally, in showing how to make the service experience useful—by moving beyond those simple insights to a social testing of which strategies can be applied with benefit to self and society.

He that will not apply new remedies must expect new evils.
—Francis Bacon

General Summary: Catalogue of Nihil Nimus Rules and Advice for New Faculty

Rule 1: Wait.

Waiting requires patience at holding back from impulsivity, rushing, and busyness. Active waiting allows clear seeing of what most needs doing and it encourages the constancy and moderation that bring the most productivity and health over the long run. Some practices of holding back are as simple as pausing before and during classes or writing. Others are as complex as waiting before committing to a mentor. All must confront the most troublesome of new faculty's tendencies: Impatience.

Franz Kafka put the solution simply in the sign over his writing desk: "WAIT."

Rule 2: Begin Early.

Active waiting supplants immediate temptations to do something easier than the essential work of newcomers to the professoriate. It fosters early, informal beginnings at tasks we might rather avoid now and do under deadlines. These early beginnings prove difficult because they require learning to start difficult tasks before we feel ready and to do them in small openings during heavily scheduled days. They prove rewarding because they increase calm, creativity, and confidence; in fact, they save time and effort compared to more traditional ways of working in academe.

So, as a teacher, begin early to collect ideas and themes for classes, amidst other activities, and stimulate imaginative teaching by linking it to real-life experiences. As a writer, generate early versions of what might be said with conceptual outlines, notes specific to the plot line, and rewriting, which eventually leads, seamlessly and painlessly, to prose. And as a socializer, start before feeling ready to learn about academic culture, in general, about new colleagues, in particular, and about usually unwritten rules for reappointment.

Who was it who said, "The early bird gets the worm"?

And who said, "Be careful about what you ask for; you might just get it"?

Rule 3: Work in Brief, Regular Sessions.

This clearest statement of the constancy and moderation of the *nihil nimus* approach has the best evidence for its effectiveness. Teachers who prepare, present, and involve students in brief, regular sessions also work with the least fatigue and with the most clarity of main points conveyed to students in memorable fashion. They also spend far less time preparing for classes than do traditional new faculty (and earn higher teaching ratings). Writers who abandon customary bingeing at writing in favor of brief, daily sessions write with less pain, with more productivity and quality, and with higher likelihood of acceptance in prestigious outlets. Socializers who interact with constancy and moderation more readily arrange friendly and substantial communication and rate best on dimensions such as approval from more senior colleagues, correct knowledge about retention/promotion criteria, and comfort in their career beginnings.

Brief, daily sessions in teaching, writing, and socializing do something else essential for new faculty: They moderate usual busyness and they allow constant attention to social life and well-being.

Ne quid nimus (moderation in all things).—TERENCE

Rule 4: Stop.

Timely stopping may be harder than timely starting because the former relies on impulse management, something largely untaught in U.S. schools. Without it, we work beyond the point of diminishing returns and displace other necessary activities. Without it, we let impatience and its mindlessness rule at a point in life where we need to be taking care of ourselves and solving the right problems.

Struggling new faculty most often have trouble stopping classes on time, holding back from activities that bring short-term relief in favor of more aversive tasks such as writing, and moderating office hours. Those of us who learn timely stopping do so by way of practice at timely pausing, at mindful contemplation, by calming and slowing begun early, and with the help of external cues. One of the most powerful strategies for augmenting this sort of holding back is pausing to notice and correct uncivil ways of communicating, including nonverbal expressions of distance, indifference, and disdain.

What is most difficult about learning to stop in timely fashion? Patience and its need for holding back, particularly in pausing or quitting while momentum and genius seem too precious to interrupt.

How poor are they that have not patience!—SHAKESPEARE

Rule 5: Balance Preliminaries with Formal Work.

Exemplary new faculty demonstrate balance most obviously. Balance proves effective for newcomers who learn to spend about the same amount of time preparing for classes as in them, to prewrite as much as they prose write, to prepare for socialization as much as they immerse themselves in collegiality.

What usually impairs balance? Inexperience at pausing and waiting, at moderating excessiveness and its close friend impatience. What most often aids it? Economies of working in mindful ways, such as clearly seeing what needs doing, what needs communicating, and what engages students, readers, and colleagues as active listeners and participants. The kinds of early beginnings in Rule 2 aim specifically at these creative economies.

Rule 6: Moderate Overattachment and Overreaction.

Struggling new faculty most commonly display excessive attachment as:

- Teachers who suppose their lecture notes must reflect the whole of current knowledge about a topic and be covered in class in complete detail
- Writers who hold to folk notions that good writing is done in a great burst and in a single draft that needs no early readers or correction
- Participants in the socialization ritual for novice professors who stick closely to preset beliefs about how best to survive, even when they are clearly suffering and failing

These excesses turn out to be issues of overcontrol and not letting go of mindless habits. What helps counter them is practice of slowing to clearly notice the effects of one's actions on others and oneself. That takes patience and self-esteem.

Slow-starting novices on campus also stand out as most overactive to inevitable criticisms, even to well-intentioned suggestions for change. Here, too, the proven correctives are as simple but difficult as learning to listen to and learn from all sorts of criticism, even to welcome it as helpful. The most pleasant exercises for moderating overreactiveness are practice at humor about your own work and at mindful standing back from your work to see it as others might. The first-order skills behind all this are patience and holding back from impulsivity; the most general curatives are slowing, calming, and pausing to switch between generating and revising. The former help direct and motivate you about what to communicate, the latter help ensure the linearity, logic, and social acceptance of what you say or write.

Remember the adages we saw much earlier in this book: "The worse the writer, the more attachment to the content of his or her writing." And, "The worse the teacher, the more the reverence of content." The third generates itself: "The poorer the involvement in socialization, the greater and more misleading the confidence that one already knows how to make a good start."

Rule 7: Moderate Negative Thoughts.

Negative self-talk usually remained unnoticed and underappreciated in the new faculty I've studied. It discourages, distracts, demoralizes, and depresses in demonic fashion. It reliably accompanies procrastination and precedes blocks and other sorts of shyness. And, it follows, negative thinking is most common to slow starters amongst new faculty.

Quick starters, in contrast, engage in far more positive thinking than negative and they learn to suspend most thinking when generating writing.

Cures for negative thinking and its pessimism are simple: Mindful noticing of usual self-talk when work seems aversive, reflecting on the worth and rationality of what is said internally, and supplanting incivilities toward oneself with more positive, constructive thoughts.

Rule 8: Moderate Emotions.

Strugglers most often rely on excessive emotions to do work they would otherwise avoid. They wait until they have large, undisrupted blocks of time. They binge by working at a fast, euphoric, and unreflective pace with few pauses so that they are unable to stop before diminishing returns set in. The hypomania they induce makes them feel brilliant and invincible in the short run, fatigued and depressed afterward. But new faculty who work with constancy and moderation:

- Evidence unmistakable superiority in producing manuscript pages, inducing student comprehension, and deriving benefit from mentoring
- Report more ease, satisfaction, and joyfulness in teaching, writing, and socialization
- Evidence less depression, pessimism, hopelessness, social distress, and illness

Who better to keep in mind with regard to costs of working amid high emotion than Joseph Conrad? Who better to recall when considering the benefits of switching to constancy and moderation?

Rule 9: Let Others Do Some of the Work.

Exemplary new faculty set the best model I've seen for mastering this difficult but essential rule: They do not hesitate to look and ask for help. They most readily engage students as helpful evaluators and collaborators—and admit mistakes and ignorances to students, while maintaining the highest standards as graders and the highest ratings from students. They share plans and prewriting early and they let others, even critics, suggest better ways to find clarity, completeness, significance, and public acceptance. They are also most proactive in learning which mentors can help them most and then in benefitting from their advice and coaching. I could add another quote about what usually hinders letting others do some of the work (pride), but I'll hold back.

Rule 10: Limit Wasted Effort.

In the end, the *nihil nimus* approach is about economy in beginning professorial careers. Good starts can't occur unless they involve holding back from wasted efforts. Good starts won't persist without the success and resilience that come with constancy and moderation. And even good starts, so far I can tell, are not optimized without the compassion of mindful patience and clear seeing that impels service for both others and oneself.

The usual problem in that last implication of advice is that readers often finish this book before they master this most mindful and self-serving rule about resilience. Without that strength, they risk not experiencing the full delights of professorial careers that I mentioned at the very beginning of this book. So I end our long journey with a wise caution:

> *People usually fail when they are on the brink of success.*
> *So give as much care to the end as to the beginning;*
> *Then there will be no failure.—LAO TSU*

Appendix:
Readings by the Numbers

These abstracts have two interrelated sources: One is referral to a reading in the text, by number, and the other is selection by new faculty in my programs as unusually interesting and useful.

#1. Sternberg, R. (1993). *The psychologist's companion: A guide to scientific writing for students and researchers.* **New York: Cambridge University Press.**

Robert Sternberg begins by dismissing eight common misperceptions about academic writing (e.g., the important thing is what you say, not how you say it; scientific writers start with clever ideas already in mind, before collecting data). He then reinforces the importance of knowing better by explaining why only the best-prepared, best-organized writing has a chance for acceptance in respected journals: space limitations require some 90 percent rejection of submitted manuscripts, and the common reason for rejection is an author taking too long to get to the point.

Sternberg first sets his advice on how to get ideas and direction in a student context, but its relevance to new faculty is immediately apparent. Too many of us trying to write, he notes, select topics that are too safe (e.g., not likely to entrance readers) or too difficult (e.g., too broad or with too little useful literature to help guide us). And, more specifically, too few of us have learned optimal ways of searching the literature. Suggestions: List each topic on a card and then organize cards into useful themes (shades of C. Wright Mills?); add notes to cards about the validity of arguments, the consistency of arguments, the basis of arguments and their implications, and the relevance of arguments to your manuscript. Sternberg excels in illustrating different ways of developing and structuring formal outlines.

When he extends his advice to faculty, he becomes more detailed: He tells readers how, exactly, to read in productive fashion, by first pursuing a few topics in depth, by noticing which topics are "leading edge," by moving from general readings/reviews to more specific sources, and, most particularly, by directing yourself to:

- Extend the theory/theme of a reading.
- Generate analogous notions.
- Challenge the assumptions in what you are reading.

For readers still uncertain about how to proceed with traditional research, Sternberg details experimental methods in succinctly useful ways (e.g., designing a project for clear outcomes, getting proper permissions to test subjects, learning incisive ways to analyze data, and using alternative conceptualizations of how to discuss what you discover).

In my observations, Sternberg puts novice professors as readers most in confidence when he lists specifics about how to:

- Interest, inform, and persuade your reader (e.g., by concisely informing readers what the manuscript is about).
- Write for your reader (e.g., do not equate traditional scientific formality with readability).
- Write clearly (e.g., be willing to go back to reread and rewrite).
- Moderate redundancies, digressions, and overexplanations.
- Avoid unnecessary qualifiers (and use them only to deliberately limit the scope of a statement).
- Opt for simple, direct sentences with concrete words and examples (and so on, through 26 useful rules of this sort).
- Be aware of commonly misused words (e.g., confusing *affect* with *effect*) (and, incredibly but usefully, 131 more cautions worth memorizing such as these).
- Properly cite/reference the literature you rely on; know ways of ensuring a thorough search of relevant precedents (e.g., membership in professional organizations and their means of communicating; access to abstracting services).
- Learn how to evaluate writing, including your own: Start by seeing how classic manuscripts are composed (e.g., the strikingly direct and memorable ways they say things) and how the work behind them was conducted (e.g., with clear measures of what mattered most). Sternberg, an unusually tough but helpful editor, includes his own formula for judging the worth of manuscripts, by asking whether it (1) contains a new result that is made sensible in a broad

context; (2) is of major theoretical or practical importance; (3) includes a new, exciting way of looking at an old problem; (4) interprets the findings unambiguously; (5) integrates precedents into a simpler framework; (6) debunks accepted ideas; (7) presents a clever method of inquiry; and (8) presents findings and theories in generally useful ways.

No, I have not come close to meeting all those standards, but I do find Sternberg's ideals a useful goal to approximate—so have many new faculty I've tracked who read the Sternberg *Guide to Scientific Writing,* including some who were not scientists. They most often put it this way: "I really like the fact that he speaks as an expert who lets me in on his personal methods for success. He makes me feel confident that I can learn how to do things right in all the details."

What I like most about the Sternberg book is its penultimate part, where he shares usually unwritten information about what writers should know before submitting a manuscript to an editor and his or her minions: Investigate the quality, content, format requirements, and editing policies of the journal; anticipate the customary review process in your field (e.g., the editor sends copies of your manuscript to reviewers who judge it without revealing their identity); and know the usual reasons manuscripts are rejected. These, not surprisingly, turn out to be the near-obverse of the ideals listed above, but in his list, Sternberg respecifies them in a manner to make sure they are understood (e.g., a manuscript that represents too little work or substance; one that is based on weak or unclear methodology; one that does not include much that is new/useful; one that reflects shoddy scholarship or misleading analyses).

Best of all, in my opinion (and in that of the readers I know), is the last part of the text, with its specific advice about making good starts with editors, grant proposal reviewers, and book publishers. I hope you will read it for yourself.

#2. Lucas, R. (1992). *The grants world inside out.* Urbana: University of Illinois Press.

Robert Lucas puts grant writing into a humorous but astute context. He often employs an "Ask Ann Granters" format:

> *DEAR ANN: I have heard that some proposals are wired. What does this mean? Is there any advantage to having a proposal wired? [signed] UNCERTAIN*

> *DEAR UNC: Some proposals are wired. You can have yours wired too. Just take your proposal to your favorite electronics store and ask for a Nobel Writing Kit. Once your proposal has been hooked up, it will glow with confidence. If you get the souped-up version with the voice synthesizer, your proposal will also sing. Proposals that sing get funded. Just don't read them in the bathtub.*

"Wired" refers to the proud sense that a proposal is exactly what an agency wants to fund, that the agency administrators actually encouraged the submission. It also tells you something else: People who depict their proposals as wired with the right connections and as so brilliant that they seem like music to the ears of reviewers are braggarts.

Another way Lucas eases entrance into the foreign culture of grants writing is with his own Ambrosian dictionary of useful grants words; for instance:

> *collaboration (ko LOB er ay shun): n. The phenomenon whereby a number of faculty members refuse to take the lead in writing a major interdisciplinary proposal, browbeat a colleague into doing so, and then later gang up on the writer because he or she hasn't adequately represented their pet areas.*

Before you quite realize it, that light-heartedness includes useful information about writing to current guidelines from agencies; knowing the essential steps behind successful proposals (thinking, discussing, searching, drafting, trimming, phoning, editing, amplifying, consulting, rewriting, polishing, reviewing, budgeting, sending, waiting, negotiating, and rebudgeting); looking at the proposals of competitors; presenting proposals to campus administrators who must eventually sign-off on them before submission to an agency—in early and orderly fashion; tempering temptations to exaggerate your prior accomplishments; getting in direct contact with the program officer before writing the proposal; and so on. Lucas also admonishes against any sentence as long as the one preceding this one.

Because all those steps sound (and are) daunting, Lucas coaches strategies of beginning by applying for small grants, seed grants, on-campus grants. In particular, he coaches readers in ways of utilizing campus grants offices. Grants offices can help new faculty write successful proposals. They can suggest fundable topics and arrange contacts with grants officers (local or distant). They inform about diverse sources of funding, about topics being funded and typical levels of funding provided, and about preparing a realistic and specific budget (including mysterious, negotiable things like indirect costs). Grants offices facilitate campus supports and sign-offs. They know ways of avoiding nomination for Golden Fleece Awards, and they steer you away from improper, unethical plans or conflicts of interest. And, among other things, they can help you get feedback from reviewers if your proposal is rejected or given a low priority for funding.

Lucas ends with another clever way of presenting valuable information inside out, with examples of how academics often write proposals but probably should not (each starts with an common phrase and is followed by what a reviewer might assume it means):

It has long been known that . . .
I can't find the reference.

It is believed that . . .
I think . . .

A statistically oriented projection of the significance of these findings . . .
A wild guess.

All jokes aside, this book has helped far more new faculty write successful proposals for funding than any other I know of.

#3. Reis, R. (1997). *Tomorrow's professor.* New York: Institute of Electric and Electronic Engineers.

The scope of Richard Reis's book is so comprehensive that I begin by abstracting its table of contents:

- Chapters on the nature of the academic enterprise (e.g., key characteristics of the culture; seven sample schools) and on science and engineering in particular (e.g., how its members collaborate)
- An optimistic chapter on new trends in the professoriate toward valuing teaching as well as research
- Key chapters on how to decide on a professorial career (e.g., getting realistic information about supply and demand), on effective ways of choosing a graduate school and then thriving therein (e.g., choosing your advisor/director), and on making good beginnings as a teacher (e.g., preparing a teaching portfolio to include with job application materials)
- More information about deciding what kind of campus you want, on preparing your formal search for positions and readying your application, and on general principles for negotiating (and specifics about special needs such as dual-career couples). For example:

It is no accident that those who apply to 60–70 places often get turned down by all of them. They cannot possibly be a match for that many different positions, and their applications show it.

Reiss also presents a wealth of advice about things like time management and effective approaches to teaching, research, and service. For example:

Other ways of simplifying your initial teaching assignment might include: Teaching a course previously taught by someone who is willing to loan you copies of their lecture notes, exams, and homework assignments. . . .

And he includes the lighter side of what he learned from the senior faculty who supplied him with advice for new faculty:

> *Although it was over 25 years ago, Paul Humke still recalls those feelings of anxiety and stress as a beginning faculty member. . . . As one would expect from a mathematician, Humke stated his point in the form of an equation:*

$$WUT = k\,exp(TL)$$

Put into words, it means that the warm-up time necessary when returning to a problem increases exponentially with time since leaving it.

My final example from this encyclopedic book is a summary of Reis's conclusions about necessities for good starts as a teacher: Rely on collegial supports and resources. Learn from and share with other teachers. Ask for advice, even for useful materials and more practical teaching assignments. And keep work at teaching moderate enough to allow time for other important activities.

#4. Bullough, R. V., Knowles, J. G., & Crow, N. (1991). *Emerging as a teacher.* New York: Routledge.

The premise of this book is that too little is known about the actual process of socialization experienced in the first few years of teaching in elementary and high schools. Bullough and colleagues support that assumption with observations of new teachers whose experiences often prove contrary to folk knowledge. First, new teachers began with the traditional belief that expert teachers possess specialized knowledge to be passed along to students. As a result, they taught over students' heads and were puzzled about the lack of student interest. Second, new teachers struggled most with a duo of problems: Controlling/disciplining and collegial isolation/loneliness. And third, senior colleagues proved unable to teach novices how to teach.

Other results of these conditions are just as understandable: New teachers suffered the frustration of feeling ineffective and the depression of having lowered their standards. Many newcomers supposed that the best teachers are the most personable (e.g., buddies to students), a bent that can induce students to do little more than play. And they struggled to be liked by *all* students. New teachers were understandably resistant to being observed by colleagues, especially those untrained as evaluators and who accomplished little more than reinforcing feelings of inadequacy.

These self-inflicted handicaps apparently began with unrealistic expectations. Many new teachers hoped they were born as teachers who needed nothing more than ideal circumstances to display their potential brilliance. And too many started by wanting foremost to be a rescuer of students, often with vague notions of the line between being helping and rescuing. As a result, they soon felt exhausted and miserable in a traditional work setting that already exacerbated self-doubts.

Three central problems in this common scenario are that schools (1) expect new teachers to learn by teaching and to exhibit skills they do not yet possess; (2) demand all this while teachers remain especially vulnerable to criticism and feelings of failure, while conceptions of themselves as teachers remain weak, confused, and often contradictory; and, (3) reward ever more conservatism (e.g., as classroom incivilities grow, teachers stick more to the text) and the growing belief that it is never acceptable to fail as a teacher. In this state of affairs, little professional development is likely to take place; instead, struggling new teachers blame their students and other external factors alone.

Bullough and colleagues take a more optimistic outlook on the potentials of fledgling school teachers by addressing the predictable stages they experience on the way to success:

- Fantasy (and high ideals/expectations)
- Survival (reality shock; struggling to gain classroom control)
- Mastery (usually slow in coming, often because of difficulties in managing classroom control, something most novices have no idea how to do)

This is Bullough's overall point in his esteemed research of this sort: The thing we usually overlook is that commitment to teaching is essential but not sufficient; teachers must also have useful information on how to begin and find satisfying experiences while doing so.

#5. Elbow, P. (1983). Embracing contraries in the teaching process. *College Teaching, 45,* 327–339.

Peter Elbow addresses the struggle inherent in teachers' conflicting loyalties, on the one hand to maintaining standards and on the other to nurturing students:

> *Our loyalty to students asks us to be their allies and hosts as we instruct and share . . . [but] our commitment to knowledge and society asks us to be guardians or bouncers: we must discriminate, evaluate, test, grade, certify.*

The result of overdoing the latter things excessively while maintaining standards can be student defensiveness that makes teaching harder. The other extreme is no better.

Some of us, Elbow observes, compromise and waffle. We sort of commit to standards and to students, but never fully to either. When we settle for a truce, we get little more than a decreasing involvement in our teaching. When we opt to care almost exclusively about standards or about nurturance, we may preserve some of our passion, but not for both.

Elbow advocates a plan that satisfies in both dimensions. The first step: Exaggerate your gatekeeping functions early, because the usual alternative, soft-pedaling the assessment, makes it seem more mysterious and worrisome for students:

> *The more I can make it clear to myself and to my students that I have a commitment to knowledge and institutions, and the more I can make it specifically clear how I am going to fulfill that commitment, the easier it is for me to turn around and make a dialectical change of role into being an extreme ally . . . the more clearly I can say what I want them to know or be able to do, the better I can figure out what I must provide to help them attain these goals.*

By addressing both kinds of loyalties (to standards and to students), Elbow puts himself at ease as a teacher:

> *I feel better about being really tough if I know I am going to turn around and be more on the student's side than usual.*

How best to act as an ally? Elbow likens his style to coaching:

> *This stance provides a refreshingly blunt but supportive way to talk to students about weaknesses. "You're strong here, you're weak there, and over here you are really out of it. We've got to find ways to work on these things so you can succeed on these essays or exams."*

In our usual role as standard keepers, Elbow notes, we do not offer information about how students need to change and develop.

At the end of this thought-provoking article, Elbow addresses the things that may make his suggestions hard to adopt: Initially, the strategy confuses students who are accustomed to teachers being hard, soft, or in the middle, both not strong in two areas. Moreover, the strategy cannot completely remove the conflict teachers feel in trying to play both roles. Elbow does, however, offer a structure and context for implementing his strategy and experiencing the improved feelings that balancing can bring:

> *It helps me understand better the pressures on me and helps me stop feeling as though there is something wrong with me for feeling pulled in two directions at once.*

#6. Erickson, B. L., & Stommer, D. W. (1991). *Teaching college freshmen.* San Francisco: Jossey-Bass.

Bette Erickson and Diane Stommer provide crucial reading for teachers of large, introductory classes and, by extension, to all others. These are their premises:

Prior efforts to strengthen the freshman year for students focused on the periphery of academic life, not on the freshman classroom; and no books prior to this one dealt extensively with instruction for freshmen students. If undergraduate education is to be improved, the change must occur largely in classrooms, first in initial survey courses.

These authors recommend that teachers of freshmen begin by understanding the transition those students have just made from high school to college. Researchers estimate that two-thirds of students are "disengaged" while in high school; in that role, students suppose that classroom success requires little academic involvement. Worse yet, many of them come to college having been part of a complex, tacit conspiracy to avoid sustained, rigorous, demanding inquiry.

Despite coming to college with profound deficits in effective ways of studying and learning (e.g., notetaking), new students expect to do B work or better. They are further handicapped because, newly freed from the imposed controls of high school, students find their new freedom hard to limit. Why should you and I care about this coming-of-age ritual, given that many people seem to survive it well enough? The first year in college [or the professoriate] is a critical time in which basic skills and attitudes will or will not be acquired. Add to that an awareness of still more ill-timed problems: Many new students find courses dull and teachers inattentive or indifferent; many classrooms are dominated by students who are more invested in jobs than in schoolwork. Even the students we say we most want to help are most often left in peril of failing—minority students often come less prepared and are then less often coached in useful ways of surviving.

Perhaps the biggest problem is that general student understanding does not come cheap; it develops gradually, as students encounter new examples and illustrations, and with extensive practice (e.g., where faculty pose the examples and students explain how they relate to the concepts under study). Students must be prompted to give something more than is customary, even to reach for learning experiences as challenging as mastering problem-solving skills.

Erickson and Strommer use their own broad experience with teachers of freshmen classes to specify many more invaluables. I abstract just two. The first advice is about the syllabus given students, with the following components at a minimum:

- Information about required texts (perhaps like the abstracts here)
- Introduction to the subject matter
- Statement of course goals
- Description of evaluation procedures
- Preview of class activities and assignments
- Course outline
- Course policies (the fine print)
- A friendly tone

The second example of specific information involves a clear depiction of how a good first meeting with a class goes. It is preceded with a humorous account of how teachers should *not* carry it off (e.g., lecture but then tell students to come prepared to discuss in the next class). Some serious advice:

- Find out about students in your class; help students connect with one another; get students to talk and to solve a problem; make an assignment for the second class
- Abandon the nonstop 50-minute lecture; it reinforces passive listening, verbatim notetaking, and superficial information-processing strategies
- Rarely present for more than 15 minutes at a stretch
- Have students work with ideas before moving on
- Plan an introduction for each class meeting to get students' attention (while pointing out your objectives)
- Highlight the major points and select appropriate examples that become gradually more complex and subtle
- Discuss examples
- Guide notetaking by providing skeletal outlines of main points, by pausing occasionally to have students paraphrase what they have put in their notes; encourage students to elaborate notes (what composition teachers call writing-to-learn), in part by your own evaluations of student notes
- Encourage student involvement by way of small-group discussion methods; visit the groups as they discuss and problem solve and help them where necessary
- Use writing-to-learn assignments to get students involved in classroom material outside class
- Make assignments that encourage regular study; call for substantial early products such as outlines; make assignments that promote thinking and understanding
- Recognize that a killer problem in large classrooms is anonymity; counter this by incorporating small-group discussions and problem-solving tasks; be assertive in inviting students to office hours
- Realize that your teaching assistants, too, need training, guidance, and support

#7. Angelo, T. (Ed.). (1998). *Classroom assessment and research: An update on uses, approaches, and research findings.* **San Francisco: Jossey-Bass.**

Notice, first of all, the extension of the title beyond the original designation of the movement as classroom research: Its leading practitioners now include careful assessment of student needs and changes. Two other things are new here. There is more attention to the philosophy and theory behind the prescriptions and the tactics are now intended for use beyond the original emphasis on single classrooms and single problems. Still, the singular approach remains most practical for faculty beginning to study ways of improving the teaching and learning in their own classes.

Chapter 1, by K. Patricia Cross, is titled Classroom Research—Implementing the Scholarship of Teaching. Patricia Cross was Tom Angelo's dissertation advisor and then collaborator; they popularized the classroom research movement together. She, perhaps because she is still Angelo's mentor, sticks to first-order actions by emphasizing beginnings with sound scholarship about what you plan to study in your classroom. This means knowing enough about specific precedents and interventions to make them productive in broadly social ways.

Cross would have you extend your usual assessments (about what is going on in class and how much students learn) to questions about why students responded as they did and how they learned what they did. To meet this goal, you will have to learn more about the learning process of your students; your classroom will become a laboratory for studying how better to teach students to learn essential things. An example of one simple device for getting useful feedback from students is the *minute paper,* a strategy we saw earlier in our own book as *one-minute papers.* This assignment—for students to write answers to, say, one or two questions for a minute each—offers several benefits for so brief a task:

- It forces students to stop and reflect on what they've just learned, perhaps even to synthesize it with a related bit of learning.
- Its regular use in classes (even when minute papers are only read by professors and not graded) prompts students to pay closer attention and ask more questions.
- It informs teachers in quick fashion of how many students are confused or comprehending, and it suggests places where teaching needs clarification.

A champion of minute papers, Richard Light (1990) concludes that no other classroom assessment device offers so much useful information for so small an investment in time, especially when that information is shared with students. Why is this probably true? Sharing the feedback gives students more timely information about how well they're learning than does sole reliance on occasional test scores such as midterms and finals. It also puts at least some of the onus on the teacher to improve the way she or he presents things commonly misunderstood in class.

Cross believes feedback from classroom assessments (CATs), like minute papers, is the first and most important step to improving teaching. I, as you know, would put moderation of classroom incivilities first, and her techniques second, at least for new faculty. In a sense, we both endorse classroom research, I for helping teachers learn which of their actions enhance or discourage student involvement and cooperation, she for checking how (and how well) students actually learn as a basis for first-order change in teaching. Which should you do? Both. You cannot excel at teaching without mastering each of them.

Chapter 2, by Mimi Steadman and Marilla Svinicki, is titled CATs—A Student's Gateway to Better Learning. These two experts show why a learning theory (something conspicuously absent in my own writing) can help teachers understand how students come to know things in classrooms. Steadman and Svinicki's Cognitive Model explains what goes on in the minds of learners when they are active participants (as opposed to passive listeners trying to do little more than memorize). Cognitive Theory uses information from research in fields like psychology and education to explain how active learning works best, in generally simple but useful ways:

- Active learning builds connections between new information and old, in ways that encode them into long-term memory as accessible forms.
- The first necessity is mindful attention to what matters in your teaching and awareness of how this new material can expand the meaning and application of other or older knowledge.
- The second step, encoding, is more than stimulus-response connection transferred to memory; when learning is active, learners consciously arrange material and create memorable images. At their most involved level, learning and memory are constructive. Active learning plays a crucial role because it keeps students reflecting and connecting before the knowledge being encoded becomes rote and rigid (see the next step).
- In the third step, active learners are aware of their own learning in ways that bring mindful control of goal setting, of broad monitoring, of learning strategies most likely to meet the goal, and of appropriate resources for the task. The result is called *metacognition*—remember that from Section II on writing?

The most important outcome may be seen in teaching students to monitor their own comprehension, consciously and metacognitively. You already know one way to initiate this mindfulness: Minute papers where students collaborate with teachers in making sense of the results and in noticing how well they learn.

Intermediate chapters in Angelo's edited book address (1) Specific ways CATs provide teachers with information that stimulates change in both teaching and learning; (2) research designs to help determine if your CATs improve student learning (e.g., in terms of students' test scores); (3) similarities between Total Quality Management (TQM) and the use of CATs; and (4) CATs applied across the disciplines and throughout a large university system.

Two of the final chapters may be most relevant to readers here.

Chapter 8, by Laurie Richlin, is titled "Using CATs to Help New Instructors Develop as Teachers." The message here, that CATs are especially helpful to novice teachers, should not surprise you. But what makes it different from what've already seen is its focus on coaching new teaching assistants as teachers. Richlin's perspective on new teachers includes these developmental steps:

- New teachers move from an initially pessimistic stance ("I'm not really a teacher") to one of teaching as a partnership with students. You intuit, I hope, how CATs would help bring that transformation—from traditional distancing as a teacher to sharing one's research-based information about intended changes as a teacher with students. That move takes optimism.
- New teaching assistants move from course- and content-planning imposed externally, and from its attendant problem of supposing that content matters most of all, to metaconcerns that go beyond requirements. One of those is seeing what students learn.
- Novices move from regarding students as idealized or unknown, then perhaps past seeing them as irrelevant or oppositional, to treating them as partners in the teaching/learning process where all of you seek improvement together.
- They progress beyond trying not to think about evaluations, past trying to fix evaluations to get good ratings, to noticing what to take responsibility for in evaluations—and taking it.
- They develop from usual worries about having enough to say to more sociable concerns, specifically to remove themselves from the center of communication to a place where the message becomes more important than the sender.

To help new teachers put her impressive insights into practice, Laurie Richlin offers new teaching assistants semester-long workshops that meet every week for the term. There, they collectively learn basics, such as writing a useful syllabus and making student assignments; most crucially, they implement CATs within the structure of a Teaching Goals Inventory. Its teaching/learning goals not only necessitate clearly specific and tested approaches for meeting them but they also provide a checklist against which to assess progress over a semester. So, for example, novice teachers are soon helped to move beyond usual concerns (e.g., "How can I get students to talk in class?") with techniques such as minute papers; but first they employ a CAT based around teaching goals (e.g., "How well do I stimulate you to ask questions and discuss things?"). Then, in most cases, they move to other mindful strategies (e.g., treating many of students' wrong answers as "alternative" answers by, say, asking for restatements of a compassionate sort from other students).

Chapter 10, by Charles Walker and Thomas Angelo, is titled, "A Collective Effort Classroom Assessment Technique [CECAT]—Promoting High Performance in Student Teams." Here, at last, CATs obviously converge with cooperative learning. And here, it figures, lies some of the most useful advice from classroom researchers.

The premise of these two classroom researchers is that CATs will teach teachers the most when carried out by student teams. Walker and Angelo begin by outlining problems of group assignments, such as social loafing because the correctives are still not well-established among college teachers. Then the authors clarify directives from their own classes for use by other teachers. Specifically, they applied CATs to understand the process experienced by students while developing collective ways of working in class. That is, they (much as I began my studies of mentoring for new faculty) looked to see what constituted naturally effective versus ineffective teams of students working collectively on a problem. One result of that empirical inquiry is a list of directives for optimal teaming: (1) evaluate students individually, independently from team scores; (2) make each individual's contribution to the group unique; (3) inform individuals and whole groups what constitutes good performance; (4) make the group's work important/meaningful; (5) pick a group assignment that cannot be done well by a single individual; (6) keep group size no larger than $N = 7$; (7) coach team members to show mutual respect; and (8) help each member to value working in a collective way.

To generate this information, Walker and Angelo devised different forms of their CECAT to assess student progress over a semester. This is a sample of one item per form:

Early: 16. _____ *I will exert a lot of effort to help the group achieve its goals.*

Midway: 3. _____ *As our work progresses, the group is becoming more cohesive.*

Summative Assessment: 19. _____ *My contribution to the group's work was unique; no one else did exactly what I did.*

Equally important, they validated their CECAT format by showing that each CECAT item differed high-scoring from low-scoring students overall (e.g., for item "The group performed excellently," $\bar{x} = 4.4$ vs. 2.2, respectively, on a 5-point scale; for item "Group outcome was valuable for me," $\bar{x} = 4.1$ vs. 2.9). Moreover, correlational analysis of these data suggested which of these items have the most influence on team success:

1. Respect for coworkers
2. Members worked equally hard
3. Group became more cohesive
4. Coworkers valued working collectively

This research-based information helps teachers know what to do and look for in setting up team projects—better yet, how to assess what works and what doesn't. It is, put simply, a nice example of how classrooms can be turned into laboratories to understand learning processes and improve teaching.

#8. Maher, F., & Tetreault, M. K. (1994). *The feminist classroom.* New York: Basic Books.

These authors address experiences and needs of faculty and students traditionally made second-class citizens because of our male-dominated educational system. Specifically, Maher and Tetreault show how serious feminists model more democratic ways of teaching.

Their ideal teacher breaks through usual silences and illusions by teaching an ever-changing culture of students and teachers to deal with traditional sexism and its exclusionism. The most compelling reasons for this change in teaching style, according to Maher and Tetreault, are (1) compassion for undergraduates who increasingly fail to graduate in four years (the percentage may now be as high as 85 percent) and (2) understanding the reason behind it—student perceptions that universities are cold, uncaring, and alien.

Is their approach a bit preachy and overconfident? Yes, at least for me. But it probably does not exceed my own evangelizing. I am invariably surprised when critics mistake my confidence and enthusiasm for arrogance or trying too hard. So how, other than "preaching to the already converted" in an academe still dominated by White males, can compassionate (i.e., feminist-oriented) teachers make a difference? By modeling an approach to teaching and learning that simply works better. In some ways this feminist style does; the key seems to lie in shifting classroom climates away from assertive, competitive, and hierarchical customs. As in the *nihil nimus* approach, feminists make compassion in relationships a first-order principle. They even label their more socialized way of teaching and learning in terms that I consider Baconian: "Connected knowing."

What these feminists emphasize that I do not are political, historical, cultural influences on universities and their teaching. Feminists have made the best effort to understand and moderate those external forces. Maher and Tetreault join them in:

- Challenging traditional paradigms about how best to arrange learning for everyone by experimenting with risky new approaches to teaching/learning
- Revising teaching philosophies to be more egalitarian in communication, more productive of diverse kinds of knowledge
- Communicating knowledge about why shared viewpoints are more generally useful than the kinds in individualized and competitive teaching
- Emphasizing ways of teaching about the disparate world views of women and men and how to mend that traditional rift via connecting principles (e.g., objectivity rooted not just in detached impartiality but on broader awareness of the social contexts that affect such "truths")
- Putting aside lecturing or Socratic dialogs (because both of those are too often authoritarian and manipulative) in favor of consciousness raising about the needs of students, including a voice of their own

To bring coherence, specificity, and shared knowledge to these approaches, Maher and Tetreault visited the campus of each of 17 model feminists to directly monitor their teaching and to interview selected students from their classes. Over time, they also observed and inquired about the classes of traditional White males. Initially, these authors/researchers framed questions around assumptions of men being more concerned with separate and rational approaches and women as more democratic and cooperative. Over time—perhaps as a result of taking their assumptions outward for public testing—they moderated their dichotomies and ideals. In the end, they chose to portray what they were shown as four critical themes of feminist teaching done well:

1. *Mastery attained by students:* This refers to mastery in relationship to internal and external standards as well as in terms of their own needs and of processes/products shared in a collaborative achievement with other students. In this view, mastery can be an interactive construction of meaning among teachers and students. What has this to do with compassion? It requires patient, mindful, and non-judgmental seeing of what views different from our own can teach us about ourselves and others. This compassion apparently grows with tolerance for conversation that may at first seem outlandish. Done well, this progression brings shared learning to a point of real competence.

2. *Voice:* At first in this study, voice seemed to be little more than awakening students to speak for themselves in making sense of educational experiences (a theme of especial value for marginalized students). But Maher and Tetreault's experience with diverse teachers on varied campuses led to a broader conception: Effective teachers help students shape voices so they can vary them depending on the environment. In this way, feminist teachers encourage voices that intersect and cooperate with each other in their classrooms. Said another way, students' voices are fashioned best when they emerge from ongoing conversations that include our information and each other's takes on it.

3. *Authority:* Feminist teachers commit to social change, and thus give themselves authority to work on behalf of people who are women and/or of color. Ironically, this often means giving up traditional authority in classrooms to make students responsible for much of their own learning.

4. *Positionality:* This means taking account of a learner's position, in any context, in terms of gender, race, class, and other dimensions relevant to social oppression. It means broad seeing of dimensions of social interactions, including teaching/learning in terms of individuals' centrality versus marginality, and oppressiveness versus oppression. It also puts special challenges to teachers regarding their own defensiveness and narrowness, both of which resist conscious awareness and require hard work to be seen in broad contexts.

A wealth of case studies accompanies these explanations of a feminist model of pedagogy. They include accounts of how exemplary teachers dealt with (1) open challenges to their authority as professors; (2) students who needed to see their own sexism/racism and its effects on others; and (3) racial tensions including usual complications with socioeconomic status.

Two things, it seems to me, stand out most in Maher and Tetreault's findings: First, teachers and students cannot fully understand what they think/believe until they appreciate what others in class reveal in their own reactions and convictions. Second, teachers and students who adopt cooperative, collaborative attitudes help make the class more valuable for everyone.

#9. Gappa, J. M., & Leslie, D. W. (1993). *The invisible faculty: Improving the status of part-timers in higher education.* San Francisco: Jossey-Bass.

Part-time faculty not only come cheap (they usually receive no benefits, no health insurance, no office space, no paid vacation or sabbatical) but they also rarely get tenure, often not even permanency. Full-time colleagues may never see them. Because of the economy they provide to campuses, part-timers now approach 40 percent of all faculty. According to Gappa and Leslie,

> *The low costs and heavy undergraduate teaching loads of the have-nots help make possible the continuation of a tenure system that protects jobs and perquisites of the haves. Because tenured faculty benefit directly and personally from this bifurcation of the academic profession, they have a vested interest in maintaining it.*

To document the tradition of disinterest in part-time faculty, Judy Gappa and David Leslie interviewed administrators, full-time faculty, and part-time faculty at 18 campuses representing the diversity of academe. They also had the timely help of data just published from national surveys about all college faculty, including 2,000 regular and temporary part-timers in the United States.

These are some of the findings: Part-timers tend to be younger, often still finishing their graduate work or else unable to find positions they wanted in beginning their careers. Racial and ethnic minorities make up only 9.2 percent of this subclass, less than in full-time positions. Women more often work as part-timers, especially when married; they are more qualified than men in part-time roles. Part-timers are generally overqualified for their positions; it is a buyer's, not a seller's, market.

While part-timers insist they love to teach, their dissatisfaction in part-time roles usually dominates their experience. They are constant victims of petty and thoughtless treatments (e.g., a general lack of appreciation for their work, an absence of power to change their classes). They often work without written contracts and their calls to teach again may come at the last minute. They usually fall outside bargaining units, even beyond benefits such as unemployment insurance.

In some ways, the increasing presence of part-timers in academe represents a false economy because it leaves fewer full-time faculty to manage departmental affairs. And, Gappa and Leslie conclude, this obviously exploitative practice demeans the campuses that engage in it. The biggest offenders are the very campuses who already suffer the lowest status in higher education: Community colleges. But just as problematic in the long run may be its reinforcement, by way of hiring more and more part-timers to teach the larger and lower-level classes that full-time faculty refuse to teach.

The same negative trends also continue to grow because of the informal, almost indifferent, ways that part-timers are recruited and monitored. Not only does academe hire part-timers with haste and without obvious concern for their qualifications, but it generally assigns them courses in evenings when departmental and faculty offices are closed. And it rarely offers them supports such as workshops or skilled evaluators of their classes.

My own studies of new faculty as part-timers corroborate Gappa and Leslie's conclusions: Feelings of loneliness, abandonment, and worthlessness exceed those of full-time newcomers, even of full-time women and minorities on the tenure track. And part-timers report far more anger, in general, particularly over the low social and professional status afforded them in comparison with full-time faculty (especially when the qualifications of full-timers were clearly no better then theirs).

Does any other subset of faculty now suffer such low esteem and support? I say no but Gappa and Leslie are more gentle in making their case. Where they and I do agree is in terms of needs for the kinds of faculty development programs proved effective for full-timers. A few campuses provide workshops that at least help make part-timers feel welcome and cared about. I, as you might expect, recommend giving them access to useful information about the plight of their kind, in general, and about ways of taking better care of themselves.

#10. Tatum, B. D. (1992). Talking about race, learning about racism: The application of racial identity development theory in the classroom. *Harvard Educational Review, 62,* 1–24.

In essence, Beverly Tatum models the ways she, herself, teaches students how racism operates in their lives and what they can do about it. She begins by noting three usual obstacles in that sort of teaching from her own experience: (1) racism is not a polite topic of serious conversation (most Whites have been raised to avoid its open discussion); (2) confronting students with their own racism elicits strong emotions and resistance; and (3) usual attempts of teachers to manage these strong defensive reactions have included little attention to the learning processes involved.

Tatum's approach begins with clear assumptions about content issues. She recommends the following clarifications in class:

- Racism is primarily about benefiting Whites as a group.
- Prejudice differs from racism in denying individualism to its victims.
- Students cannot be blamed for learning what they have been taught.
- Change is possible; even some Klansmen have seen the light.
- Facing these issues, usually amid the assumption that others are racist but we are not, will be emotional and exhausting but eventually worth the effort.

Then Tatum moves to process issues. She finds the best way of inducing awareness and change in regard to racism lies in casting the learning experience in terms of predictable stages of progress toward antiracism:

1. *The preencounter stage:* This is the usual, unenlightened state of most White students in class, one that reflects internalized (and sometimes unconscious awareness of) racist stereotypes. Until White students join African Americans in assignments, such as hunting for apartments together, they might not appreciate the subtle kinds of racism that people of color encounter on a daily basis—nor, for that matter, may some students of color.

2. *The encounter stage:* Once *all* students begin to acknowledge the impact of racism on their own and other's lives and are bothered by it, they begin to make progress. The primary encounters with racism often occur in class discussions where students listen to the racist experiences of others, tolerantly and compassionately. This is where emotions can rise to surprising heights in class, where the professor not only needs to act as a moderator but also as a teacher who puts students' comments and reactions into this framework of racial development. The result is a mindful stepping back to observe how racism and the anger/guilt that usually surround it are more understandable and forgivable when seen in terms of where the person stands in relation to the developmental stages.

3. *The immersion/emersion stage:* This is where resistance and other mindlessly excessive reactions may be strongest. African Americans, for example, may experience immersion as avoidance of White symbols and strong attraction to African American culture. But with continued encounters that broaden students' views, immersion begins to turn into emersion from so narrow an orientation.

4. *The internalization stage:* Here, at last, students display less defensiveness about discussing racism or accepting their own. They show more respect for their own self-definition and they make more effort to establish meaningful relationships toward members of other racial groups.

5. *The internalization/commitment stage:* The final transformation, one that Tatum works hard to implant in students and other teachers, is commitment and action sustained over time. She doesn't insist on action, but she does demand that students at least think about ways in which they could actively interrupt racism.

In this classic article, Tatum brings those developmental stages and the struggles that accompany them to life with quotes from a diversity of students in her classes. This excerpt from student notes represents a larger report in which all the developmental stages appear in one reflection:

> *I have been aware for a long time that I am Korean. But through this class I am beginning to really become aware of my race. . . . I grew up wanting to be accepted and ended up almost denying my race and culture. I don't think I did this consciously, but the denial did occur. . . . This is when I went through my "Korean friend" stage. . . . In our class, I feel that everyone is trying to sincerely find the answer of abolishing racism. I knew that people like this existed, but it's nice to meet with them weekly.*

If this sounds as if the students did all the work, consider the active and necessary roles that Tatum played. She tempered emotions and mindless statements. She informed her classes, at length, about reasons why people of color often feel powerless and angry in our society (e.g., by overviewing a study in which young African American students drew pictures of themselves without arms). She coached students to move beyond excessive guilt to more constructive action. And, again, she cast the class in a broad perspective of developmental stages to help students see where they stood and where they might want to go. She also, of course, coaches other teachers about the social responsibility of addressing and moderating racism. In the end, Tatum reminds us why this responsibility grows harder and harder to ignore. Classes at college campuses are becoming more multiracial and those classes need more attention to matters of race if all students in class are to be fully involved, valued, and likely to learn.

References

Ackroyd, P. (1990). *Dickens.* New York: HarperCollins.

Amabile, T. M. (1983). *The social psychology of creativity.* New York: Springer-Verlag.

Amada, G. (1992). Coping with the disruptive college student: A practical model. *Journal of American College Health, 40,* 203–215.

Amar, J. (1919). *The physiology of industrial organizations.* New York: Macmillan.

American Psychiatric Association. (1994). *Diagnostic and statistical manual of mental disorders* (4th ed.). Washington, DC: American Psychiatric Association.

Andreasen, N. C. (1987). Creativity and mental illness: Prevalence rates in writers and their first-degree relatives. *American Journal of Psychiatry, 144,* 1288–1292.

Angelo, T. (1990). Classroom assessment: Improving learning where it matters most. *New Directions for Teaching and Learning, 42,* 71–82.

Angelo, T. (Ed.). (1999). Classroom assessment and research: An update on uses, approaches, and research findings. *New Directions for Teaching and Learning, 75.*

Appleby, D. C. (1990, Spring). Faculty and student perceptions of irritating behaviors in the college classroom. *Journal of Staff, Program, & Organization Development,* 41–46.

Associated Press. (1994). Becoming American, bad habits and all. *New York Times,* p. B7.

Astin, A. W. (1984). Student involvement: A development theory for higher education. *Journal of College Student Personnel, 40,* 288–305.

Austin, A. E., & Baldwin, R. G. (1991). *Faculty collaboration: Enhancing the quality of scholarship and teaching.* Washington, DC: ASHE ERIC.

Baldwin, R. G., & Blackburn, R. T. (1981). The academic career as a development process. *Journal of Higher Education, 52,* 598–614.

Bandura, A. (1990). Conclusion: Reflections on nonability determinants of competence. In R. J. Sternberg & J. Kolligan (Eds.), *Competence considered* (pp. 315–362). New Haven, CT: Yale University Press.

Banks, W. M. (1984). Afro-American scholars in the university: Roles and conflicts. *American Behavioral Scientist, 27,* 325–329.

Baringer, F. (1993, June 2). School hallways as gantlets of sexual taunts. *New York Times,* p. B7.

Barrios, M. V., & Singer, J. L. (1981). The treatment of creative blocks: A comparison of waking imagery, hypnotic dream, and rational discussion techniques. *Imagination, Cognition, and Personality, 1,* 89–101.

Barron, F. (1963). *Creativity and mental health.* Princeton, NJ: Van Nostrand.

Bartlett, S. J. (1993, Summer). Barbarians at the door. *Modern Age,* 296–311.

Bate, W. J. (1977). *Samuel Johnson.* New York: Harcourt Brace Jovanovich.

Baumeister, R. F. (1991). *Meanings of life.* New York: Guilford.

Baumeister, R. F., Heatherton, T. F., & Tice, D. M. (1994). *Losing control: How and why people fail at self-regulation.* New York: Academic Press.

Baumeister, R. F., & Scher, S. J. (1988). Self-defeating behavior patterns among normal individuals: Review and analysis of common self-destructive tendencies. *Psychological Bulletin, 104,* 3–22.

Becker, H. (1986). *Writing for social scientists—How to start and finish your thesis, book, or article.* Chicago: University of Chicago Press.

Bem, S. (1974). The measurement of psychological androgyny. *Journal of Consulting and Clinical Psychology, 42,* 155–162.

Berg, A. S. (1978). *Max Perkins: Editor of genius.* New York: Dutton.

Bergler, E. (1950). *The writer and psychoanalysis.* Garden City, NY: Doubleday.

Blackburn, R. T., Beiber, J. P., Lawrence, J. H., & Trautvetter, L. (1991). Faculty at work: Focus on research, scholarship, and service. *Research in Higher Education, 32,* 385–413.

Blackburn, R. T., & Havighurst, R. J. (1979). Career patterns of male social scientists. *Higher Education, 8,* 553–572.

Block, L. (1984, August). Fear of writing. *Writer's Digest,* pp. 52–54.

Bluedorn, A. C., Kaufman, C. F., & Lane, P. M. (1992). How many things do you like to do at once? An introduction to monochronic and polychronic time. *Academy of Management Executive, 6,* 17–26.

Boice, R. (1982). Increasing the productivity of blocked academicians. *Behaviour Research and Therapy, 20,* 197–207.

Boice, R. (1983a). Contingency management in writing and the appearance of creative ideas. *Behaviour Research and Therapy, 21,* 534–537.

Boice, R. (1983b). Experimental and clinical treatments of writing blocks. *Journal of Consulting and Clinical Psychology, 21,* 183–191.

Boice, R. (1983c). Observational skills. *Psychological Bulletin, 93,* 3–29.

Boice, R. (1985a). Cognitive components of blocking. *Written Communication, 2,* 91–104.

Boice, R. (1985b). Psychotherapies for writing blocks. In M. Rose (Ed.), *When a writer can't write* (pp. 182–218). New York: Guilford.

Boice, R. (1986). Faculty development via field programs for middle-aged, disillusioned faculty. *Research in Higher Education, 25,* 115–135.

Boice, R. (1987). Is released time an effective device for faculty development? *Research in Higher Education, 26,* 311–326.

Boice, R. (1989). Procrastination, busyness, and bingeing. *Behaviour Research and Therapy, 27,* 605–611.

Boice, R. (1990). Mentoring new faculty: A program for implementation. *Journal of Staff, Program, & Organizational Development, 8,* 143–160.

Boice, R. (1990–1991). Countering common misbeliefs about student evaluations of teaching. *Teaching Excellence, 2* (2), 1–2.

Boice, R. (1991). Quick starters. *New Directions for Teaching and Learning, 48,* 111–121.

Boice, R. (1992a). Combined treatments for writing blocks. *Behaviour Research and Therapy, 30,* 107–116.

Boice, R. (1992b). Lessons learned about mentoring. *New Directions for Teaching and Learning, 50,* 51–61.

Boice, R. (1992c). *The new faculty member.* San Francisco: Jossey-Bass.

Boice, R. (1993a). New faculty involvement of women and minorities. *Research in Higher Education, 34,* 291–341.

Boice, R. (1993b). Primal origins and later correctives for midcareer disillusionment. *New Directions for Teaching and Learning, 55,* 33–41.

Boice, R. (1993c). Writing blocks and tacit knowledge. *Journal of Higher Education, 64,* 19–54.

Boice, R. (1994). *How writers journey to comfort and fluency: A psychological adventure.* Westport, CT: Praeger.

Boice, R. (1995a). Developing writing, then teaching amongst new faculty. *Research in Higher Education, 36,* 415–456.

Boice, R. (1995b). Writerly rules for teachers. *Journal of Higher Education, 66,* 32–60.

Boice, R. (1996a). Classroom incivilities. *Research in Higher Education, 37,* 453–486.

Boice, R. (1996b). *First-order principles for college teachers.* Bolton, CT: Anker.

Boice, R. (1996c). *Procrastination and blocking.* Westport, CT: Praeger.

Boice, R. (1997a). What discourages research-practitioners in faculty development. In J. C. Smart (Ed.), *Higher education: Handbook of theory and research.* New York: Agathon Press.

Boice, R. (1997b). Which is more productive, writing in binge patterns of creative illness or in moderation? *Written Communication, 14,* 435–459.

Boice, R., & Myers, P. E. (1986). Two parallel traditions: Automatic writing and free writing. *Written Communication, 3,* 471–490.

Boice, R., Scepanski, J. M., & Wilson, W. (1987). Librarians and faculty members: Coping with pressures to publish. *College & Research Libraries, 48,* 494–503.

Boice, R., & Turner, J. L. (1989). The FIPSE-CSULB mentoring project for new faculty. *To Improve the Academy, 8,* 117–139.

Bond, M. J., & Feather, N. T. (1988). Some coordinates of structure and purpose in the use of time. *Journal of Personality and Social Psychology, 55,* 321–329.

Boorstein, S. (1996). *Don't just do something, sit there.* New York: HarperCollins.

Borne, L. (1858). *Gesmmelte schriften.* Milwaukee, WI: Bickler.

Boswell, J. (1934). *Boswell's life of Johnson.* Oxford: Clarendon Press.

Bova, B. M. (1995). Mentoring revisited: The Hispanic woman's perspective. *Journal of Adult Education, 23* (1), 8–19.

Bowen, D. D., Seltzer, J., & Wilson, J. A. (1987). Dealing with emotions in the classroom. *The Organizational Behavior Teaching Review, 7* (20), 1–14.

Bowers, P. (1979). Hypnosis and creativity: The search for the missing link. *Journal of Abnormal Psychology, 88,* 564–572.

Boyer, E. L. (1987). *College teaching: The undergraduate experience in America.* New York: Harper and Row.

Boyer, E. L. (1990). *Scholarship reconsidered.* Princeton, NJ: Carnegie Foundation.

Boyle, P. (1995). *Socialization experiences of new graduate students.* Dissertation, State University of New York at Stony Brook.

Boyle, P., & Boice, B. (1998). Systematic mentoring for new faculty teachers and graduate teaching assistants. *Innovative Higher Education, 22,* 157–179.

Brand, A. G. (1986). *The psychology of writing: The affective experience.* Westport, CT: Greenwood.

Brande, D. (1934). *Becoming a writer.* New York: Harcourt, Brace.

Brandon, B. (1986). *The passion of Ayn Rand.* Garden City, NY: Doubleday.

Braxton, J. M. (Ed.). (1996). *Faculty teaching and research: Is there a conflict?* New Directions for Educational Research, Number 90. San Francisco: Jossey-Bass.

Brookfield, S. D. (1995). *Becoming a critically reflective teacher.* San Francisco: Jossey-Bass.

Brown, R. M. (1988). *Starting from scratch: A different kind of writer's manual.* New York: Bantam.

Bruer, J. T. (1993). The mind's journey from novice to expert. *American Educator, 17* (2), 6–16, 38–45.

Bruffee, K. A. (1984). Collaborative learning and the "conversion of mankind." *College English, 46* (7), 635–652.

Bullough, R. V., Knowles, J. G., & Crow, N. (1991). *Emerging as a teacher.* New York: Routledge.

Burka, J. B., & Yuen, L. M. (1983). *Procrastination.* Reading, MA: Addison-Wesley.

Charlton, J. (1986). *The writer's quotation book.* New York: Viking Penguin.

Chickering, A. W. (1974). *Commuting versus resident students.* San Francisco: Jossey-Bass.

Chodrin, P. (1997). *When things fall apart: Heart advice for difficult times.* Boston: Shambhala.

Chopra, D. (1993). *Ageless body, timeless mind.* New York: Harmony Books.

Clark, B. R. (1987). *The academic life: Small worlds, different worlds.* Princeton, NJ: Carnegie Foundation for the Advancement of Teaching.

Clark, S. M., & Corcoran, M. (1986). Perspectives on the professional socialization of women faculty: A case of academic disadvantage? *Journal of Higher Education, 57,* 20–43.

Claxton, G. (1999). *Hare brain, tortoise mind: Why intelligence increases when you think less.* Hopewell, NJ: Ecco Press.

Cohen, A. G., & Gutek, B. A. (1991). Sex differences in the career experiences of members of two APA divisions. *American Psychologist, 46,* 1292–1298.

Cohen, P. (1981). Student ratings of instruction and student achievement: A meta-analysis of multisection validity studies. *Review of Educational Research, 51,* 281–309.

Coles, R. (1993). When volunteers are sorely tested. *Chronicle of Higher Education, 39* (35), A52.

Cooper, J. L. (1996). Research on cooperative learning in the mid-1990s: What the experts say. *Cooperative Learning and College Teaching, 6* (2), 2–3.

Cooper, J., Prescott, S., Cook, L., Smith, L., Mueck, R., & Cuseo, J. (1990). *Cooperative learning and college instruction: Effective use of student learning teams.* Long Beach: California State University.

Cornford, F. M. (1978). *Microcomsographia academia, being a guide for the young academic politician.* London: Bowes & Bowes. (Originally published in 1908.)

Crowther, J. G. (1960). *Francis Bacon: The first statesman of science.* London: Crisset Press.

Csikszentmihalyi, M. (1990). *Flow: The psychology of optimal experience.* New York: Harper and Row.

Cuseo, J. B. (1996). *Cooperative learning: A pedagogy for addressing contemporary challenges and critical issues in higher education.* Stillwater, OK: New Forums Press.

Daly, J. A. (1985). Writing apprehension. In M. Rose (Ed.), *When a writer can't write* (pp. 43–82). New York: Guilford.

Darley, J. M., & Zanna, M. P. (1987). *The compleat academic: A practical guide for beginning social scientists.* New York: Random House.

DeJonge, P. (1993, June 6). Talking trash. *New York Times Magazine,* pp. 30–38.

Didner, J. (1992, February 10). Survey reveals high level of academic fraud. *Stony Brook Statesman,* pp. 1–2.

Dorsey, L. (1982). *Space, time and medicine.* Boulder, CO: Shambhala.

Durant, W., & Durant, A. (1977). *A dual autobiography.* New York: Simon and Schuster.

Edgerton, R., Hutchings, P., & Quinlan, K. (1991). *The teaching portfolio.* Washington, DC: American Association for Higher Education.

Eisenberger, R. (1992). Learned industriousness. *Psychological Review, 99,* 248–267.

Elbow, P. (1973). *Writing without teachers.* New York: Oxford University Press.

Elbow, P. (1983). Embracing contraries in the teaching process. *College Teaching, 45,* 327–339.

Elledge, S. (1984). *E. B. White.* New York: Norton.

Ellenberger, H. (1970). *The discovery of the unconscious.* New York: Basic Books.

Ellis, A., & Knaus, W. J. (1977). *Overcoming procrastination.* New York: Institute for Rational Living.

Epstein, M. (1995). *Thoughts without a thinker: Psychotherapy from a Buddhist perspective.* New York: Basic Books.

Erickson, B. L., & Stommer, D. W. (1991). *Teaching college freshmen.* San Francisco: Jossey-Bass.

Ericsson, K. A., & Charness, N. (1994). Expert performance: Its structure and acquisition. *American Psychologist, 49,* 725–747.

Exline, J. J., & Lobel, M. (in press). The perils of outperformance: Sensitivity about being a target of a threatening upward comparison. *Psychological Bulletin.*

Exum, W. M. (1983). Climbing the crystal stair: Values, affirmative action, and minority faculty. *Social Problems, 30,* 301–324.

Farhi, D. (1996, March/April). Holding your breath. *Yoga Journal,* pp. 76–81, 140–145.

Feibleman, P. J. (1993). *A Ph.D. is not enough! A guide to survival in science.* Reading, MA: Addison-Wesley.

Feldman, K. (1976). The superior college teacher from the students' view. *Research in Higher Education, 5,* 43–48.

Feldman, K. A. (1987). Research productivity and scholarly productivity of college teachers as related to their instructional effectiveness. *Research in Higher Education, 26,* 227–298.

Field, J. (1981). *A life of one's own.* Los Angeles: J. P. Tarcher. (Originally published in 1936.)

Finkelstein, M. J. (1984). *The American academic profession.* Columbus: Ohio State University Press.

Finn, R. (1995). Career-building on the Internet: Hunting for jobs electronically. *The Scientist, 9,* 23.

Flower, L. (1990). The role of task representation in reading-to-write. In L. Flower, V. Stein, J. Ackerman, M. J. Kantz, K. McCormick, & W. C. Peck (Eds.), *Reading-to-write* (pp. 35–75). New York: Oxford University Press.

Fogarty, J. L., Wang, M. C., & Creek, R. (1983). A descriptive study of experienced and novice teachers' interactive thoughts and actions. *Journal of Educational Research, 77,* 22–32.

Fox, M. F. (1985). Publication, performance, and reward in science and scholarship. In J. C. Smart (Ed.), *Higher education: Handbook of theory and research* (vol. 1, pp. 255–282). New York: Agathon Press.

Fremont, S. K., & Anderson, W. (1988). Investigation of factors involved in therapists' annoyance with clients. *Professional Psychology: Research and Practice, 19,* 330–335.

Gaff, J. G. (1994). Reform agendas of college campuses: Survey results. *Connections, 1* (2), 6–7.

Gaff, J. G., & Simpson, R. D. (1994). Faculty development in the United States. *Innovative Higher Education, 18* (3), 167–176.

Gappa, J. M., & Leslie, D. W. (1993). *The invisible faculty: Improving the status of part-timers in higher education.* San Francisco: Jossey-Bass.

Gardner, H. (1993). *Creating minds.* New York: Basic Books.

Garfield, P. L. (1974). *Creative dreaming.* New York: Ballantine.

Gladwell, M. (1999, January 11). Six degrees of Lois Weisberg. *New Yorker,* pp. 52–63.

Glendinning, V. (1992). *Anthony Trollope.* New York: Knopf.

Gmelch, W. (1993). *Coping with faculty stress.* London: Sage.

Goldberg, N. (1994). *Long quiet highway: Waking in America.* New York: Bantam Books.

Goleman, D. (1993, August 19). Schools try to tame violent pupils one punch and taunt at a time. *New York Times,* p. B11.

Gunaratana, H. (1992). *Mindfulness in plain English.* Boston: Wisdom.

Hall, E. T. (1992). *An anthropology of everyday life: An autobiography.* New York: Doubleday.

Hayes, J. P. (1984). *James A. Michener.* New York: Bobbs-Merrill.

Hayes, J. R. (1990). Individuals and environments in writing instruction. In B. F. Jones & I. Idol (Eds.), *Dimensions of thinking and cognitive instruction* (pp. 241–263). Hillsdale, NJ: Erlbaum.

Hayes, J. R. (1996). A new framework for understanding cognition and affect in writing. In C. M. Levy & S. Ransdell (Eds.), *The science of writing* (pp. 1–27). Mahwah, NJ: Erlbaum.

Hayes, J. R., & Flower, L. S. (1986). Writing research and the writer. *American Psychologist, 41,* 1106–1113.

Heiberger, M. M., & Vick, J. M. (1992). *The academic job search handbook.* Philadelphia: University of Pennsylvania Press.

Highet, G. (1950). *The art of teaching.* New York: Knopf.

Hilgard, E. R. (1977). *Divided consciousness.* New York: Wiley.

hooks, bell. (1997, May–June). The wisdom of hopelessness. *UTNE Reader,* pp. 61–63, 96–98.

Horney, K. (1945). *Our inner conflicts.* New York: Norton.

Jamison, K. R. (1993). *Touched with fire.* New York: Free Press.

Jarvis, D. K. (1991). *Junior faculty development: A handbook.* New York: Modern Language Association of America.

Jasen, D. A. (1981). *P. G. Wodehouse: A portrait of a master.* New York: Continuum.

Johnson, D. W., Johnson, R. T., & Smith, K. (1991). *Cooperative learning: Increasing faculty instructional productivity.* Washington, DC: Association for the Study of Higher Education.

Johnsrud, L. K., & Atwater, C. D. (1993). Scaffolding the ivory tower: Building supports for faculty new to the academy. *CUPA Journal, 44* (1), 1–14.

Kabat-Zinn, J. (1994). *Wherever you go, there you are.* New York: Hyperion.

Kapleau, P. (1969). *The three pillars of Zen.* Boston: Beacon.

Kearney, P., & Plax, T. G. (1992). Student resistance to control. In V. P. Richmond & J. C. McCroskey (Eds.), *Power in the classroom* (pp. 85–99). Hillsdale, NJ: Erlbaum.

Kellogg, R. T. (1994). *The psychology of writing.* New York: Oxford.

Kurfiss, J. G. (1988). *Critical thinking: Theory, research, practice, and possibilities.* Washington, DC: Association for the Study of Higher Education.

Lama, D., & Carriere, J. C. (1996). *Violence and compassion.* New York: Doubleday.

Lamb, R. (1977). *Booknotes: America's finest authors on reading, writers, and the power of ideas.* New York: Random House.

Lamott, A. (1994). *Bird by bird: Some instructions on writing and life.* New York: Pantheon.

L'Amour, L. (1989). *Education of a wandering man.* New York: Bantam Books.

Landino, R. A., & Owen, S. V. (1988). Self-efficacy in university faculty. *Journal of Vocational Behavior, 33,* 1–14.

Langer, E. J. (1989). *Mindfulness.* Reading, MA: Addison-Wesley.

Lao Tse. (1972). *Tao te ching.* Translated by G. F. Feng & J. English (Trans.). New York: Knopf. (From sixth century, B.C.).

Larson, R. (1985). Emotional scenarios in the writing process. In M. Rose (Ed.), *When a writer can't write* (pp. 19–42). New York: Guilford.

Lee, F. R. (1993). Disrespect rules. *New York Times* Education Supplement (Section 4A): 16.

Lenze, L. F., & Dinham, S. M. (1994). *Examining pedagogical knowledge of college faculty new to teaching.* Paper presented at the American Educational Research Association, New Orleans, April.

Levine, S. (1989). *A gradual awakening.* New York: Anchor.

Lieberman, E. J. (1993). *Acts of will: The life and work of Otto Rank.* Amherst: University of Massachusetts Press.

Light, R. J. (1990). *The Harvard assessment seminars.* Cambridge, MA: Harvard University.

Lodge, D. (1975). *Changing places: A tale of two campuses.* London: Specker & Warburg.

Lodge, D. (1995). *Small world: An academic romance.* New York: Penguin Books. (Originally published in 1984.)

Logue, A. W. (1994). *Self-control.* Englewood Cliffs, NJ: Prentice-Hall.

Lombroso, C. (1891). *The man of genius.* London: Scott.

London, M. (1993). Relationships between career motivation, empowerment, and support for career development. *Journal of Occupational Development, 66,* 55–69.

Lucas, R. A. (1992). *The grants world inside out.* Chicago: University of Illinois Press.

Ludwig, A. M. (1992). Creative achievement and psychopathology: Comparisons among professions. *American Journal of Psychotherapy, 46,* 330–356.

Maher, F. A., & Tetreault, M. K. (1994). *The feminist classroom.* New York: HarperCollins.

Mandel, R. D. (1977). *The professor game.* Garden City, NY: Doubleday.

Manegold, C. S. (1993, April 8). To Crystal, 12, school serves no purpose. *New York Times,* pp. A1, B7.

Mathews, N. (1996). *Francis Bacon: A history of character assassination.* New Haven, CT: Yale University Press.

McGaughey, R. A. (1993). But can they teach? In praise of college teachers who publish. *Teachers College Record, 95,* 242–257.

McKeachie, W. (1994). *Teaching tips.* Lexington, MA: D. C. Heath.

Meichenbaum, D. (1985). Teaching thinking: A cognitive-behavioral perspective. In S. F. Chipman & J. W. Segal (Eds.), *Thinking and learning skills* (vol. 2, pp. 407–426). Hillsdale, NJ: Erlbaum.

Meichenbaum, D. (1993). Changing conceptions of cognitive behavior modification: Retrospect and prospect. *Journal of Consulting and Clinical Psychology, 61,* 202–204.

Mencken, H. L. (1942). *A new dictionary of quotations.* New York: Knopf.

Meyers, J. (1991). *Joseph Conrad.* New York: Scribner.

Mills, C. W. (1959). *The sociological imagination.* New York: Grove Press.

Moffat, M. (1989). *Coming of age in New Jersey: College and American culture.* New Brunswick, NJ: Rutgers University Press.

Moore, D. M. (1992). *The accidental Buddhist.* Chapel-Hill, NC: Algonquin Books.

Morris, E. (1979). *The rise of Theodore Roosevelt.* New York: Coward, McCann & Geoghegan.

Moxley, J. (1992). *Publish, don't perish.* Westport, CT: Praeger.

Murray, D. M. (1978). Write before writing. *College Composition and Communication, 29,* 375–381.

Murray, D. M. (1995). *The craft of revision.* Orlando: Harcourt Brace.

Nitzsche, J. C. (1978). The junior professor's dilemma—How to save your own career. *Change, 10,* 40–43.

Nixon, H. K. (1928). *Psychology for the writer.* New York: Harper.

Murray, D. (1995). *The craft of revision.* New York: Harcourt Brace.

Murray, D. M. (1978). Write before writing. *College Composition and Communication, 29,* 375–381.

Oatley, K. (1992). *Best laid schemes: The psychology of emotions.* New York: Cambridge University Press.

Ochse, R. (1990). *Before the gates of excellence.* New York: Cambridge University Press.

Olsen, T. (1965). *Silences.* New York: Delacorte.

Olson, G. A. (1992). Publishing scholarship in humanistic disciplines: Joining the conversation. In J. Moxley (Ed.), *Writing and publishing* (pp. 49–69). New York: University Press of America.

Oxford Dictionary of Quotations (2nd ed.). (1966). London: Oxford University Press.

Pascarella, E. T., & Terenzini, P. (1991). *How college affects students.* San Francisco: Jossey-Bass.

Paulsen, M. B., & Feldman, K. A. (1995). *Taking teaching seriously: Meeting the challenge of instructional improvement.* Washington, DC: ASHE-ERIC Higher Education Report No 2.

Pear, J. J. (1977). Self-control techniques of famous novelists. *Journal of Applied Behavior Analysis, 10,* 515–525.

Perkins, D. N. (1981). *The mind's best work.* Cambridge, MA: Harvard University Press.

Perl, J. (1994). *Sleep right in five nights.* New York: Morrow.

Perry, R. P., Hechter, F. J., Menec, V. H., & Weinberg, L. E. (1993). Enhancing achievement motivation and performance in college students: An attributional retraining perspective. *Research in Higher Education, 34,* 687–723.

Plax, T. G., & Kearney, P. K. (1992). Teacher power in the classroom. In V. P. Richmond & J. C. McCroskey (Eds.), *Power in the classroom* (pp. 67–84). Hillsdale, NJ: Erlbaum.

Rabinbach, A. (1990). *The human motor.* New York: Basic Books.

Rachlin, H. (1995). Self-control: Beyond commitment. *Behavioral and Brain Sciences, 18,* 109–159.

Reis, R. M. (1997). *Tomorrow's professor.* New York: IEEE.

Rheingold, H. L. (1994). *The psychologist's guide to an academic career.* Washington, DC: American Psychological Association.

Ribot, T. (1906). *Essay on the creative imagination.* Chicago: Open Court.

Rothblum, E. D. (1988). Leaving the ivory tower: Factors contributing to a women's voluntary resignation from academia. *Frontiers, 10,* 236–241.

Rothblum, E. D. (1990). The fear of failure: The psychodynamic, need achievement, fear of success, and procrastination models. In H. Leitenberg (Ed.), *Handbook of social and evaluation anxiety* (pp. 387–394). New York: Plenum.

Rubin, J. (1996). *Psychotherapy and Buddhism.* New York: Plenum.

Rushton, J. P. (1990). Creativity, intelligence, and psychoticism. *Personality and Individual Differences, 9,* 1009–1024.

Schoen, L. G., & Winokur, S. (1998). An investigation of the self-efficacy of male and female academics. *Journal of Vocational Behavior, 32,* 307–328.

Schoenfeld, A. C., & Magnan, R. (1992). *Mentor in a manual: Climbing the academic ladder to tenure.* Madison, WI: Magna Publications.

Seligman, M. E. P. (1991). *Learned optimism.* New York: Knopf.

Shanker, A. (1995). Classrooms held hostage. *American Educator, 19* (1), 8–13, 47–48.

Simonton, D. K. (1988). *Scientific genius.* New York: Cambridge University Press.

Simonton, D. K. (1994). *Greatness.* New York: Guilford.

Singer, J. L. (1988). Sampling ongoing unconsciousness and emotional implications for health. In M. J. Horowitz (Ed.), *Psychodynamics and cognition* (pp. 297–348). Chicago: University of Chicago Press.

Skinner, B. F. (1981). How to discover what you have to say—A talk to students. *The Behavior Analyst, 4,* 1–7.

Smiley, J. (1995). *Moo.* New York: Fawcett Columbine.

Smith, A. (1776). *The wealth of nations.* Oxford: Clarendon Press.

Smith, K. A., & Walker, A. A. (1997). Cooperative leaning for new teachers. In W. E. Campbell & K. A. Smith (Eds.), *New paradigms for college teaching* (pp. 185–209). Edina, MN: Interaction Book Company.

Snyder, C. R., & Higgins, R. L. (1988). Excuses: Their effective role in the negotiation of reality. *Psychological Bulletin, 104,* 23–35.

Sternberg, R. J. (1994). *The psychologist's companion: A guide to writing for students and researchers.* Cambridge: Cambridge University Press.

Sternberg, R. J., Okagaki, L., & Jackson, A. S. (1990). Practical intelligence for success in school. *Educational Leadership, 42,* 35–39.

Strunk, W., & White, E. B. (1979). *The elements of style.* New York: Macmillan.

Tatum, B. D. (1992). Talking about race, learning about racism: The application of racial identity development theory in the classroom. *Harvard Educational Review, 62,* 1–24.

Thompson, R. (1985). *Bibliography on service.* Unpublished manuscript, Western Washington University.

Tierney, W. G., & Bensimon, E. M. (1996). *Promotion and tenure: Community and socialization in academe.* Albany: State University of New York Press.

Tinto, V. (1975). Dropout from higher education: A theoretical synthesis of recent research. *Review of Educational Research, 45,* 89–125.

Tobias, S. (1990). *They're not dumb, they're different.* Tucson, AZ: Research Corporation.

Toby, J. (1993). Everyday school violence: How disorder fuels it. *American Educator, 17* (4), 4–9, 44–47.

Tremmel, R. (1989). Investigating productivity and other factors in the writer's practice. *Freshman English News, 17,* 19–25.

Tremmel, R. (1993). Zen and the art of reflective practice in teacher education. *Harvard Educational Review, 63,* 434–468.

Trollope, A. (1883). *Anthony Trollope: An autobiography.* New York: Penguin Books. (Reprinted in 1983.)

Wagner, R. K., & Sternberg, R. J. (1986). Tacit knowledge and intelligence in the everyday world. In R. J. Sternberg & R. K. Wagner (Eds.), *Practical intelligence: Nature and origin of competence in the everyday world.* New York: Cambridge University Press.

Wain, J. (1975). *Samuel Johnson.* New York: Viking Press.

Walker, C., & Angelo, T. (1998). A collective effort classroom technique: Promoting high performance in student teams. In T. Angelo (Ed.), *Classroom assessment and research: An update on uses and research findings* (pp. 101–112). San Francisco: Jossey-Bass.

Wallace, I. (1968). *The writing of one novel.* New York: Simon and Schuster.

Weimer, M. (1990). *Improving college teaching.* San Francisco: Jossey-Bass.

Weimer, M., & Lenze, L. F. (1991). Instructional interventions: A review of the literature on efforts to improve instruction. In J. C. Smart (Ed.), *Higher education: Handbook of theory and research* (pp. 294–333). New York: Agathon.

Weissman, J. (1993). *Of two minds: Poets who hear voices.* Hanover, CT: Wesleyan University Press.

Whicker, M. L., Kronefeld, J. J., & Strickland, R. A. (1993). *Getting tenure.* Newbury Park, CA: Sage.

Winckler, K. J. (1988, November 9). Minority students, professors tell of isolation, anger in graduate school. *Chronicle of Higher Education, 35,* pp. A15, A19.

Wyatt, G. (1992). Skipping class: An analysis of absenteeism among first-year students. *Teaching Students, 20,* 201–207.

Name Index

Subject Index